# JavaScript

## Hands-on Learning for Beginners

Jie Wang

JavaScript: Hands-on Learning for Beginners

: interactive front-end web development

Jie Wang

ISBN-10: 0-9982738-0-5

ISBN-13: 978-0-9982738-0-8

# Preface

This book provides a concise, practical and problem-oriented guide for JavaScript. Being designed for beginners, no prior programming experience is required except for basic knowledge of HTML and CSS. For anyone who is interested in web programming, this book does not only teach you basic programming concepts through a number of concrete examples, case studies and hands-on exercises, but also makes it easy for you by breaking down each example into steps.

Developed from a study guide that the author had previously created for an online web programming course at college level, this book mainly targets readers who demonstrate a wide variety of prior programming knowledge. The book contains twelve chapters covering topics from basic programming concepts to interactive web application development. Each chapter is built upon the previous one. For beginners, it is recommended to read through from the first chapter to the last chapter without skipping pages or chapters.

After working through this book, you will have a strong foundation in web development and become an expert in creating interactive, versatile web pages. The book serves equally well as a text for online web programming classes or for self-study.

Downloading the source code in this book: https://github.com/JagerAxolotl/JavaScriptBookCode.

Errata: Although the author has taken every effort to ensure the correctness of the content, mistakes do happen. If you find errors in the text or the code, please send a note to: wangjiemn@gmail.com.

# CONTENTS

Contents

Contents

Contents

# Chapter 1  SETTING UP JAVASCRIPT ENVIRONMENT

To write and run JavaScript programs, the minimum software requirement is a source code editor and a web browser. A source code editor provides a place where program can be written. A web browser runs a web page that hosts JavaScript code. JavaScript code can also be executed in a JavaScript runner without being embedded in a web page.

This chapter guides you to set up an environment in your computer for learning JavaScript Programming. You can definitely stay with what you previously have used, either some editor or integrated development environment (IDE). In the following we describe briefly a recommended environment featuring a JavaScript code editor in combination with either the Firefox web browser or its developer edition.

The relevant files for this chapter are stored in the subfolder ch1 of the book data file.

## Table of Contents

# Web Browsers

A web browser is needed to render or interpret program code written in HTML, CSS, JavaScript and other languages for web development. In this book, we use Firefox or Firefox Developer Edition (the first browser made for developers which was released by Mozilla in 2014). Both browsers contain many built-in gadgets in the *Web Developer Tools*, including a JavaScript editor "*Scratchpad*", a style editor "*Style Editor*" and a debugger.

To install Firefox, go to https://www.mozilla.org/en-US/firefox/new/. To install Developer Edition, go to https://www.mozilla.org/en-US/firefox/developer/.

# Editors

Presently, editors can be divided into two categories: simple source code editors and complex development environments.

## Source Code Editors

A source code editor is a computer program, easy to use and lightweight, for editing text. Such editors typically support multiple programming languages so that we can use the same editor for different programming language assignments. A disadvantage of the editors is that you may need to use the command line for running the compiler or use an interpreter for rendering the code. In addition, a code editor lacks functions for managing large programming projects.

Some popular source code editors for Microsoft Windows are *Notepad++*, *Sublime Text*, *UltraEdit*, *jEdit* and *Brackets*.

Mac users have options with *Brackets*, *TextMate*, *TextWrangler* or *jEdit*. Brackets is a relatively new open source editor, which you may install and explore its features via the link http://brackets.io/.

There also are many online code editors such as JSFiddle Code Editor that tests JavaScript, CSS, HTML or CoffeeScript online.

We recommend the following editors for managing source code in HTML, CSS and JavaScript:

- **Notepad++** is a free code editor supporting multiple languages.
- **Brackets** is a modern open source text editor for web design.
- **Sublime Text** is a colorful editor with unlimited time for evaluation.
- **Scratchpad** is a JavaScript editor which is bundled in an installation of Firefox and Firefox Developer Edition.

There is no restriction on the editor you can use as long as you are able to edit program code.

## Installing a Source Code Editor in Your Computer

If you choose to install Notepad++, Sublime Text or Brackets go to their official web sites at https://notepad-plus-plus.org/, https://www.sublimetext.com/ and http://brackets.io/index.html. Download the installer suitable for the operating system running in your computer. Install and then start to use.

Scratchpad does not need to be installed as this editor is a built-in tool in Firefox and Firefox Developer Edition. The part "Using Web Console and Scratchpad" will show you how to open and use this tool.

## Integrated Development Environments

Most professional developers use an IDE (Integrated Development Environment) which combines a source code editor with many other advanced tools for software development. These environments make it easy to edit, debug, compile and run a program through a graphical user interface rather than a command line interface. IDEs are superior to plain editors for project management. Some popular IDEs are NetBeans (open source), Eclipse (open source) and WebStorm (commercial software). Feel free to use any IDE for running the code, just note that using IDE will not be discussed in this book.

# Debugging

A beginner rarely writes computer code successfully in the first attempt. Believe it or not, we are frequently struggling with tiny problems such as typos, opening brackets and unpaired quotation marks, inconsistent names from letter cases and wrong punctuations. Everyone learns programming by trial-and-error. The errors or defects in the code are referred to as bugs as they prevents the program from performing correct operations. Experienced programmers use **debugging** techniques to identify and remove bugs from computer programs.

One technique that we recommend to you is doing programming together with your peer or experienced programmers.

> According to the Wikipedia page, **pair programming** is an efficient technique in which two programmers work as a pair together on a single computer. One, the driver, writes code while the other, the observer, pointer or navigator, reviews each line of code as it is typed in. The two programmers switch roles frequently.

While debugging is not discussed in this book, the following part briefly introduces debugging JavaScript.

Assuming that a web page has been created in an HTML file, `example.html`. The JavaScript code is written in an external file, `example.js` which is stored in a subfolder `'js'`.

Link the script in `example.js` to the web page by simply inserting the following statement within `example.html`:

```
<script src="js/example.js"></script>
```

To run and debug the JavaScript code, open `example.html` in the browser. If the result appearing on the page is not correct, open `example.js` in a code editor and identify errors. Modify the code. Refresh the web page in the browser. If the page shows the correct result, it is completed; otherwise, repeat modifying the code until seeing the right page. Refer to the next part "Using Web Console and Scratchpad" for using Scratchpad in code editing and testing.

As a program becomes more and more complex with advanced programming concepts, such as events, functions and objects, web developers need to use standard and advanced debugging techniques to help them identify bugs quickly. Firefox Developer Edition provides a built-in debugger for JavaScript.

# Using Web Console and Scratchpad

Recall that Scratchpad and the web console are two built-in developer tools in Firefox and Firefox Developer Edition. Both provide an environment which enables an interaction with a web page by executing JavaScript *expressions* or *statements* in the context of the web page. Later, we will illustrate how to use these two tools.

> In computer programming, a statement is the smallest standalone element written in a computer programming language that commands the computer to perform a specified action.

> In computer programming, an expression is a finite combination of symbols that can be evaluated as to produce a single value.

## Opening Scratchpad and Web Console

Follow the instructions below to open a Scrachpad window and the Web Console window on a computer running Windows operating system.

In Firefox Developer Editon,

> → At the top right corner, click the wrench/screw spanner icon "Open Web developer tools (Ctrl+Shift+I)" In the popup menu, select "Web Console (Ctrl+Shift+K)" and "Scratchpad (Shift+F4)".

In Firefox,

> → On the top menu bar, open the menu Tools. Expand Web Developer. Check "Web Console (Ctrl+Shift+K)" and "Scratchpad (Shift+F4)".

Or simply use the following shortcut keys:

- ■ Press Ctrl+Shift+K to open Scratchpad.

- ■ Press Shift+F4 to open the web console.

On a computer running Mac OS, use the shortcut key Option+Command+K to open Scratchpad and Command+F4 to open the web console.

## Using Scratchpad and Web Console to Edit and Run JavaScript Code

The following workout will guide you through the steps which you can follow to learn how to use Scratchpad and web console for editing, running and saving JavaScript code. At this moment, you should have a solid knowledge of HTML and CSS, but you do not need to understand JavaScript code in this workout.

## Workout 1-1

1.    Open a new Firefox or Firefox Developer Edition window.

2.    To open a new Scratchpad window, press `Shift+F4` for PC or `Command+F4` for Mac. Or in the browser window, click the icon 'Web Developer Tools' at the top right, then select Scratchpad.

3.    A new Scratchpad window pops up. The following shows the default content in the window.

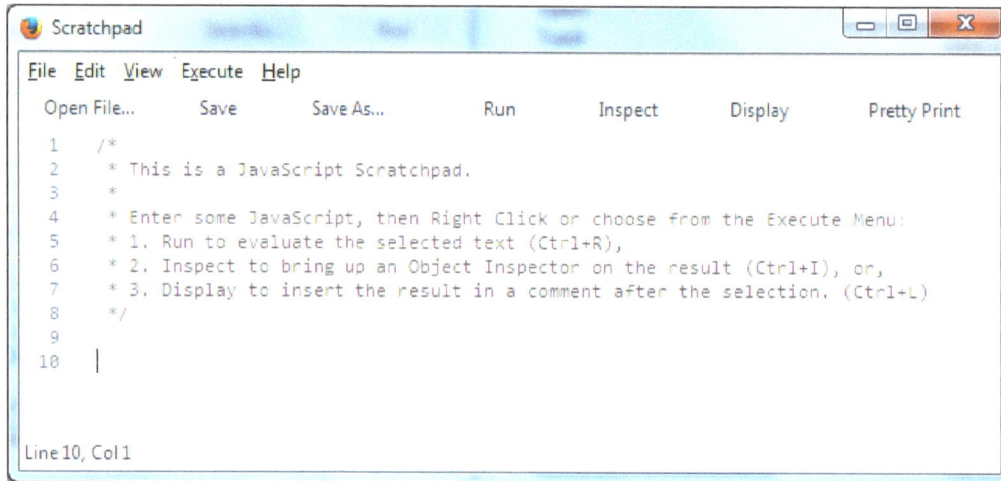

The default content is written in a comment block. A JavaScript comment block begins with the symbol '/\*' and ends with the symbol '\*/'. A JavaScript inline or single line comment begins with '//'.

> **NOTE**
>
> In computer programming, comments are not executed as regular code by a compiler or an interpreter such as a web browser. Comments are inserted to make the program easier to read and understand. Special symbols are used to distinguish comments from code. A JavaScript comment block begins with the symbol '/\*' and ends with the symbol '\*/'. A JavaScript inline or single line comment begins with '//'.

4.    In the window, you can edit and run JavaScript code without having to create a web page as a host program. Read the comments in the window to know three actions that you can take on the code, `Run`, `Inspect` and `Display`, as well as a shortcut key for each.

```
/*
 * Enter some JavaScript, then Right Click or choose from the Execute Menu:
 * 1. Run to evaluate the selected text (Ctrl+R),
 * 2. Inspect to bring up an Object Inspector on the result (Ctrl+I), or,
 * 3. Display to insert the result in a comment after the selection. (Ctrl+L)
 */
```

5.    You can delete the comment block at lines 1 through 8 if not needed.

6.    Now open the web console by pressing `Ctrl+Shift+K` for PC or `Option+Command+F4` for Mac.

The following Toolbox window will appear at the bottom of the browser, with the Web Console tab activated.

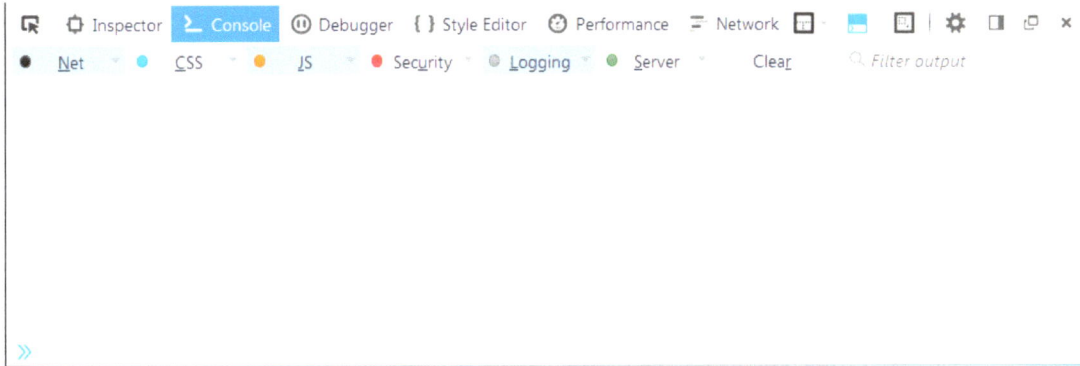

[1]    The Toolbox window is split into four parts from top to bottom: a tool bar, a sub-tool bar, a display pane and a command line bar.

Be sure that the Logging in the sub-tool bar is selected in order to see the log message from the log function.

[2]    By default, the Toolbox window is docked to the bottom of the browser window. To separate the Toolbox window from the browser window, click the overlapping window icon 'show in separate window' on the top right corner.

[3]    In the command line bar, we can enter JavaScript expressions and the console will run the expression and display the result in the display pane.

[4]    To customize the appearance of the window, clicking the steering wheel icon (Toolbox Options) on the top right corner. The settings pane shows up. Check or uncheck to enable or disable an option.

[5]    The default theme is light theme in Firefox and dark theme in Firefox Developer Edtion. You can swtich between two themes to determine the one that is more comfortable for your eyes.

[6]    To close the settings pane, activate the console tab by clicking `> Console` button on the top tool bar.

## Edit a new script in Scratchpad

7.    In the Scratchpad window, enter the code in the following box. (Note: <u>Do NOT type the line numbers followed by a dot in front of each line</u> as they are not the JavaScript code. They are only used in the book to specify one or more lines in a script.)

```
1.  var colors = ['white', 'black', 'custom'];
2.  console.log(colors[2]);
3.  colors[2] = 'beige';
4.  alert(colors[2]);
```

8.    After entering the code, you should see the code displayed in different colors.

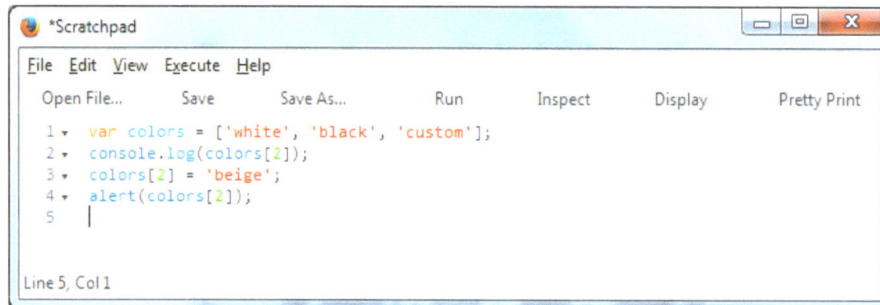

The color scheme in Scratchpad uses the following colors:

- o   black:           syntax characters ([, <, >, =, ], (, ), ;, .)
- o   orange:         JavaScript keywords
- o   blue:            variables, objects
- o   lightblue:      methods, functions
- o   red:             strings
- o   green:           numbers
- o   gray:            comments

9.    Computer programs should be well-formed for better readability. The well-formed code also helps us easily and quickly locate errors and typos. To do so, press `Pretty Print` button, the code becomes

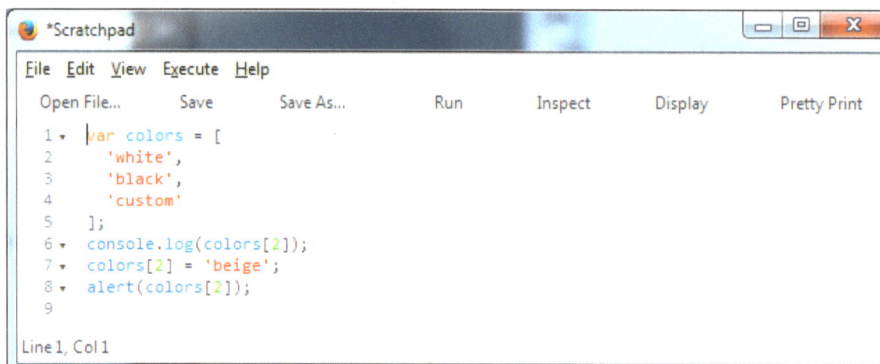

## Run script in Scratchpad

10.   In the Scratchpad window, press Run button on the top tool bar. As a result, the statement

```
console.log(colors[2]);
```

calls a function `console.log()` which writes the current value in `colors[2]`, `'custom'`, to the web console.

Afterwards, an alert box pops up after running the statement

```
alert(colors[2]);
```

The alert box shows the new value of `colors[2]`, `'beige'` (You can press OK to close this alert box.).

```
                              beige


                                    OK
```

NOTE

In web programming, when a programmer says writing code to "print a variable" or "display a variable" or "write a variable to", often it means printing the value that is stored in the variable to a web page, web console or a web browser.

11.   Now press Ctrl+N to open a new Scratchpad window. In the new Scratchpad window, enter the following code.

```
1.      var colors = ['white', 'black', 'custom'];
2.      colors[2] = 'beige';
3.      var times = colors.length;
4.      for (var i=0; i<times; i++){
5.          console.log(colors[i]);
6.      }
```

A program structure, loop, is used here to scan the array `colors` and print, in the web console, the value stored in each item of `colors`. Arrays will be covered in Chapter 2. The loop structure will be discussed in Chapter 8.

After applying Pretty Print, the script becomes

12.     Run the code. The web console will display all of three items in the array `colors`.

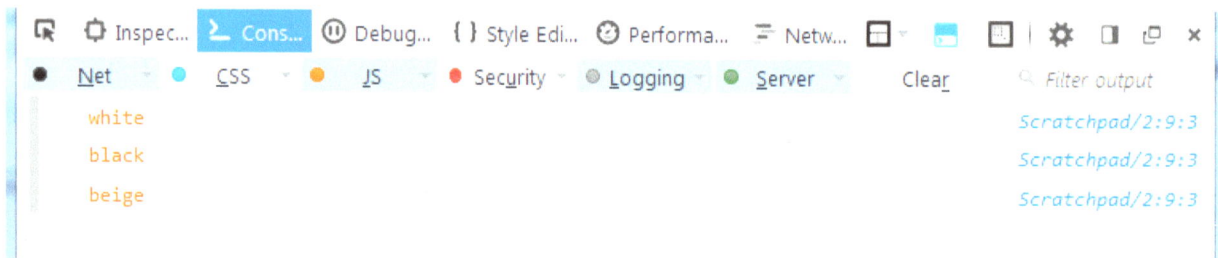

## Save script in Scratchpad

13.     After completing the script, to save the script in a file, press `Save As...` button or choose the submenu
        item `File->Save As...`

        In the `Save File As` dialog box, choose "JavScript Files (*.js;*jsm;*.json)" in the field "Save as
        type". In the field "File name:", enter `c1w1.js`.

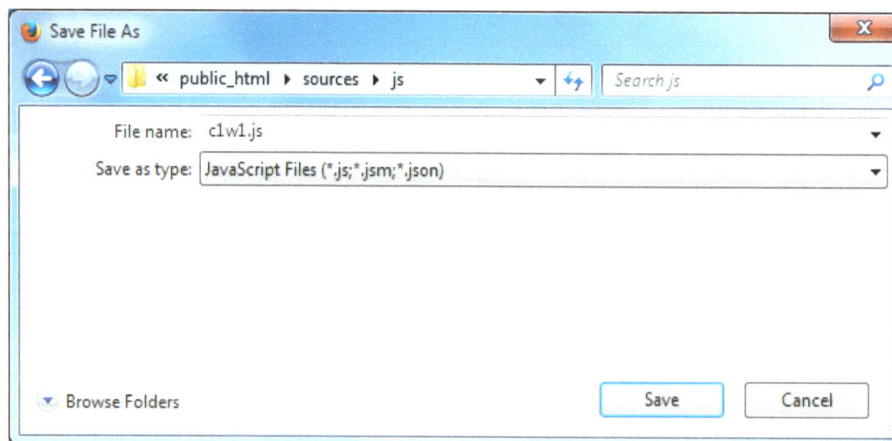

14.     Close the Scratchpad window.

## Open an existing script in Scrachpad

15.     To open an existing `js` file, say, `c1w1.js` from step 13, open a new Scratchpad window.

16.     In the new Scratchpad window, press `Open File...` button. Navigate to the file `c1w1.js` and select the file to open. The same code as the screen shot in step 11, should display in the window.

17.     Run the code in the Scratchpad window.

## Run expressions in web console

18.     Now let us run JavaScript expressions in the web console. In the browser window, place the cursor in the command line bar at the bottom of the Toolbox window. Enter the expression `colors` and press the key `Enter`.

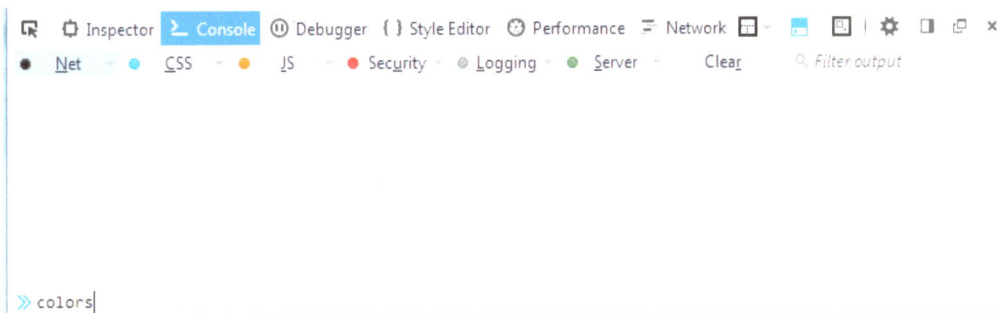

The expression you have entered will be echoed in the display pane. The browser will evaluate the expression and print the result below the expression.

19.     To clear the history output in the display pane: press the `Clear` button in the tool bar underneath the `>Console` tab. If ther is no `Clear` button, click the trash can icon on the leftmost of the tool bar.

20.     Let us try other expressions. In the command line bar, enter and run the following five expressions one after the other in the order, without clearing the display pane,

        1)      `alert(colors)`

        2)      `2 + 3`

        3)      `10 * (-2)`

        4)      `colors[0]`

        5)      `'The first color is ' + colors[0]`

The results in the browser window should be similar to the screen shot below.

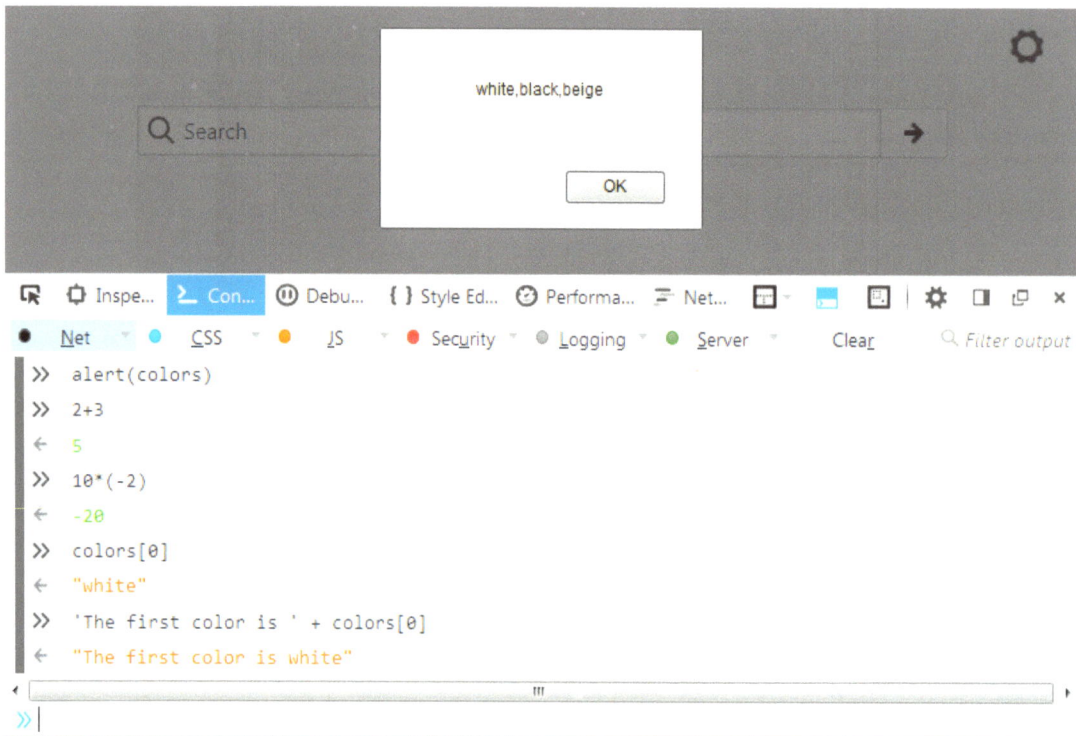

## Workout 1-2

Open a new web browser window.

Open the web console tool.

In the command line bar, enter and run each of the following expressions. Describe what each expression does as best you can.

1.  Enter and run the statement:

    ```
    window.print();
    ```

2.  Enter and run the expression:

    ```
    window.screen.width
    ```

3.  In a web browser window, open the site, google.com. In the command line bar, enter and run the statement:

    ```
    window.document.write("Erasing the Current Web Page");
    ```

4.  Open the site, google.com. Enter and run the expression:

    ```
    window.location
    ```

5.  Enter and run the statement:

    ```
    'hotel'.toUpperCase();
    ```

6.  Enter and run the expression:

    ```
    Math.random()
    ```

7.  Enter and run the expression:

    ```
    Math.random()*10
    ```

## Workout 1-3

Open a new Scratchpad window.

Enter the code in the following box.

```
1.    var number = Math.floor(Math.random() * 50) + 1;
2.  for (var i = 1; i <= 6; i++)
3.  {
4.    var guess = window.prompt('Enter guess #' + i + ' (an integer between 1 and 50)');
5.    if (guess < number)
6.    {
7.      alert('Too small');
8.    }
9.    else if (guess > number)
10.   {
11.     alert('Too big');
12.   }
13.   else {
14.     alert('Got it');
15.     break;
16.   }
17.   if (i === 6)
18.   {
19.     alert('You have tried 6 times.');
20.   }
21. }
```

Apply Pretty Print to the code.

Save the code to the file 'c1w3.js'.

Run the script a few times until you figure out what the script does.

Note:

- If the code that you have entered is not exactly the same as the given program in the box above, typos, syntax errors or running errors may prevent the program from working correctly.

- If the program runs without any error, you should see a dialog box that displays a dialog with a message prompting the user to enter an integer.

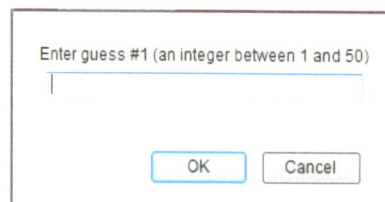

> Enter guess #1 (an integer between 1 and 50)
>
> |
>
> OK        Cancel

- If you want to terminate an execution, close the current browser tab or window.

Submit the file c1w3.js and describe the function of this script.

# Using Scratchpad and Web Console to Edit JavaScript Code with a Web Page

In this part, we will introduce how to use Scratchpad for experimenting with JavaScript code from an existing `.js` file that is associated with a web page.

## Example 1.1

Assuming that you have the following files in your computer.

---

`File Listing`

```
ex-0.html,
css/ex-0.css,
js/ex-0.js,
img/nespresso.jpg, img/kinderegg.jpg, img/capsule.jpg
```

NOTE

The file notation `css/ex-0.css` indicates `ex-0.css` is stored in a subfolder named `'css'`. The notation `js/ex-0.js` indicates `ex-0.js` is stored in the subfolder `'js'`. The notation `img/nespresso.jpg` indicates `nespresso.jpg` is stored in the subfolder `'img'`.

By default, we group all of the book files in a folder. Inside the folder, each chapter or case has its own subfolder. Within each chapter or case folder, we store JavaScript code in the subfolder `js`, style files in the subfolder `css` and image files in the subfolder `img`. The following shows the file structure in the folder `ch1` for Chapter 1.

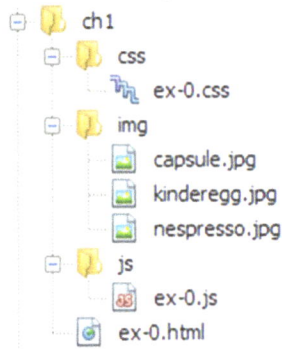

```
ch1
    css
        ex-0.css
    img
        capsule.jpg
        kinderegg.jpg
        nespresso.jpg
    js
        ex-0.js
    ex-0.html
```

You are free to choose a different file structure to store program files. However, if there is any `<link>`, `<script>` or `<image>` tags in a given HTML file from the book file collection, in order for web browsers to be able to locate these external resources, you must update the `src` or `href` values with the actual file paths in your computer.

1.  Open `ex-0.html` in a code editor, such as Notepad++ or Brackets. Read the source code as shown below.

```
1.    <!DOCTYPE html>
2.    <html lang="en">
3.        <head>
4.            <meta content="text/html; charset=utf-8" http-equiv="Content-Type">
5.            <title>A Page Having Three Boxes</title>
```

```
6.            <link rel="stylesheet" href="css/ex-0.css">
7.        </head>
8.
9.        <body>
10.          <div class="center">
11.          <ul>
12.              <li>Box 1</li>
13.              <li>Box 2</li>
14.              <li>Box 3</li>
15.          </ul>
16.          </div>
17.          <script src="js/ex-0.js"></script>
18.        </body>
19.    </html>
```

ex-0.html

2. Line 6 links the web page to style sheets from an external file, `css/ex-0.css`.

```
<link rel="stylesheet" href="css/ex-0.css">
```

The web browser will fetch this `css` file and apply the style rules to render the web page.

In `css/ex-0.css`, listed in the following box, the element style `li` makes each `li` element a square box and three class selectors, `.b0`, `.b1` and `.b2`, specify the `url` value for three distinct background images.

```
1.    @import url(https://fonts.googleapis.com/css?family=Oswald);
2.  body {
3.      background-color: cadetblue;
4.      font-family: 'Oswald', 'Futura', sans-serif;
5.  }
6.  .center {
7.      position: absolute;
8.      margin: auto;
9.      top: 0;
10.     right: 0;
11.     bottom: 0;
12.     left: 0;
13.     height: 420px;
14. }
15. li {
16.     list-style-type: none;
17.     display: inline-block;
18.     background-color: #F4EBC3;
19.     width: 300px;
20.     height: 300px;
21.     margin: 5px;
22. border: 10px solid #FFFFFF;
23. }
24. .b0 {
25.     background-image: url(../img/nespresso.jpg);
26. }
27. .b1 {
28.     background-image: url(../img/kinderegg.jpg);
29. }
```

```
30. .b2 {
31.     background-image: url(../img/capsule.jpg);
32. }
```

css/ex-0.css

(If we open a CSS file in the code editor, Sublime Text, the style rules are displayed in colors which not only makes rule editing vivid but also easily identify different names.)

3.  Now let us load ex-0.html in a browser window.
    The page will dynamically respond to the user input in such a way as programmed in the script from the external file js/ex-0.js. The script is linked to the web page by the following HTML statement in line 17 of ex-0.html.

    ```
    <script src="js/ex-0.js"></script>
    ```

    In the beginning, a prompt window pops up, asking for an integer between 1 and 3.

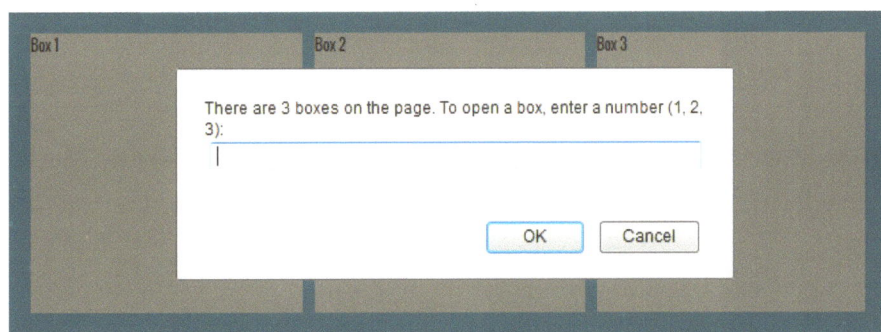

4.  Enter 1 in the text field and press OK button. The prompt window closes and a picture displays in the first box on the page.

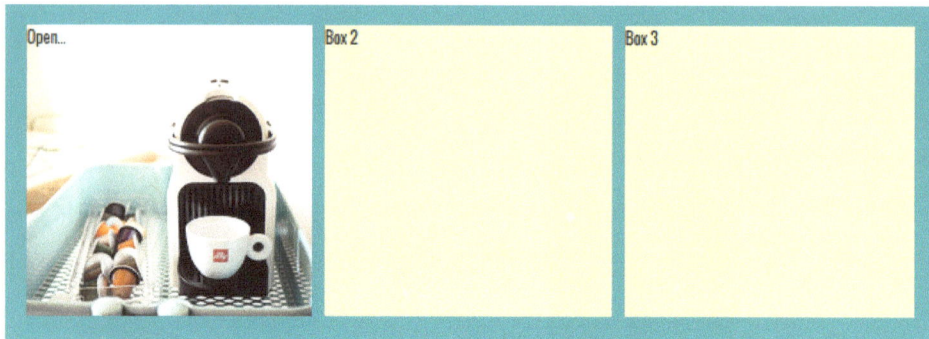

5.  Reload the page. This time, enter 2 in the prompt window. A picture will display in the second box.

6.  Reload the page. Enter 3 in the prompt window. This time, you will see a picture in the third box.

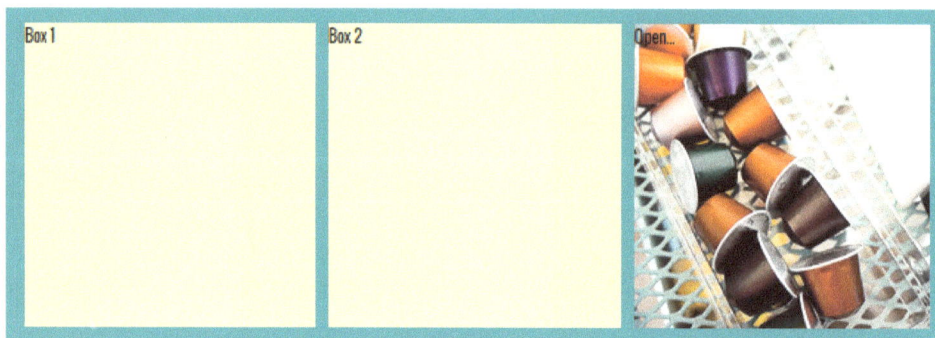

## Open the associated script with active web page in Scratchpad

7.  Now let us press Shift+F4 to open a new Scratchpad window.

8.  In the Scratchpad window, press the key Ctrl+o, or the Open File... button, or use the menu File →Open File, to open js/ex-0.js. The script is displayed in the window.

```
File  Edit  View  Execute  Help

Open File...      Save       Save As...        Run        Inspect       Display        Pretty Print
  1    // Search HTMl elements with the tag 'li'
  2    var items = document.getElementsByTagName('li');
  3
  4    // Prompt the user for an integer between 1 and 3
  5    var input = window.prompt('There are 3 boxes on the page. To open a box, enter a number (1, 2, 3): ');
  6
  7    // Repeat prompting until the user enters a valid value
  8    while ( Number.isNaN(parseInt(input)) || (parseInt(input) > 3 || parseInt(input) < 1) )
  9 ▾ {
 10      input = window.prompt('Invalid input. You must enter a number (1, 2, 3). Try again: ');
 11    }
 12
 13    // Locate the selected li element and apply a class selector
 14    var select = parseInt(input) - 1;
 15 ▾ items[select].innerHTML = 'Open...';
 16    var name = 'b'.concat(select);
 17 ▾ items[select].setAttribute('class', name);

Line 1, Col 1
```

9.  Alternatively, we can open a JavaScript file in any source code editor. Scratchpad is advantageous to be a simple tool for JavaScript. We can modify and save the JavaScript code in the Scratchpad window, read the errors and debug the code in the web console, then refresh the page in the web browser to find whether the page behaves as expected or not.

    For instance, replace the text value "Open…" in line 6 with "Open the box…", then press Save button. Reload ex-0.html. After a box is open, the new text is written into the box.

10. When a web page does not work as expected, we can examine the values in JavaScript variables by running expressions in the web console. This helps us locate the lines which causes the errors.   (For instructions of using the web console, refer to steps 18-20 in *Workout 1-3*.)

    Run the following expressions in the web console:

    1) items

    2) items[0]

    3) items[1]

    4) items[2]

    5) items[0].getAttribute('class')

    6) items[1].getAttribute('class')

    7) items[2].getAttribute('class')

# Chapter 2　STORING DATA

Computer programs store data in containers which typically are termed variables. A variable stores one or more values that can be reused, modified and computed during its lifetime within its effective range in a computer program. Before writing JavaScript programs, we must understand variables and their uses.

## Table of Contents

# Variable Basics

## Declare a Variable

In JavaScript, we create a new variable by using the keyword **var** followed by a name. For instance, the following **declaration statement** creates a new variable named message.

```
var message;
```

NOTE A statement in a computer program is the smallest standalone element. All JavaScript statements end with a semicolon.

The name of a variable serves as an identifier. A JavaScript **variable** must be **identified** with **unique name** within its valid scope where this variable is accessible.

Other general rules for naming a variable are listed in the following:

- A name can contain letters, digits, underscores, and dollar signs.

- A name must begin with a letter.

- A name can also begin with $ and _ (not used in this book.)

- A name is case sensitive (For example, JavaScript reads y and Y as two different characters.)

- Reserved words that are used by JavaScript should be avoided in variable names.

For a list of the words and names reserved for JavaScript, see Appendix B. *Reserved Words and Names used by JavaScript*.

After declaring the variable message, we can perform some common operations such as storing a value, displaying the value, replacing the old value with a new value and performing calculations.

In JavaScript, we can redeclare a variable more than one time. For instance, we can declare the same variable in two consecutive statements:

```
var message;
var message = 'You declared me again!';
```

However, redeclaration is not common for other programming lanuages. In other programming languages, the variable cannot be redeclared in the same scope where it is effective. A redeclaration will generate syntax error.

## Assign Values to the Variable

To **store a value in a variable**, use the assignment operator which is an equal sign. The following assignment statement assigns a string "Fun Education Fun" to the variable message.

```
message = "Fun Education Fun";
```

A string value must be enclosed with either double quotes or single quotes.

The declaration statement and the assignment statement can also be combined into one statement:

```
var message = "Fun Education Fun";
```

To replace the current value with a new value in `message`, simply use the same assignment operator:

```
message = "<h1>Fun Education Fun</h1>";
```

# Know Data Types

A variable can store a single value for a string, a numerical value, a Boolean value, `null` or `undefined`.

A string is a sequence of characters and symbols.

A numerical value can be an integer or a floating point number.

The Boolean data type supports two possible values, `true` and `false`. A Boolean value is either `true` or `false`, which is usually generated by evaluating an expression or a condition. If the condition holds, it produces a Boolean value `true` and `false` otherwise.

`null` is considered as a value representing absence of any value.

`undefined` is a special value to be assigned to an uninitialized variable.

Run the following statements in Scratchpad. Inspect each variable in the web console. (Refer to Chapter 1 *Run Expressions in Web Console*)

```
var star = "Alpha";
var score = 95;
var confirm = true;
var type;
var status = null;
```

The variable `star` stores a string `"Alpha"`.

The variable `score` holds a number which is `95`.

The variable `confirm` has a Boolean value `'true'`.

The variable `type` is left uninitialized and by default, its value is `undefined`.

The variable status is assigned with `null`.

# Inspect the Variable

After the declaration and assignment, we can **print or inspect the current value** in the variable. When a program does not produce the right result, programmers often need to debug the program. To debug source code of a web page that runs JavaScript code, the simplest way is to inspect variables to watch how the values of variables change dynamically.

To inspect a variable in the web console, refer to Chapter 1 *Run Expressions in Web Console*.

To inspect a variable in a Scratchpad window, in the Scratchpad window, enter the script

```
var message = "Fun Education Fun";
```

Click Run button to execute the statement. Then highlight message in the statement, click Inspect button. A new column appears on the right where the current value of the selected variable is displayed.

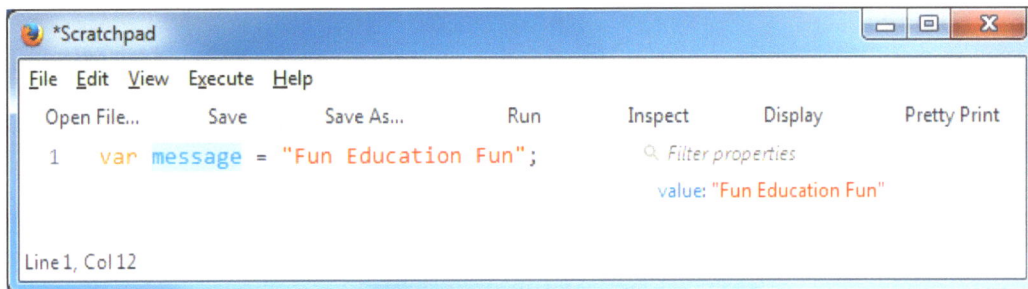

Now add the second statement to the script

```
message = "<h1>Fun Education Fun</h1>";
```

Then run the script and inspect message. You will see the current value is updated to the new value.

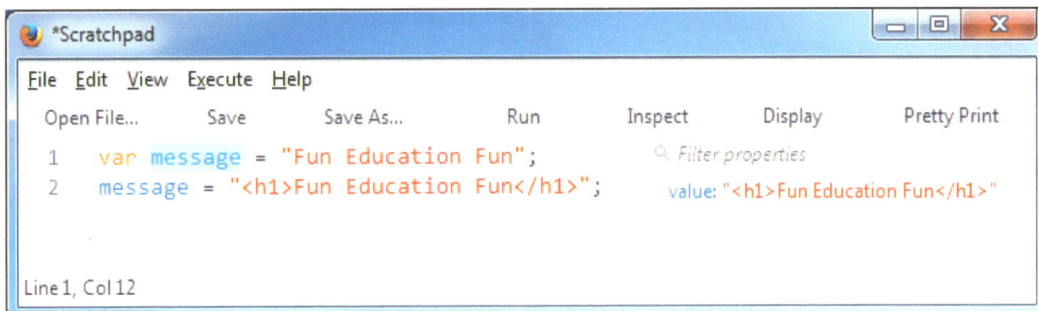

# Display the Variable

To display a variable in a JavaScript program, use any of the following three functions.

```
window.alert
window.confirm
console.log
```

Place a variable name inside the parenthesis and the functions will print the current value in the variable. All of the following three statements print `message`.

```
console.log(message); //show the value in a web console

window.alert(message); //show the value in an alert box

window.confirm(message); //show the value in a confirmation box
```

**NOTE**

A JavaScript function is a script block to perform a specific task. To complete a task, a function may require zero, one or more input values termed arguments. The argument(s) are enclosed in a pair of parenthesis. Chapter 3 will discuss functions.

Now let us run these statements.

## Example 2.1

First, open a new web browser window or tab. Remind that operational instructions and screenshots in this book are based on Firefox or Firefox Developer Edition. The tools are the same in both Firefox and Firefox Developer Edition except for different color settings.

Next, open the Web Console window (Ctrl+Shift+K) and a Scratchpad window (Shift+F4) (See instructions in Chapter 1).

In the Scratchpad window, enter the following script

```
1.    var message = "Fun Education Fun";
2.    console.log(message);
3.    window.alert(message);
4.    window.confirm(message);
```

Click Run button to run the script.

**NOTE**

A web browser processes and interprets statements in the same order as they appear in the script unless the script contains some special programming structures like loops and decisions.

The browser interprets these four statements one by one.

1.  Declare a new variable `message` and assign a value to it;

2.  Print `message` in the web console.

3.  Create an alert box to display the value of `message`. To close the alert box, press OK.

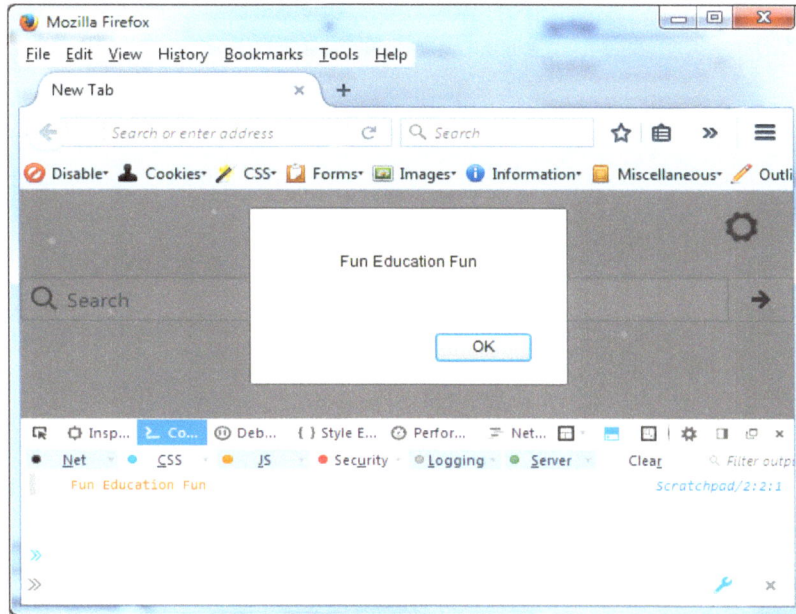

4.  After closing the alert box, a confirmation box appears. Press the OK button to confirm what displayed in the box and close the confirmation.

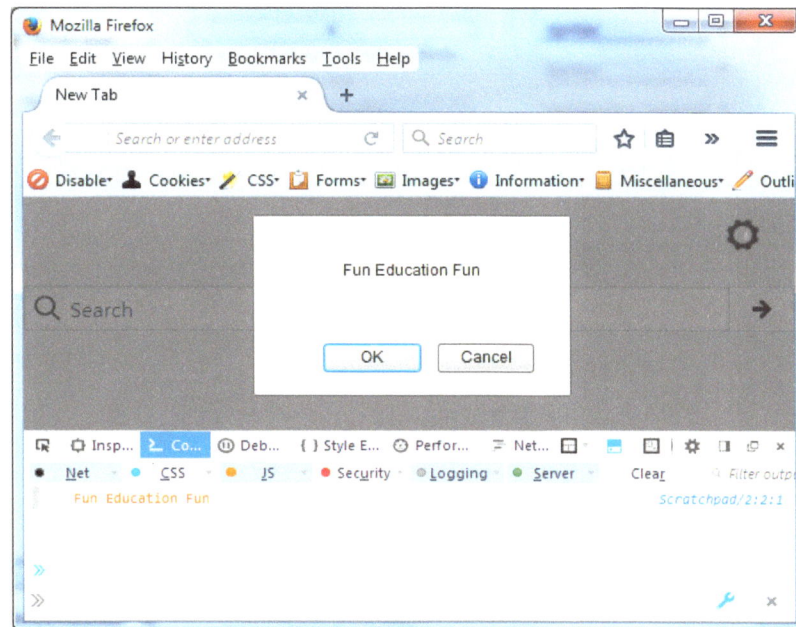

## Workout 2-1

In a Scratchpad window, write a script to perform the following tasks in order:

1. Declare a variable today,

2. Assign a string value 'Friday' to today

3. Display today in a confirmation box.

4. Assign a new value 'Monday' to today

5. Print today in the web console.

Save the script to a file named c2w1.js.

## Workout 2-2

Two scripts are given below which are supposed to declare a variable, assign a value and print the value in the console. Both scripts should print "Fun Education Fun" in the web console.

Instead, after running each script in Scratchpad, you will see both have an error which is displayed below each script.

Script 1:

```
var message = "Fun Education Fun";
console.log(mesage);
```

The error is

```
/*
Exception: ReferenceError: message is not defined
@Scratchpad/1:11:1
*/
```

Script 2:

```
var message = 'Fun Education Fun";
console.log(message);
```

The error is

```
/*
Exception: SyntaxError: unterminated string literal
@Scratchpad/1:10
*/
```

You need to discover and correct the error for both scripts. Submit the new scripts without errors.

# Linking JavaScript File to a Web Page

In the previous parts, we have discussed Scratchpad for debugging and testing a JavaScript script. JavaScript was designed as an object-oriented language to support dynamical web pages that enables a user to interact with the pages. This language has been augmented with many powerful libraries and frameworks including jQuery, D3.js, Ajax, Node.js and Dojo.

- jQuery (https://jquery.com/) is a JavaScript library that performs functions to make it much simpler for HTML document traversal and manipulation, event handling, animation and Ajax.

- Ajax (http://api.jquery.com/jquery.ajax/) uses the XMLHttpRequest object to communicate with server-side scripts.

- D3.js (https://d3js.org/) is a library for data visualization that illustrates and animates data.

- Node.js (https://nodejs.org/en/) is an asynchronous event driven framework for building a scalable network applications.

- Dojo (https://dojotoolkit.org/) is a toolkit that provides source modules for building a web application.

Before we can utilize these tools, we must understand JavaScript basics including its syntax, keywords, objects and functions.

**From the perspective of a web designer**, HTML and CSS are client-based script languages; we use HTML elements to place static content, texts and images, on a web page and use style sheets in CSS to render the page with its layout and look. A web designer must master the art of CSS.

**From the perspective of a web developer**, JavaScript can manipulate HTML elements, perform data processing and update the page with new look and content. These changes can be triggered by users' actions, event occurrences, HTML form submissions as well as input validations.

Applying JavaScript to a web page requires both HTML and CSS coding skills.

From *Example 1.1* of Chapter 1, we has seen that a web page can render style sheets and run JavaScript code that are stored in an external file. Below, by following an example, we will learn building such a web page that runs external JavaScript code.

## Example 2.2

Below is a list of the files that will be used in this example.

---

```
File Listing
        ex-1-nojs.html, css/ex-1.css,
        ex-1.html, js/ex-1.js,
        ex-1-append.html, js/ex-1-append.js
```

---

The purpose of this example is to produce a web page which contains three embedded squares; the outermost square is colored in cadetblue, the middle square is colored in white and the innermost square is colored in burlywood. A text "Add me to the div grandfather" is displayed on the top left corner of the outermost square. The following picture shows a sample view after loading ex-1.html in a web browser.

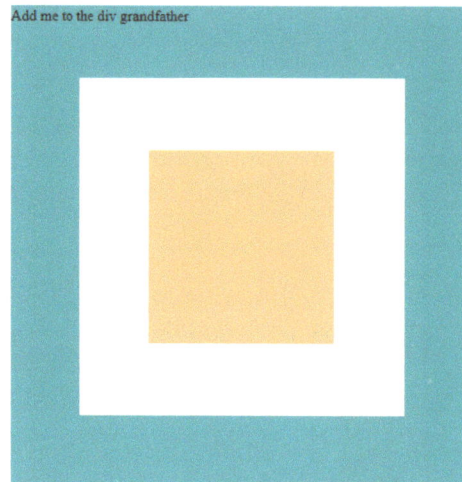

To implement this example, we follow the steps listed in the following.

## Step 1. Create a Web Page

You can use a source code editor to open a program or edit a new program. Refer to the section "Editors" in Chapter 1. For this example, the web page has been created in an HTML file, ex-1-nojs.html, which contains three nested div elements. The style rules are declared in css/ex-1.css that is linked to the HTML file.

The HTML code, in ex-1-nojs.html, is listed in the following.

```
1.  <!DOCTYPE html>
2.  <html lang="en">
3.      <head>
4.          <meta content="text/html; charset=utf-8" http-equiv="Content-Type">
5.          <title>A Page Having Nested div Elements</title>
6.          <link rel="stylesheet" href="css/ex-1.css">
7.      </head>
8.      <body>
9.      <div id="grandfather">
10.         <div id="father">
11.            <div id="son"></div>
12.         </div>
13.     </div>
14.     </body>
15. </html>
```

ex-1-nojs.html

NOTE

When web browsers encounter errors in an HTML file that does not conform to the rules of the language, they are tolerant with the errors and proceed with rendering the page as best as they can. Even though browsers always render any page no matter it contains errors or not, using HTML parser to validate source can help us make a well-formed HTML source file and detect typos. An HTML Code Validation Tool is located at https://validator.w3.org/#validate_by_input .

Each HTML element can have a number of attributes including id, class and name. We can distinguish the HTML elements by their HTML tag name, name, class or id value. In this example, we will identify three div elements by their id value that is grandfather, father and son, respectively.

The element div#grandfather contains the element div#father. The element div#father embraces the element div#son.

The notation div#grandfather represents an HTML element with the tag <div> and it has the id attribute whose value is 'grandfather'.

If an HTML <div> element has the class name 'news', its representing notation is div.news.

> The class name is prefixed with a dot sign. The prefix of the id value is a pound sign #.

Normally, an id selector rule is applied to one and only one HTML element while a class selector can be applied to multiple HTML elements. Though web browers still renders an HTML file where multiple elements have the same id value; however, the practice of assigning the same id value to multiple elements should be avoided as this may cause issues in web applications where the id value is used in JavaScript code for identifying a specific element.

## Step 2. Link the Page to Style Sheets

In line 6 of ex-1-nojs.html,

```
<link rel="stylesheet" href="css/ex-1.css">
```

The href value indicates that the linked style sheets are stored in an external file css/ex-1.css, which is displayed below.

```
1.      div {
2.          position: absolute;
3.          margin: auto;
4.          top: 0;
5.          right: 0;
6.          bottom: 0;
7.          left: 0;
8.      }
9.      #grandfather {
10.         width: 500px;
11.         height: 500px;
12.         background-color: cadetblue;
13.     }
14.     #grandfather p {
15.         font-size: 25px;
16.         color: white;
17.         text-align: center;
18.     }
19.     #father {
20.         width: 350px;
21.         height: 350px;
22.         background-color: white;
23.     }
24.     #son {
25.         width: 200px;
```

```
26.          height: 200px;
27.          background-color: burlywood;
28.     }
```

css/ex-1.css

In `css/ex-1.css`, there are five selectors.

- The element selector `div` centers every `div` element.

- Three `id` selectors, `#grandfather`, `#father` and `#son`, are declared to distinguish three `div` elements, each of which is assigned with specific size and background color.

- The decendent selector, `#grandfather p,` declare style rules for `p` elements that are anywhere inside an element with the `id` value `grandfather`.

Now Let us open `ex-1-nojs.html` in a browser window. On the page is a set of three embedded squares.

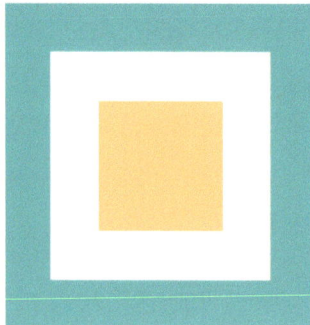

Next, Let us link this web page to JavaScript code.

## Step 3. Link the Page to JavaScript Code

There are two ways of running JavaScript code in a web page.

A `script` tag can directly embed a JavaScript code block within the `HTML` code. The syntax is given below.

Syntax

```
<script type="text/javascript">
    //[JavaScript code block]
</script>
```

In this book, we use the other way by storing JavaScript code in an external file and linking the web page to the file. An advantage of storing JavaScript code in an external file is that we can reuse the same code in multiple web pages as long as we link the page to that external file.

### *Edit JavaScript code*

Refer to Chapter 1 *Using Web Console and Scratchpad* for editing and saving JavaScript code in Scratchpad.

Firstly, in a Scratchpad window, enter the following script.

```
1.    var message = "<p>Add me to the div grandfather</p>";
2.    var grandfatherHandle = document.getElementById("grandfather");
3.    var fatherHandle = document.getElementById("father");
4.    var sonHandle = document.getElementById("son");
5.    grandfatherHandle.innerHTML = message;
```

The expression, `document.getElementById`, is a method (function) associated with a special JavaScript object, `document`. The `document` object represents the web page that has been loaded into the current browser window. This object carries properties and methods. These concepts will be covered with more details in later chapters.

The method, `getElementById`, takes a string value as argument, compares this value with the `id` value of every element on the page and returns a reference to the first element whose `id` value matches the given string.

Thus, the statement

```
var grandfatherHandle = document.getElementById("grandfather");
```

declares a new variable `grandfatherHandle`; looks up the element whose `id` value is `grandfather` and if there is the one, then stores its reference into the variable `grandfatherHandle`. By this reference, `grandfatherHandle`, we can access and manipulate the element `div#grandfather`.

Similarly, in order to access two other `div` elements, retrieve their references by using `getElementById` with their `id` values, respectively.

```
var fatherHandle = document.getElementById("father");

var sonHandle = document.getElementById("son");
```

### *Save the code to a File*

After editing the JavaScript code, save the code to the subfolder `js`, in a file named `ex-1.js`. If needed, refer to Chapter 1 *Using Web Console and Scratchpad* for the instructions about saving JavaScript code in Scratchpad.

If you use a code editor other than Scratchpad, when saving the script into a file, be sure that the file extension is set to `js`. The following shows a sample Save As dialog box in Notepad++.

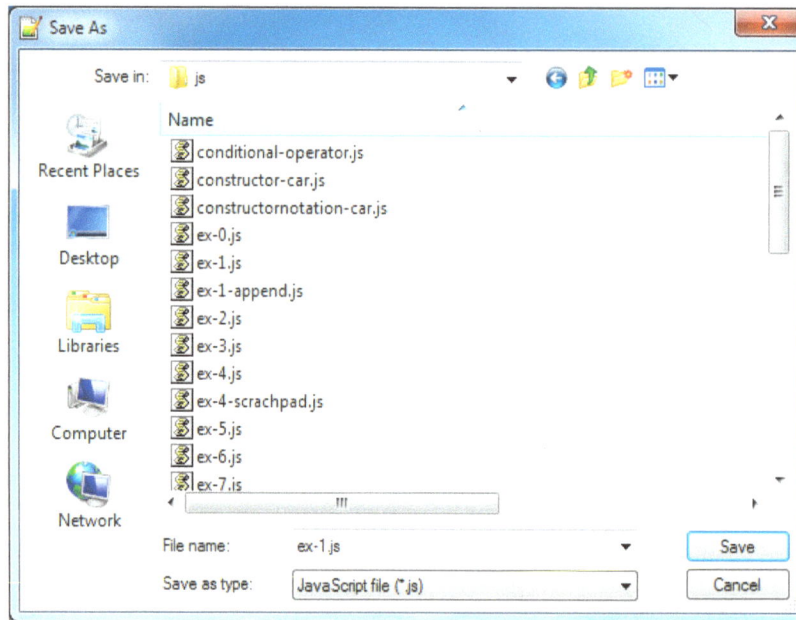

## Insert the script tag

After saving the JavaScript code to js/ex-1.js, we can create a script link in the HTML source.

Open ex-1-nojs.html, below the closing div tag of the element div#grandfather and above the closing body tag, insert the following script statement with the src attribute.

```
<script src="js/ex-1.js"></script>
```

When the browser executes this statement, it will read the src value for a file path, navigate along the path to the file folder js and look up the file ex-1.js. If the browser finds the file successfully, the browser executes the script; otherwise, the script will not be executed due to the error type "File Not Found".

Though web browser will not alert the error, it will print the error silently to the web console under the JS tab. In order to see the errors that are relevant to the JavaScript code, keep the web console open in the browser window.

After inserting the script link, save the HTML source to a new file named ex-1.html.

```
1.    <!DOCTYPE html>
2.    <html lang="en">
3.      <head>
4.        <meta content="text/html; charset=utf-8" http-equiv="Content-Type">
5.        <title>A Page Having Nested div Elements</title>
6.        <link rel="stylesheet" href="css/ex-1.css">
7.      </head>
8.      <body>
9.        <div id="grandfather">
10.         <div id="father">
11.           <div id="son"></div>
12.         </div>
13.       </div>
14.       <script src="js/ex-1.js"></script>
15.     </body>
```

```
16. </html>
```

## Step 4. Test the Page

After linking both CSS and JavaScript files to the web page, let us open ex-1.html in the browser. What is on the page?

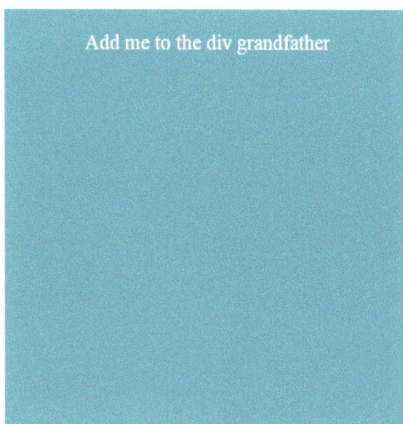

message has successfully been written into the outermost square whose id is grandfather, but two inner squares disappear. This result is not correct.

Why? Because the assignment statement

```
grandfatherHandle.innerHTML = message;
```

recursively removes the entire HTML content within the element grandfather, then write new content in message into div#grandfather. Before this assignment statement is executed, the HTML content wrapped by the element div#grandfather is

```
<div id="father">
    <div id="son"></div>
</div>
```

After executing the statement

```
grandfatherHandle.innerHTML = message;
```

innerHTML resets the entire HTML content in div#grandfather by message, which is

```
<p>Add me to the div grandfather</p>
```

Thus, inside the div#grandfather, there is only one paragraph. To fix this problem, instead of replacing the HTML content, we need to append the new content to the current HTML content. This can be done with multiple ways.

> **NOTE**
>
> Assigning a new value to the attribute innerHTML will replace everything in an element with the new value. Due to this unsafe operation from innerHTML, we should be very careful of assigning this attribute a new value. Improper use of this attribute can open a cross-site scripting (XSS) attack.

## Step 5. Debug the Code

Now let us modify js/ex-1.js so as that two inner squares will not be removed.

1. Copy js/ex-1.js to a new file js/ex-1-append.js.

2. Open js/ex-1-append.js in a code editor or a Scratchpad window. Replace the statement

   ```
   grandfatherHandle.innerHTML = message;
   ```

   with two statements

   ```
   var currentHTML = grandfatherHandle.innerHTML;
   grandfatherHandle.innerHTML = message + currentHTML;
   ```

   → In the first statement, grandfatherHandle.innerHTML returns the current HTML content that is wrapped by the div#grandfather.

   ```
   <div id="father">
       <div id="son"></div>
   </div>
   ```

Then store the content to a variable currentHTML.

   → The second statement joins the current HTML content with message. The plus sign, +, is an operator which joins multiple strings into one string. Here, the expression, message + currentHTML, will produce a new string. By placing message as the first operand, the new string appends message before the beginning of current content.

3. The final code in js/ex-1-append.js is listed below.

```
1.   var message = "<p>Add me to the div grandfather</p>";
2.   var grandfatherHandle = document.getElementById("grandfather");
3.   var fatherHandle = document.getElementById("father");
4.   var sonHandle = document.getElementById("son");
5.   var currentHTML = grandfatherHandle.innerHTML;
6.   grandfatherHandle.innerHTML = message + currentHTML;
```

js/ex-1-append.js

An alternate to `Element.innerHTML` is `Element.insertAdjacentHTML`. This method will be explained in Chapter 8.

4. Copy `ex-1.html` to a new file `ex-1-append.html`.

5. Open `ex-1-append.html`, locate the line

   ```
   <script src="js/ex-1.js"></script>
   ```

   Change the `src` value to `"js/ex-1-append.js"`.

6. Load `ex-1-append.html` in the browser window. The page displays all of three squares and the new message as well.

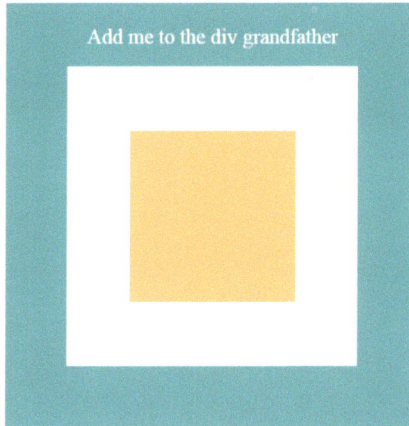

## Step 6. Inspect the Variables

There are several ways of inspecting variables. The Inspect function in Scratchpad was introduced in the section "*Inspecting the Variable*" of this chapter.

After loading `ex-1-append.html` in the browser, we can inspect `currentHTML` and `message`. Here we inspect a variable by running a few statements in Scratchpad. To do so, open a Scratchpad window. Enter and run the statement

```
alert("The value in currentHTML is" + currentHTML);
```

You will see the value of `currentHTML` in an alert box.

```
The value in currentHTML is
<div id="father">
  <div id="son"></div>
</div>

                                    OK
```

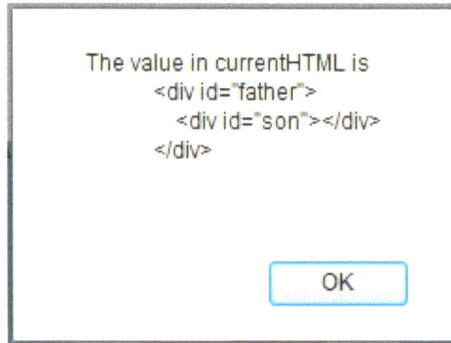

Also, you can alert the result from joining two variables by runnning the statement

```
alert(message + currentHTML);
```

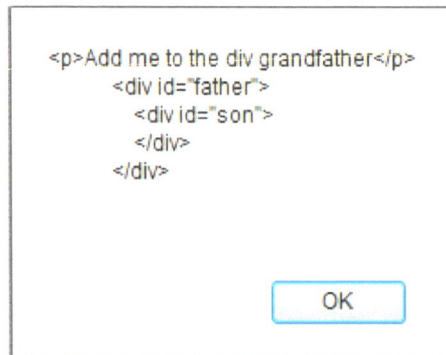

```
<p>Add me to the div grandfather</p>
<div id="father">
  <div id="son">
  </div>
</div>

                                    OK
```

NOTE

Programmers often examine intermediate values of variables while the program is running. There are many ways to do this. For this example, after the statement, `var currentHTML = grandfatherHandle.innerHTML;` we can verify the value claimed above by inserting a statement, `console.log(currentHTML);` or `alert(currentHTML);` or `window.confirm(currentHTML);`

## Positioning the script Tag

Before ending this example, one important thing that must be mentioned is the position of the `script` tag. Can we insert an external script file anywhere within the `body` element?

Let us read again the code in `ex-1-append.html`.

```
1.    <!DOCTYPE html>
2.    <html lang="en">
3.        <head>
4.            <meta content="text/html; charset=utf-8" http-equiv="Content-Type">
5.            <title>A Page Having Nested div Elements</title>
6.            <link rel="stylesheet" href="css/ex-1.css">
7.        </head>
```

```
8.          <body>
9.             <div id="grandfather">
10.                <div id="father">
11.                   <div id="son"></div>
12.                </div>
13.             </div>
14.             <script src="js/ex-1-append.js"></script>
15.          </body>
16.    </html>
```

ex-1-append.html

Let us move the `script` tag to the place between the opening `body` tag and the opening `div` tag for `grandfather`, like below.

```
<body>
    <script src="js/ex-1-append.js"></script>
    <div id="grandfather">
```

Test the page in the browser and you will find that this position change will disable the script to access the `div#grandfather` and the message will not be written to the outermost square.

This is caused by a very important rule that a web browser complies with for rendering `HTML` code.

> A web browser interprets HTML source sequentially in top-down approach. When a JavaScript script runs, it can only access to HTML elements that are written above its insertion point.

Before moving the `script` tag, the browser parses the `HTML` elements in the following order:

```
<div>: grandfather
<div>: father
<div>: son
<script>: js/ex-1-append.js
```

Because the script runs after the browser has parsed all of the three `div` elements, the script has access to all of them.

After moving of the `script` tag, the rendering order becomes

```
<script>: js/ex-1-append.js
<div>: grandfather
<div>: father
<div>: son
```

With this new sequence, the web browser runs the script before parsing the `div` elements. Thus, the script has no access to any of these `div` elements as they have not been parsed yet. As a consequence, the statement

```
var grandfatherHandle = document.getElementById("grandfather");
```

will not be able to get any element with the `id` value 'grandfather' because it has not been created yet. grandfatherHandle is set to `null` by the statement

```
var grandfatherHandle = document.getElementById("grandfather");
```

As a result, the subsequent processing would not be effective to a `null` reference.

To summarize, keep in mind that a web browser runs HTML source sequentially from top to down and a JavaScript script can only access to HTML elements which have been programmed above the opening `script` tag `<script>`.

> **NOTE**
>
> A rule of thumb is to place the script tag directly above the closing body tag </body>.

## Workout 2-3

Open a Scratchpad window, enter the following statements:

```
var newline = "<br>";
var string1 = "<h1>Today is Sunday.<h1>";
var string2 = "Enjoy!";
var string3 = string1 + newline + string2;
alert("After joining, the new string is " + string3);
```

Run the script. Describe the result.

## Workout 2-4

Based on three files from *Example 2.2*,

**File Listing**

```
ex-1-append.html, css/ex-1.css, js/ex-1-append.js
```

Do the following tasks:

1. Save ex-1-append.html as a new file named c2w4.html.

2. Save css/ex-1.css as a new file named css/c2w4.css.

3. Save js/ex-1-append.js as a new file named js/c2w4.js.

4. Open ex-1-append.html,

   → Locate the line

   ```
   <link rel="stylesheet" href="css/ex-1.css">
   ```

Replace the `ref` value `js/ex-1.css` with `js/c2w4.css`. Save the file.

$\rightarrow$ Locate the line

```
<script src="js/ex-1.js"></script>
```

Replace the `src` value `js/ex-1.js` with `js/c2w4.js`. Save the file.

5.  Now you need to modify `js/c2w4.js` to write a random number after the text "`Add me to the div grandfather`" in the `div grandfather`.

    Hint: In JavaScript, a random number can be generated by the statement

    ```
    var randomNumber = Math.random();
    ```

The expected page should show a picture similar to the this one:

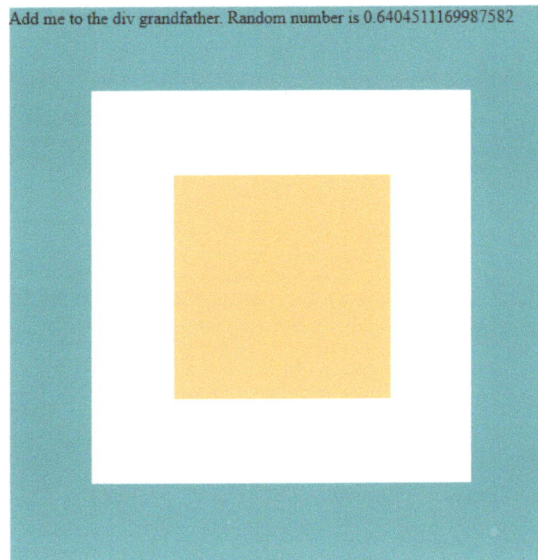

# Using Arrays

As previously discussed, a variable can store a string, a numerical value, a Boolean value or `null`. Very often, we need to store a list of related values in a single unit. JavaScript has the primitive array type and the `Array` object; both support this data storage requirement.

## Creating an Array

For instance, rather than making ten individual variables for storing ten star names, we can construct an array of ten elements/items; each stores one star name.

To create such an array and initialize each item with a star name, write the statement

```
var stars = ["Alpha", "Beta", "Gamma", "Delta", "Epsilon", "Theta", "Chi", "Zeta", "Mu",
"Eta"];
```

This statement uses the keyword `var` to declare an array named `stars`. On the right hand side of the statement, the initial values are enclosed in square brackets; the values are separated by commas. These initial values are sequentially assigned to each array item.

### Example 2.3

Sometimes, we need to create an empty array without any value for the time being and at a later time, add new items to the array. To do this, on the right hand side of the assignment, put a pair of square brackets with no value inside. In the following, the 1$^{st}$ statement shows declaring an empty array. The 2$^{nd}$ statement assigns `10` values to the array.

```
var stars = [];
stars = ["Alpha", "Beta", "Gamma", "Delta", "Epsilon", "Theta", "Chi", "Zeta", "Mu", "Eta"];
```

Open a Scratch window. Enter two statements above. Click Run button. Hightlight `stars` in either statement. Click Inspect button. A new pane opens on the right of the window, as shown below.

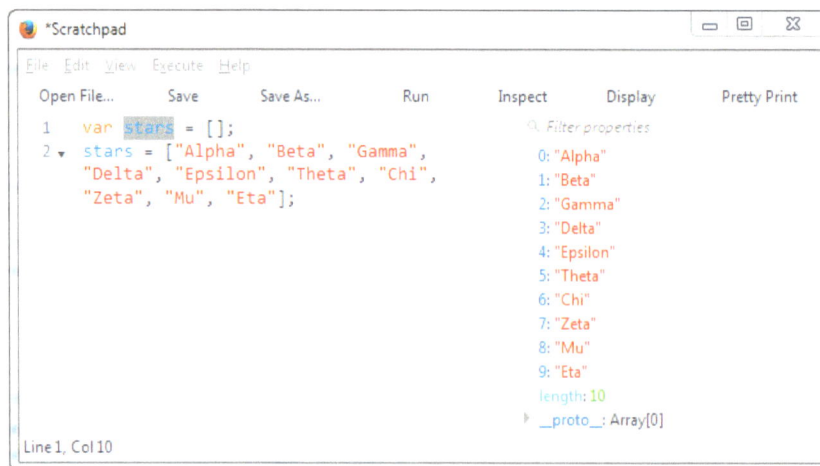

In this pane, the array is printed in a list of **11** key-value pairs. In the first **10** pairs, the key is an integer and the value is the value of an array item. The last key is `length` and its value is **10** from counting the items.

The integer keys 0~9 indicate the position of items in an array. We can use these integer keys to access array items. Next, we will discusss array notation for accessing array items.

## Accessing Array Items

To access the items in an array, use array notation.

### Syntax

```
ArrayName[indexValue]
```

This notation consists of an array name `ArrayName,` followed by an integer key `indexValue` inside a pair of square brackets. It returns the `(indexValue+1)-th` item.

`indexValue` is the key indicating position of the item to be visited. In JavaScript, the position index begins with zero and increments consecutively from the first item to the last one.

For example, with the previous declaration for the array `stars`, `stars[0]` returns the $1^{st}$ item in `stars`. To access the value in the $5^{th}$ element, the notation is `stars[4]`. The following table shows the relationship between the index, the array notation and the array item.

| position | 0 | 1 | 2 | 3 | 4 | 5 | 6 | 7 | 8 | 10 |
|----------|----------|----------|----------|----------|------------|----------|----------|----------|----------|----------|
| notation | stars[0] | stars[1] | stars[2] | stars[3] | stars[4] | stars[5] | stars[6] | stars[7] | stars[8] | stars[9] |
| value | "Alpha" | "Beta" | "Gamma" | "Delta" | "Epsilon" | "Theta" | "Chi" | "Zeta" | "Mu" | "Eta" |

### Example 2.4

Read the following statements:

```
var stars = [];
stars[0] = 'Alpha';
stars[4] = 'Epsilon';
```

In the beginning, the $1^{st}$ statement declares an empty array `stars`. Then the $2^{nd}$ statement assigns a string `"Alpha"` to the $1^{st}$ array item and the $3^{rd}$ statement writes a string `"Epsilon"` to the $5^{th}$ array item, respectively.

Run the statements above in Scratchpad. Inspect `stars` and the following is the resulting window.

```
*Scratchpad                                              ─ ▢ ✕

File  Edit  View  Execute  Help

  Open File...      Save        Save As...      Run      Inspect      Display      Pretty Print
  1    var stars = [];                            🔍 Filter properties
  2 ▾  stars[0] = 'Alpha';                              0: "Alpha"
  3 ▾  stars[4] = 'Epsilon';                            4: "Epsilon"
                                                        length: 5
                                                      ▸ __proto__: Array[0]

Line 1, Col 10
```

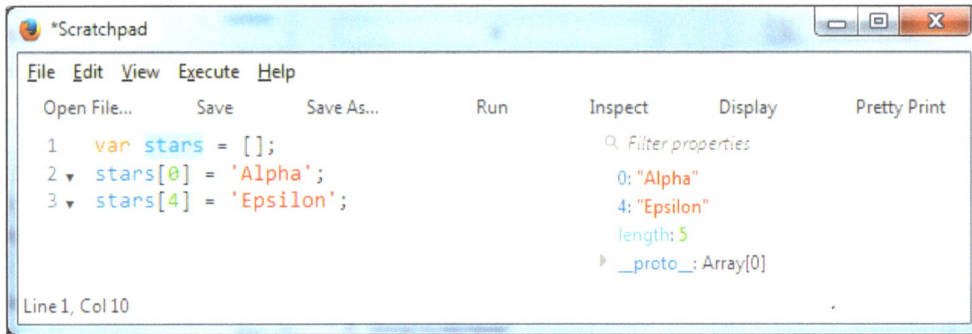

In the right pane of the screen capture above, it shows that in stars, only two items are defined with the key 0 and the key 4.

To examine the status of other items which have not been initialized with a specific value, say the item with the key 1, type stars[1] in line 4. Hightlight stars[1] and click Inspect. The result in the right pane shows the item under inspection is undefined. This implies that an array item is undefined until we assign it a value.

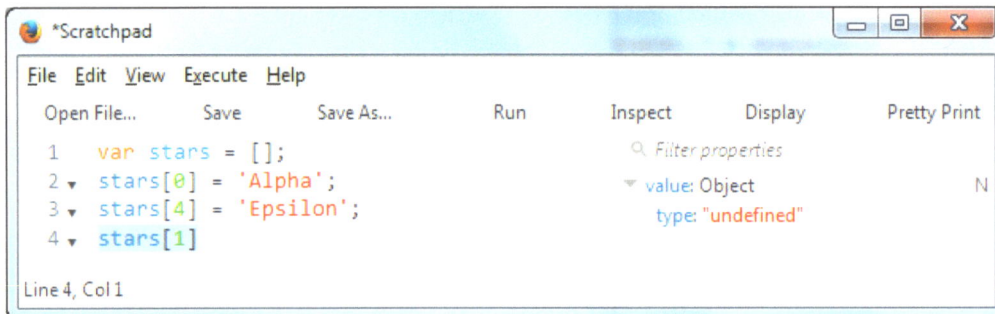

```
*Scratchpad                                              ─ ▢ ✕

File  Edit  View  Execute  Help

  Open File...      Save        Save As...      Run      Inspect      Display      Pretty Print
  1    var stars = [];                            🔍 Filter properties
  2 ▾  stars[0] = 'Alpha';                            ▾ value: Object                    N
  3 ▾  stars[4] = 'Epsilon';                              type: "undefined"
  4 ▾  stars[1]

Line 4, Col 1
```

NOTE

> An array item is undefined until it has been assigned with a specific value.

So far, the array that we have declared is primitive. In addition, JavaScript has the Array object. The Array object has a property 'length' which returns the total number of items or the current capacity of the array. To access a property of a JavaScript object, use a dot to connect the object name and the property name, for example, stars.length.

## Example 2.5

**File Listing**

        js/ex-2.js

Open a Scratchpad window and the web console. Enter and run the following code block in Scratchpad.

```
1.    // Declare an array and initialize 10 items
2.    var stars = [
3.       'Alpha',
4.       'Beta',
```

```
5.         'Gamma',
6.         'Delta',
7.         'Epsilon',
8.         'Theta',
9.         'Chi',
10.        'Zeta',
11.        'Mu',
12.        'Eta'
13.    ];
14.    // Print the 1st item in the web console
15.    console.log('The 1st item in stars: ' + stars[0]);
16.    // Print the 5th item in the web console
17.    console.log('The 5th item in stars: ' + stars[4]);
18.    // Find the total of items and print the total
19.    var size = stars.length;
20.    console.log('The total items in stars is ' + size);
21.    // Declare a variable as the array index
22.    var index = 6;
23.    // Use the variable in the array notation
24.    console.log('The item indexed by ' + index + ' is ' + stars[index]);;
```

js/ex-2.js

Four `console.log` statements print four lines in the console, as shown in the console window below.

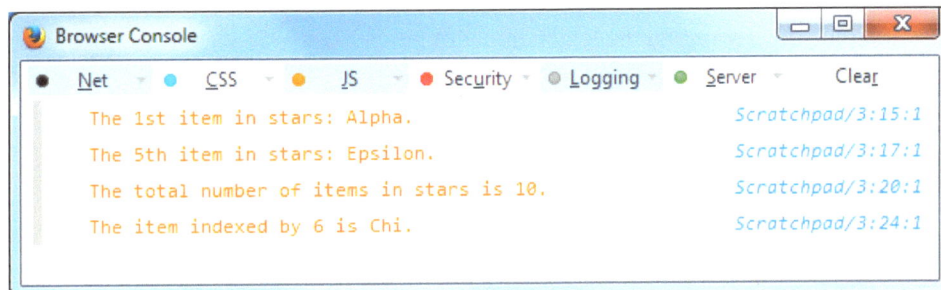

```
Browser Console

  Net      CSS      JS      Security   Logging   Server      Clear

    The 1st item in stars: Alpha.                    Scratchpad/3:15:1

    The 5th item in stars: Epsilon.                  Scratchpad/3:17:1

    The total number of items in stars is 10.        Scratchpad/3:20:1

    The item indexed by 6 is Chi.                    Scratchpad/3:24:1
```

## Workout 2-5

In Scratchpad, enter the following statement.

```
var combatPower = [10, 200, , , 15, , 187, ];
```

Run the statement. Inspect the array combatPower.

Based on the inspection result, answer the following questions:

1.  How many items in combatPower have been initialized with a number?

2.  Is the 3$^{rd}$ item defined in the array?

3.  To find the total number of items in the array, write an expression to access to the property length.

## Workout 2-6

Write a script to

1.  Declare an array named movies,

2.  Initialize the first 5 items with 5 movie names.

3.  Print each item in the web console.

4.  Access the length property to find the total number of movies in movies. Print the total in the console.

## Workout 2-7

Write a script to

1.  Declare an array named unitPrices,

2.  Initialize the array with 5 unit product price. Each price is a numerical value.

3.  Print each array item in the web console.

4.  Use the length property to find the total number of items in unitPrices. Print the total in the web console.

# Applying Array Methods

The `Array` object provides gadgets for processing array items. These tools are accessible by the methods with the `Array` object. JavaScript objects will be covered in Chapter 4.

> **NOTE**
>
> JavaScript is an object-oriented language. An object is described by properties and behavior. The behavior is represented by methods. A **method** is a procedure associated with an object. We access and use a method by its name. Calling/invoking a method is a term in programming to describe such cases. Some methods require input data as parameters and generate a result as well as returning it.

To access a method for an array, **dot** notation places a dot symbol between an array name and a method name. The following part shows several array methods and their use.

To add a new item, `"Iota"`, to the end of the array stars,

```
stars.push("Iota");
```

Add a new item, `"Iota"`, to the front of the array stars,

```
stars.unshift("Iota");
```

Remove an item from the end of the array stars,

```
stars.pop();
```

Remove an item from the front of the array stars,

```
stars.shift();
```

Find the index of the item, `"Beta"`, in the array stars. If the value is not found, it returns `-1`.

```
star.indexOf("Beta")
```

## Example 2.6

---

```
File Listing
        js/ex-3.js
```

The following script, in `js/ex-3.js`, provides examples of applying these `Array` methods to the array `stars`.

```
1.   var stars = [];
2.   stars.push("Beta");
3.   stars.push("Gamma");
4.   stars.push("Delta");
5.   var size = stars.length;
6.   console.log("Now we have pushed " + stars.length + " items into stars.");
7.   var position = stars.indexOf("Gamma");
```

```
8.    console.log("Gamma is at the position " + position + ".");
9.    stars.unshift("Alpha");
10.   console.log("After this addition, stars[0] = " + stars[0]);
11.   stars.shift();
12.   stars.pop();
13.   size = stars.length;
14.   console.log("Now stars has " + size + " item(s).");
```

js/ex-3.js

# Sorting an Array

If we want to sort array items in certain order, ascending or descending, `Array` object has the built-in method `sort` to sort all items in place and return the sorted array.

To sort an array by default comparing rules, use the following syntax:

Syntax

```
arrayName.sort();
```

The default `sort` function will convert all items in `arrayName` into strings and sort them by their Unicode value in ascending order.

The default JavaScript `sort` method will not be able to sort values numerically. To sort by numerical values, a custom comparing function needs to be given. This will be discussed in Chapter 4.

Unicode is an encoding standard that assigns each symbol a unique code.

In the Unicode chart, refer to http://unicodelookup.com/#latin, alphabets in uppercase take the code 65 to 90 in decimal notation and the set in lowercase take the code 97 to 122. The code of letters increases in alphabetical order. As in the chart at http://unicodelookup.com/#digit/1, the digits 0 through 9 are encoded from 48 through 57 in decimal notation.

## Example 2.7

Run the following script in Scratchpad.

```
var cityNames = ['Malaga', 'Florence', 'Paris', 'Chicago', 'Prague', 'Heidelberg'];
cityNames.sort();
```

`cityNames.sort()` will sort all the names and return the sorted array back to `cityNames`. Enter `cityNames` in the command line of the web console. You will see the names in `cityNames` are sorted alphabetically in ascending order.

```
>>  cityNames
←   Array [ "Chicago", "Florence", "Heidelberg", "Malaga", "Paris", "Prague" ]
```

## Example 2.8

Run the following script in Scratchpad.

```
var numbers = [20, -2, 100, 35];
numbers.sort();
```

Enter `numbers` in the command line of the web console. The display pane shows the array `numbers` after sorting.

```
>> numbers
← Array [ -2, 100, 20, 35 ]
```

It indicates that the default `sort` method always compare values as characters from left to right by Unicode. For numerical sorting, see "*Customizing the Sort Method*" of Chapter 7.

## Workout 2-8

Write a script to do the following tasks

1. Declare an array named `movies`;

2. Initialize the first 5 items with 5 movie names;

3. Print each movie by their index values in increasing order in the web console;

4. Access the `length` property to find the total number of movies in `movies` and print the total in the console;

5. Sort movie names;

6. After sorting, print each movie by their index values in increasing order in the web console.

# Chapter 3    BUILDING FUNCTIONS

What is a function? Are functions indispensable in computer programs? How do we create a function? Functions present a very important programming concept. This chapter covers functions and their importance to functionality of a computer program.

In the last chapter, we have discussed variables and arrays for storing data. Data is stored to be processed in order to complete target requirements. If any processing operations need to be repeated, instead of copying the same source code every time when the operations need to be performed, a function can be declared to group the operations into a special unit. Once declared, a function can be called whenever needed. Functions can be identified by their names.

> Frequently repeated computations and operations are grouped into a block, referred to as function. A function is a named block or section of statements that performs a specific task.

## Table of Contents

# Repeated Operations

Let us first introduce an example which illustrates one of the motivations to use functions. In this example, an array `stars` is declared by the following statement:

```
var stars = [
    'Alpha',
    'Beta',
    'Gamma',
    'Delta',
    'Epsilon',
    'Theta',
    'Chi',
    'Zeta',
    'Mu',
    'Eta'
];
```

The declaration above tells us that `stars` has `10` star names of type `string`. The purpose of this example is to display, on a web page, each star in one `HTML` paragraph within a `div` element.

## Example 3.1

We start this example with the following two script files.

---

`File Listing`

       `ex-4-nojs.html, css/ex-4.css, img/star.png`

### *Create and style a web page*

The web page is given in the `HTML` file `ex-4-nojs.html`. Initially, the page only contains one `div` element which has the `id` value `stars`.

```
1.  <!DOCTYPE html>
2.  <html lang="en">
3.      <head>
4.          <meta content="text/html; charset=utf-8" http-equiv="Content-Type">
5.          <title>Learn Functions</title>
6.          <link rel="stylesheet" href="css/ex-4.css">
7.      </head>
8.      <body>
9.          <div id ="stars"></div>
10.     </body>
11. </html>
```

ex-4-nojs.html

The associated style sheets are declared in `css/ex-4.css`. It has one `@import` at-rule, three element selectors, one `id` selector and one `::before` rule.

```css
1.    @import url(https://fonts.googleapis.com/css?family=Oswald);
2.    body {
3.        background-color:#666666;
4.        font-family: 'Oswald', 'Futura', sans-serif;
5.    }
6.    div {
7.        position: absolute;
8.        margin: auto;
9.        width: 500px;
10.       top: 0;
11.       right: 0;
12.       bottom: 0;
13.       left: 0;
14.   }
15.   p {
16.       border-bottom: 1px #F4EBC3 dotted;
17.       margin-left: 5px;
18.       margin-right: 5px;
19.       font-size: 150%;
20.   }
21.   p::before {
22.       content: "";
23.       display: inline-block;
24.       background-image: url(../img/star.png);
25.       width: 40px;
26.       height: 40px;
27.       margin-right: 20px;
28.   }
29.   #stars {
30.       color: #F4EBC3;
31.   }
```

css/ex-4.css

### *Load the web page*

Load `ex-4-nojs.html` in a browser window. The file displays a blank dark gray page.

### *Display the first star*

Now, we start to edit the JavaScript code to print each star on the page.

Open a Scratchpad window. Enter the following script in the Scratchpad window.

```javascript
1.  var stars = ["Alpha", "Beta", "Gamma", "Delta", "Epsilon", "Theta", "Chi", "Zeta", "Mu",
    "Eta"];
2.  var place = document.getElementById("stars");
3.  var index = 0;
4.  var line0 = "<p>The star indexed by " + index + " is " + stars[index] + ".</p>";
5.  place.innerHTML = line0;
```

Line 1 declares and initializes the array `stars`.

Line 2 gets a reference to the first HTML element whose `id` value is `stars`.

Line 3 defines an array `index` and set it to zero.

Line 4 makes a new string `line0` whose value is the HTML source content for printing a star with the key `index` in a paragraph. Read the following note for the plus sign.

> **NOTE**
>
> **The plus sign '+' is an operator which joins multiple strings into one string.** If index is 1, then `stars[index]` returns `'Beta'` and the statement
>
> `var line1 = "<p>The element indexed by " + index + " is " + stars[index] + ".</p>";`
>
> will join five strings to generate the following HTML source content in a new string
>
> `"<p>The element indexed by 1 is Beta.</p>"`
>
> Also, assign the new string to the variable `line1`.

Line 5 sets the `innerHTML` attribute of the `div` `stars`, to `line0`. Recall that setting a new value to the `innerHTML` attribute of an element will trigger the browser to render the element with the new `innerHTML` value.

The following window capture shows the script after applying Pretty Print.

```
*Scratchpad
File  Edit  View  Execute  Help

Open File...    Save      Save As...      Run      Inspect      Display      Pretty Print

 1 ▾ var stars = [
 2      'Alpha',
 3      'Beta',
 4      'Gamma',
 5      'Delta',
 6      'Epsilon',
 7      'Theta',
 8      'Chi',
 9      'Zeta',
10      'Mu',
11      'Eta'
12    ];
13    var place = document.getElementById('stars');
14    var index = 0;
15 ▾ var line0 = '<p>The star indexed by ' + index + ' is ' + stars[index] + '.</p>';
16    place.innerHTML = line0;

Line 16, Col 25
```

Keep `ex-4-nojs.html` open in the browser window. In the Scratchpad window, click Run button. A new text line "The element indexed by 0 is Alpha" appears on the page.

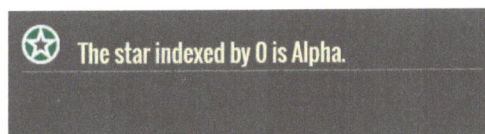

After printing the 1st star, to display the 2nd star, we need to increment `index` by one and `stars[index]` will return the 2nd star. The statement for incrementing `index` is

```
index = index + 1;
```

The statement, `index = index + 1`, updates `index` by incrementing its value by one. For instance, if `index` is 1, after the statement is executed, the value of `index` becomes 2.

Create a new paragraph and store its HTML content in `line1` by the following statement

```
var line1 = "<p>The star indexed by " + index + " is " + stars[index] + "</p>";
```

Then append the new paragraph `line1` to the last paragraph `line0`, and assign the joining content to the `div` stars. The following statement will generate the new content and print both paragraphs on the page.

```
place.innerHTML = line0 + line2;
```

After adding the above three statements, the new script becomes

1. `var stars = ["Alpha", "Beta", "Gamma", "Delta", "Epsilon", "Theta", "Chi", "Zeta", "Mu", "Eta"];`
2. `var place = document.getElementById("stars");`
3. `var index = 0;`
4. `var line0 = "<p>The star indexed by " + index + " is " + stars[index] + ".</p>";`
5. **`place.innerHTML = line0;`**
6. `index = index + 1;`
7. `var line1 = "<p>The element indexed by " + index + " is " + stars[index] + ".</p>";`
8. **`place.innerHTML = line0 + line1;`**

The script updates the HTML source content for the `div` stars twice in line 5 and line 7.

Run the script and two stars will display on the page.

Similarly, repeat adding the block for the rest of stars. In the end, the script becomes

```
1.    var stars = [
2.    'Alpha',
3.    'Beta',
4.    'Gamma',
5.    'Delta',
6.    'Epsilon',
7.    'Theta',
8.    'Chi',
9.    'Zeta',
10.   'Mu',
11.   'Eta'
12.   ];
13.   var place = document.getElementById('stars');
14.   var index = 0;
15.   var line0 = '<p>The star indexed by ' + index + ' is ' + stars[index] + '.</p>';
16.   place.innerHTML = line0;
```

```
17.    index = index + 1;
18.    var line1 = '<p>The star indexed by ' + index + ' is ' + stars[index] + '.</p>';
19.    place.innerHTML = line0 + line1;
20.    index = index + 1;
21.    var line2 = '<p>The star indexed by ' + index + ' is ' + stars[index] + '.</p>';
22.    place.innerHTML = line0 + line1 + line2;
23.    index = index + 1;
24.    var line3 = '<p>The star indexed by ' + index + ' is ' + stars[index] + '.</p>';
25.    place.innerHTML = line0 + line1 + line2 + line3;
26.    index = index + 1;
27.    var line4 = '<p>The star indexed by ' + index + ' is ' + stars[index] + '.</p>';
28.    place.innerHTML = line0 + line1 + line2 + line3 + line4;
29.    index = index + 1;
30.    var line5 = '<p>The star indexed by ' + index + ' is ' + stars[index] + '.</p>';
31.    place.innerHTML = line0 + line1 + line2 + line3 + line4 + line5;
32.    index = index + 1;
33.    var line6 = '<p>The star indexed by ' + index + ' is ' + stars[index] + '.</p>';
34.    place.innerHTML = line0 + line1 + line2 + line3 + line4 + line5 + line6;
35.    index = index + 1;
36.    var line7 = '<p>The star indexed by ' + index + ' is ' + stars[index] + '.</p>';
37.    place.innerHTML = line0 + line1 + line2 + line3 + line4 + line5 + line6 + line7;
38.    index = index + 1;
39.    var line8 = '<p>The star indexed by ' + index + ' is ' + stars[index] + '.</p>';
40.    place.innerHTML = line0 + line1 + line2 + line3 + line4 + line5 + line6 + line7 + line8;
41.    index = index + 1;
42.    var line9 = '<p>The star indexed by ' + index + ' is ' + stars[index] + '.</p>';
43.    place.innerHTML = line0 + line1 + line2 + line3 + line4 + line5 + line6 + line7 + line8 +
       line9;
```

js/ex-4-scratchpad.js

Now, click Run button, the web page should display all of 10 stars as below.

The star indexed by 0 is Alpha.

The star indexed by 1 is Beta.

The star indexed by 2 is Gamma.

The star indexed by 3 is Delta.

The star indexed by 4 is Epsilon.

The star indexed by 5 is Theta.

The star indexed by 6 is Chi.

The star indexed by 7 is Zeta.

The star indexed by 8 is Mu.

The star indexed by 9 is Eta.

## *Save the script*

After the script draft in the Scratchpad window has been successfully tested, we can save the script to a file. Name it js/ex-4.js.

## *Link the page with the script*

To link the web page to js/ex-4.js, in ex-4-nojs.html, insert a script tag before the closing body tag.

```
<script src="js/ex-4.js"></script>
```

Save the page to a new HTML file named ex-4.html.

At this point, we have completed this example. The complete script files are listed below.

## File Listing

```
ex-4.html, css/ex-4.css, js/ex-4.js, img/star.png
```

## *Observe the script*

Let us read the code in js/ex-4.js. Noticeably, the same operations are repeated for each star. The lines declaring variables, line0 through line9, have the same right hand side

```
"<p>The star indexed by " + index + " is " + stars[index]+".</p>"
```

Each time this part is run, it generates a new value because index has been incremented by one and stars[index] returns the next star.

If stars has 100 elements, we have to repeat typing the same block for 100 times. Is this repetition pratical for an array having thousands of elements? Definitely, it is not a good programming style to make such an amount of repetitions. Additionally, repetition of code deteriorates the visual appearance of a program, which may make it harder for others to read it.

We can resolve this issue easily by using a function or a loop. Next we will study the concept of function.

The concept of loop will be covered in Chapter 8.

# Function Declaration

In the previous example, there are many repeated code lines in `js/ex-4.js`. A function can reduce the lines in a program by grouping repeatedly-used code into a block. A function should have an objective.

There are two ways in JavaScript to create a function: function declaration and function expression.

*Function expression is covered in a later section "Function Expression".*

A function declaration uses the keyword `function` and it consists of a signature and a body. A function signature distinguishes one function from others.

Syntax

```
function functionName([parameter1, parameter2,…])
{
    [function body]
    [return statement]
}
```

## Function Signature

The *signature* part, highlighted in yellow, provides the information for identifying the function.

A function signature consists of three parts:

→ The keyword `function`

→ A function name that should describe the objective of the function.

By convention, a function name is a verb or a verb phrase, such as "calculateAverage", or just "average", with the first letter in lowercase for the first word and in uppercase for the following words if any.

→ A pair of parentheses with zero or more parameters inside.

The prior information to be needed for starting a function is termed "parameter". Parameters are listed inside parentheses and appears as variable names. No declaration is needed for function parameters. When the function is triggered in the program, the parameters will transport the information from outside into the function.

*Function parameters are names of the values that a function must be provided prior to execution.*

## Function Body

The *body* part contains statements that implement the steps for accomplishing the objective. The function body is enclosed in curly brackets. After the function is executed, it may return the processing result at the end of the function body. Imagine a function as a self-contained box, then its function parameters are the input into the box and returned data are the output flowing out of the box.

In the following, we declare two functions by using the keywords **function** and **return**.

## Example 3.2

A function, `reminder`, is declared to open an alert box displaying a specific reminder "Clock out!"

```
function reminder() {
    window.alert("Clock out!");
}
```

The first line, the signature line, tells us the function name `reminder`.

The function name is always followed by a pair of parentheses. As this function does not need any prior information in the signature line, there is no parameter listed inside the parentheses.

After making the signature line, a *left curly bracket* begins the function body in blue and a *right curly bracket* ends the body. All of the operations that belong to this function must be enclosed in the function body.

This function is very simple and it only does one operation, namely opening an alert box for a message "Clock out!"

Often, functions are more complex than `reminder`. They usually contain more than one statement and require parameters for passing input data into the function body.

## Example 3.3

This example declares a function `calcArea` that calculates the area of a given rectangle and returns the area. To calculate the area of a rectangle, we need two numbers for width and height.

To declare such a function, we write the following statement block.

```
function calcArea(width, height) {
    return width*height;
}
```

Separated by a comma, two parameters, `width` and `height`, are listed in the signature line.

Parameters are used within the function body in the same way as variables. By means of these two parameters, we can use this function to calculate the area of any rectangle as long as width and height are correctly passed to the function.

> A function does not run itself. The next section "Function Call" will explain how to run a function.

If a function is expected to produce a result, the keyword **return** can return the result at the end of the function body. The `return` statement should be placed above the closing curly bracket.

In the function body, the calculated area is returned as a product of `width` and `height`. Following the keyword `return`, it can be a local variable, an expression, an array or other data structures.

Where is the result returned to? This will be explained in the next section "Function Call".

**NOTE**

There are many ways of describing a function. We can briefly describe the function calcArea as "The function `area` takes two numbers, width and height, calculates the area and returns it.

All roads lead to Rome. There are differenct ways to declare a function. The following is an alternative to declaring `calcArea`. A local variable `area` is created to store the area and the `return` statement returns `area`.

```
function calcArea (width, height) {
    var area = width * height;
    return area;
}
```

This alternative shows an important programming concept: variable scope. JavaScript has two scopes, local and global. If a variable is declared inside a function, the variable is local which means it is only visible within the function while invisible in the area outside the function. We will discuss more about the scope in the section "*Code Reconstruction*".

# Function Call

A function will not be executed by itself until a statement is written to call or invoke the function. A programmer often uses these two terms `'call'` and `'invoke'` exchangeably even though they were coined initially for slightly different use.

## Example 3.4

This example shows how to call a function that has been declared.

---

`FileListing`

        js/ex-3-4.js

In the following script, the first part in lines 1 through 7 include two function declarations from *Example 3.2* and *Example 3.3*. The second part, in lines 8 through 12, shows the examples of calling a function.

```
1.    function reminder(){
2.        window.alert("Clock out!");
3.    }
4.    function calcArea(width, height) {
5.        var area = width * height;
6.        return area;
7.    }
8.    reminder();
9.    var area = calcArea(3, 4);
10.   console.log("The area of a rectangle 3 by 4 is " + area + ".");
11.   area = calcArea(10, 15);
12.   console.log("The area of a rectangle 10 by 15 is " + area + ".");
```

js/ex-3-4.js

The first thing that you should do is test the script in Scratchpad. Enter the script and run the script. You can also inspect the variables and functions in the web console.

If the script has been correctly entered in Scratchpad, you will see the message `'Clock out!'` in an alert box. Press OK to close this alert, then the two following logs appear in the web console:

        The area of a rectangle 3 by 4 is 12.
        The area of a rectangle 10 by 15 is 150.

The result above indicates that both functions have been executed successfully.

When the JavaScript interpreter finds, in lines 1 through 3, a function declaration named `reminder`, the interpreter will invisibly pull the declaration to the top of the script, but does not run the function body until seeing a calling statement to the function in line 8. The same procedure happens to the function `calcArea`.

Line 8 shows a statement that invokes a function having no parameter or return. Simply write its name followed by a pair of parentheses.

        reminder();

The statement in line 9

```
var area = calcArea(3, 4);
```

shows a statement that calls a function with two parameters and a return value. The numbers 3 and 4 in the function call are often referred to as `arguments`. They are values to be passed in order to the function parameters. In the above example, 3 is passed to the parameter `width` and 4 to the parameter `'height'`.

> The parameters in a function call are referred to as arguments.
>
> In a function call, arguments are values to be passed to a function's parameters.

The function call, `var area = calcArea(3, 4)`, does the following steps:

Step 1.   Invoke the function `calcArea`;

Step 2.   Pass two argument values, 3 and 4, to the parameters `width` and `height`;

Step 3.   Run the function body of `calcArea`

Step 4.   Write the function return into the global variable `area`.

A function can be used whenever needed in a program. Line 11 calls the function `area` again to calculate the area for another rectangle with a width `10` and a height `15`.

# Function Expression

In JavaScript, a function can be anonymous without a name. An anonymous function is treated as an expression, known as a function expression. A function expression can be assigned to a variable. See the following syntax to assign an anonymous function to a variable `myfunction`.

### Syntax

```
var myfunction = function([parameter1, parameter2,…]){
    [function body]
};
```

Pay attention to the ending mark ';' because this is an assignment statement and a JavaScript statement ends with a semicolon.

## Example 3.5

The following code gives an example which assigns an anonymous function as an expression to a variable `area` and calls the function with the variable name `area`.

```
1.    var area = function(width, height) {
2.      return width*height;
3.    };
4.    console.log("The area of a rectangle 3 by 4 is " + area(3,4) + ".");
```

The first line assigns a function expression to a variable `area`. The function expression begins with the keyword `function` and ends at the closing curly bracket. Line 4 shows we can use the variable name to invoke the anonymous function.

Enter the code in Scratchpad. Run the code and it will display `12` in the web console.

If you move line 4 to the top of the script before the function expression, run the script again. A type error will be generated in Scratchpad:

```
/*
Exception: TypeError: area is not a function
@Scratchpad/1:1:52
*/
```

This is caused by the way that the JavaScript interpreter renders function expressions. The following paragraph will give an explanation.

## Positioning Issue with Function Calls

If a function is created in a function declaration, a statement that calls the function can be placed before or after the function declaration. When a JavaScript script is interpreted, all of the declarations including variable names and functions with their bodies are always invisibly moved to the top, therefore a function call can be written either below or above the function declaration.

However, this is not the case with function expression. The JavaScript interpreter does not move the assignment part to the top. Therefore, if <u>a function is created in a function expression, a statement that calls the function must be written below the function expression</u>.

## Workout 3-1

Write a script which

1. creates a function expression to compute and return the average of two numbers;

2. Assigns the function expression to a variable;

3. Calls the function to compute the average of 99.98 and -15.68 and

4. Prints the average in the web console.

Test the script in Scratchpad.

# Restructure Code

After getting familiar with the concept of function, let us revisit the script `js/ex-4.js` of *Example 3.1* in the section "*Repeated Operations*". In *Example 3.1*, we have concluded that a function should be created to remove the repeated blocks in the code.

In the following example, we will describe the steps that will be taken for improving the script `js/ex-4.js` by using a function.

## Example 3.6

We start with *Example 3.1* in the files: `ex-4.html`, `css/ex-4.css`, `js/ex-4.js`, `img/star.png`.

### *Create a function*

First, declare a function that contains the statements which are repeated for each star in `js/ex-4.js`.

```
1.  function makeLine(index) {
2.      var index = index;
3.      var line = "<p>The element indexed by " + index + " is " + stars[index] + ".</p>";
4.      return line;
5.  }
```

In the function declaration above, the first line makes a function signature. The function name is `makeLine` and this function has a parameter `index`.

The function body includes two assignment statements and one `return` statement.

⟶ Line 2 declares a variable `index` and assigns it with the parameter `index`.

⟶ Line 3 declares a variable `line` which has an assignment part for the HTML source of printing the star name with the key `index` in an HTML paragraph.

⟶ At the end, the keyword `return` returns `line`.

### *Understand variable scope*

Before continuing work with the stars, it is good for us to know the following rules underlying the variable scope.

- The **scope of a variable** outlines the area where the variable is accessible.

- Two most common JavaScript scopes are **local scope (function scope)** and **global scope**.

- Variables in the same scope cannot have the same name.

- Variables can have the same name if their scopes are different.

- Each function defines its own local scope. Any variables that are declared within a function is only visible locally inside the function, so they are **local variables or function variables**.

- All local variables in a function are destroyed immediately after the function terminates. The computer memory they have taken is freed up.

- A variable declared outside any function is visible globally in the context of the entire program, referred to as **global variable**.

- A global variable is visible and accessible within any function.

- Inside a function, we can declare a local variable having the same name with a global variable which has been declared. In such as case, in the function scope,

    a. Every time we write the name, the name only points to the local variable. The global variable of the same name becomes invisible within the function.

    b. The local variable will take precedence over the global variable inside a function.

Applying these concepts to the function declaration `makeLine`, we know that

→ There is a function parameter `index`;

→ There are two local variables, `index` and `line`;

→ In line 2, the statement

```
var index = index;
```

assigns the parameter `index` to the local variable `index`.

## *Call the function*

Recall that in `js/ex-4.js`, the variable `index` has been declared as a global variable for being the array index.

Now let us write a statement to call `makeLine` with the global `index` being the argument. The following statement meets this need and assigns the function return to a variable `line`

```
var line = makeLine(index);
```

`makeLine(index)` calls the function `makeLine`, passing the value of the global variable `index` as the argument to the function parameter `index`.

Prior to calling `makeLine`, if the global `index` is 0, `makeLine` will make an HTML paragraph for the 1st star. After calling, increment `index` and the next call will make a paragraph for the 2nd star, and so on until the last star.

By this idea, we can restructure `js/ex-4.js`.

In `js/ex-4.js`, add the function declaration of `makeLine` and substitute each of ten paragraph generating statements with a function call. Save the restructured code in `js/ex-5.js`.

```
1.  var stars = ["Alpha", "Beta", "Gamma", "Delta", "Epsilon", "Theta", "Chi", "Zeta", "Mu",
    "Eta"];
2.  var place = document.getElementById("stars");
3.  var index = 0;
4.  var line0 = makeLine(index);
```

```
5.      index = index + 1;
6.      var line1 = makeLine(index);
7.      index = index + 1;
8.      var line2 = makeLine(index);
9.      index = index + 1;
10.     var line3 = makeLine(index);
11.     index = index + 1;
12.     var line4 = makeLine(index);
13.     index = index + 1;
14.     var line5 = makeLine(index);
15.     index = index + 1;
16.     var line6 = makeLine(index);
17.     index = index + 1;
18.     var line7 = makeLine(index);
19.     index = index + 1;
20.     var line8 = makeLine(index);
21.     index = index + 1;
22.     var line9 = makeLine(index);
23.     place.innerHTML = line0 + line1 + line2 + line3 + line4 + line5 + line6 + line7 + line8 +
        line9;
24.     function makeLine(index) {
25.         var line = "<p>The element indexed by " + index + " is " + stars[index] + ".</p>";
26.         return line;
27.     }
```

js/ex-5.js

At the same time, change the script tag in ex-4.html. Copy the HTML source to a new HTML file, ex-5.html.

```
1.      <!DOCTYPE html>
2.      <html lang="en">
3.          <head>
4.              <meta content="text/html; charset=utf-8" http-equiv="Content-Type">
5.              <title>Use functions</title>
6.              <link rel="stylesheet" href="css/ex-4.css">
7.          </head>
8.          <body>
9.              <div id ="stars"></div>
10.             <script src="js/ex-5.js"></script>
11.         </body>
12. </html>
```

ex-5.html

Open ex-5.html in the browser. It should prints the same 10 lines as ex-4.html does.

Two completed script files are listed below.

## File Listing

        ex-5.html, js/ex-5.js, css/ex-4.css, img/star.png

### *Use the array*

In term of visual appearance, `js/ex-5.js` can be further improved. As far as we know, ten variables, `line0` through `line9`, all store the same type of data, a string representing the HTML source that creates a paragraph.

Therefore, we can move them into an array, which makes data management in a program more systematic and effective.

We declare a new array, `lines`. Each item in `lines` will store a returned paragraph upon calling the function `makeLine` over a star with a specific index.

The modified code is in the file `js/ex-6.js`. The associated web page file is `ex-6.html`.

## File Listing

```
        ex-6.html, js/ex-6.js, css/ex-4.css, img/star.png
```

```
1.   var stars = ["Alpha", "Beta", "Gamma", "Delta", "Epsilon", "Theta", "Chi", "Zeta", "Mu",
     "Eta"];
2.   var lines = [];
3.   var place = document.getElementById("stars");
4.   var index = 0;
5.   lines[index] = makeLine(index);

6.   index = index + 1;
7.   lines[index] = makeLine(index);
8.   index = index + 1;
9.   lines[index] = makeLine(index);
10.  index = index + 1;
11.  lines[index] = makeLine(index);
12.  index = index + 1;
13.  lines[index] = makeLine(index);
14.  index = index + 1;
15.  lines[index] = makeLine(index);
16.  index = index + 1;
17.  lines[index] = makeLine(index);
18.  index = index + 1;
19.  lines[index] = makeLine(index);
20.  index = index + 1;
21.  lines[index] = makeLine(index);
22.  index = index + 1;
23.  lines[index] = makeLine(index);

24.  place.innerHTML = lines[0] + lines[1] + lines[2] + lines[3] + lines[4] + lines[5] + lines[6] +
     lines[7] + lines[8] + lines[9];
25.  function makeLine(index) {
26.      var index = index;
27.      var line = "<p>The element indexed by " + index + " is " + stars[index] + ".</p>";
28.      return line;
29.  }
```

Obviously, lines 6 through 23 make nine copies of a set of two statements. There is space for further improvements. In the last section of this chapter, after introducing a special function related to the `Array` object, we will revisit the above example.

## Workout 3-2

Declare a function which meets the following requirements:

1. The function name is `calcAverage`.

2. Takes two parameters, named `number1` and `number2`.

3. Returns the average of `number1` and `number2`.

## Workout 3-3

Declare a function `printSlogan` that

1. Takes two string parameters;

2. Joins two given strings

3. Returns the resulting string after joining.

Hint: Enter the function declaration in Scratchpad. Test it in the web console.

For example, if the statement `printSlogan('Every day is", "Friday")` is entered in the command line bar, a string `'Every day is Friday'` will be displayed.

## Workout 3-4

Write a script to

1. Declare a function, `calcAverage(number1, number2)`, which takes two numbers, computes their average and returns the average. The JavaScript expression to calculate the average of two numbers a and b is `(a + b)/2`.

2. Declare two variables, `num1` and `num2`. Initialize each with a numerical value (either an integer or a decimal number).

3. Call `calcAverage` to find the average of `num1` and `num2`.

4. Display the average in the web console.

## Workout 3-5

Write a script to

1. Create an array `unitCosts`.

2. Initialize the array with 5 unit product prices.

3. Declare a function, `listPrice(index)`, which displays the item `unitCosts[index]` in the web console. For example, if the first element is `20.59`, then the function call `listPrice(0)` should write the following text in the console.

```
The unit price at position 0 is $20.59.
```

4. Call the function `listPrice` for each item in `unitCosts`.

Run the script in Scratchpad. It should print all the prices in the web console.

# Immediately Invoked Function Expression

If a function is written for an ad-hoc purpose and it is executed whereever the function is in the program, the function can be written in an **IIFE**, an acronym for *immediately invoked function expression*. The syntax of an IIFE is in the following:

Syntax

```
var result = (function() {
    [function body]
    [return statement]
}());
```

The variable `result` will store the return value from the `IIFE`. Pay attention to the syntax, featuring multiple pairs of various parentheses. Leaving any parenthesis open will cause a syntax error.

## Example 3.7

```
1.    var area = (function() {
2.        var width = 3;
3.        var height = 4;
4.        var size = width*height;
5.        var message = "The area of a rectangular with a width " + width + " and a height " +
          height + " is " + size;
6.        return message;
7.    }());
8.    console.log(area);
```

Run the script in Scratchpad.

The script above uses an `IIFE` to construct a string. The script runs the function expression within the curly brackets, assigns the return a string to the variable `area`, and print `area` in the web console.

> An `IIFE` is a JavaScript function that runs immediately right after it is declared.

## Workout 3-6

Write a script which creates an `IIFE` to compute and return the average of two numbers, `99.98` and `-15.68`, stores the average in a variable and prints the average in the web console.

For this exercise, you may apply the `toPrecision` method of the `Number` object to specify the number of significant digits for a number. The `toPrecision` method returns a string representing a `Number` object to the specified precision.

For instance, the expression

```
(5.1234).toPrecision(2)
```

produces a string `'5.1'`.

The statement

```
console.log((5.1234).toPrecision(2));
```

will output 5.1 in the web console.

The following script

```
var num = 5.123456;
console.log(num.toPrecision(4));
```

will print 5.123 in the web console.

# The Array Method forEach & Callback

It is common practice to apply the same operations to every item of an array. For example, if we want to determine whether the items in an array match a specific word, we scan the whole array and make a comparison per each item. In programming, this process is referred to as iterating or looping through an array, which is supported in JavaScript by `for` loops, `do-while` loops and `while` loops. These loop structures will be discussed in Chapter 8. Here, we introduce a specific JavaScript `Array` method, `forEach`.

It should be pointed out that when a web page interacts with a user, the user input may introduce changes to data, i.e., inserting a new item, deleting an existing item or modifying the item. Therefore, in many cases, the total number of items in an array is subject to change during the course of execution.

The `forEach` method automatically loops over every array item and executes a provided function. The provided function is referred to as *callback*. By associating `forEach` with a callback, we need neither to count the items in the array nor use array notation.

Syntax

```
array.forEach(callback);
```

where `callback` is a function to be passed as an argument to the `forEach` method. The `forEach` method will run the `callback` once for each array item.

> In general, a callback function is a function that is passed to another function.

NOTE

> When using the `forEach` method, keep in mind that this method is nonstandard and it may not be supported in some JavaScript implementations such as IE8.

## Example 3.8

With `forEach`, we are able to work with the stars again. Based on *Example 3.6* in the following files:

```
ex-6.html, js/ex-6.js, css/ex-4.css, img/star.png,
```

we will apply the `forEach` method to `js/ex-6.js`. This can significantly decrease the statement lines. The function `makeLine` needs modifications to become a valid callback.

### Apply forEach method

To apply the `forEach` method to run `makeLine` for each `stars` item, write the statement

```
stars.forEach(makeLine);
```

where a callback, `makeLine`, is passed to `forEach` and `forEach` invokes the callback for every `stars` item.

## Construct a callback

To make a valid callback function, rewrite the previous function `makeLine` to the following:

```
function makeLine(element, index) {
    lines[index] = "<p>The element indexed by " + index + " is " + element + "</p>";
}
```

The callback function has two parameters, `element` and `index`.

> No matter what parameter names are used in the callback, the first parament returns the current array item and the second parameter is the index of the current item.

Every time when the callback is triggered by `forEach` with an item, `forEach` will automatically pass the item to the first parameter and its index to the second parameter.

Instead of a `return` statement, we change `makeLine` to make it assign the result directly into a global array, `lines`. Because `lines` is declared outside the function, it is a global array which is accessible and changable inside the function.

After the `forEach` statement is completed, `lines[0]` through `lins[9]` are all set.

The new code is shown below, as in `js/ex-7.js`.

```
1.  var stars = ["Alpha", "Beta", "Gamma", "Delta", "Epsilon", "Theta", "Chi", "Zeta", "Mu",
    "Eta"];
2.  var lines = [];
3.  stars.forEach(makeLine);
4.  var place = document.getElementById("stars");
5.  place.innerHTML = lines[0] + lines[1] + lines[2] + lines[3] + lines[4] + lines[5] + lines[6] +
    lines[7] + lines[8] + lines[9];
6.  function makeLine(element, index) {
7.      lines[index] = "<p>The element indexed by " + index + " is " + element + "</p>";
8.  }
```

*js/ex-7.js*

After making these changes, the completed example is in the following files:

```
File Listing
        ex-7.html, css/ex-4.css, js/ex-7.js, img/star.png
```

## Use IIFE

Instead of declaring a callback in a named function, we also can provide the callback as an anonymous function by moving the function declaration into the `forEach` statement. Pay attention to the syntax when using anonymous functions.

```
1.  var stars = ["Alpha", "Beta", "Gamma", "Delta", "Epsilon", "Theta", "Chi", "Zeta", "Mu",
    "Eta"];
2.  var lines = [];
```

```
3.    stars.forEach(function (element, index){
4.        lines[index] = "<p>The element indexed by " + index + " is " + element + "</p>";
5.    });
6.    var place = document.getElementById("stars");
7.    place.innerHTML = lines[0] + lines[1] + lines[2] + lines[3] + lines[4] + lines[5] + lines[6] +
       lines[7] + lines[8] + lines[9];
```

*js/ex-8.js*

Comparing `js/ex-4.js` with `js/ex-8.js`, the code becomes more concise.

Now we have done with processing the stars. The final files are:

## File Listing

ex-8.html, css/ex-4.css, js/ex-8.js, img/star.png

## Workout 3-7

Use `js/ex-8.js` as an example. Create a web page where you place a `div` element whose `id` value is `'list'`. Write a script to create an array consisting of 5 movie names and display movie names alphabetically with each movie name in one `HTML` paragraph inside the `div` element `'list'`.

# Chapter 4     MODELING REAL-WORLD OBJECTS

From the previous chapters, we have learned that *variables* and *arrays* are two data storage structures, and a *function* is a sequence of activities to complete a task. Besides, JavaScript is an object-oriented language and it supports *objects*.

A real world object can be modeled in a JavaScript object. For instance, in a web catalog which lists items of various types, such as books, photos, hotels, and cars, each type must have a name as well as other properties that are specific to the type. In this case, we can represent these item types in JavaScript objects.

An object has a composite structure that is made up of two components types, properties and methods. A JavaScript object packs a set of properties and methods together.

> The variables within an object is referred to as *properties* and the functions with an object is termed *methods*.

The properties describe what the object is. The methods shows what the object can do and the operations that can be fulfilled by the object.

The names of properties and methods in an object are termed *key*.

    → A *key* is a name which identifies either a property or a method.

    → A *key* must be unique within the object scope.

    → A *key* can have a value, which makes a *key/value* pair.

Another concept related to object is *instance*.

> An instance is a concrete occurrence or implementation by assigning specific values to property keys.

In this book, the name 'object' implies *abstract* object type and 'instance' means *concrete* object examples. From an abstract object, we can produce many instances. For example, to distinguish a car model from other models, we must know about make, model, year and possibly, more other properties. So, the property keys for a car object can be make, `model` and `year`. For a `2010 Cruze from Chevrolet`, it makes an instance of three key/value pairs.

```
make: 'Chevrolet'
model: 'Cruze'
```

```
year: 2010
```

This chapter describes objects and instances for their creation and use.

## Table of Contents

# Creating an Instance

In JavaScript, an instance is created either using *literal notation* or *constructor notation*. Literal notation is mostly used if a program only needs a few instances. Introduced in the next section, constructor notation, is preferred for creating, especially on the fly, many instances of the same object type.

## Literal Notation

Example 4.1

This example shows syntax of *literal notation*.

---

**File Listing**

        js/literalnotation-car.js

The script file contains only one assignment statement which carries out two tasks:

1) Creates an instance with night key/value pairs including

    a.   Seven property keys: make, model, avatar, year, color, safety, currentSpeed

    b.   Two method keys: accelerate, brake

2) Assign the instance to a variable mycar.

See the statement in the following:

```
1.    var mycar = {
2.        make: 'Dodge',
3.        model: 'Charger',
4.        avatar: 'dodge.png',
5.        year: 2010,
6.        color: 'white',
7.        safety: 5,
8.        currentSpeed: 0,
9.        accelerate: function(mph) {
10.          this.currentSpeed += mph;
11.       },
12.       brake: function() {
13.          this.currentSpeed = 0;
14.       }
15.   };
```

js/literalnotation-car.js

When using literal notation, take into account the following rules:

- The content of instance must be enclosed in a pair of curly brackets.

- Key/value pairs can be in a single line or split into multiple lines.

- Key/value pairs are separated by a comma except for the last one.

- Each key/value pair represents either a property or a method.

- The keys must be unique within the instance.

- The key and its value are separated by a colon.

- If a key identifies a method, its value takes the form of an anonymous function.

In mycar, both method keys, accelerate and brake, are assigned with an anonymous function.

```
accelerate: function(mph) {
        this.currentSpeed += mph;
}
brake: function() {
        this.currentSpeed = 0;
}
```

## The Keyword this

Pay attention to the keyword this appearing in both anonymous functions.

> NOTE
>
> Within the context of this object instance, the keyword **this** refers to the current object, mycar.
> In the instance scope, to access a key, place a dot/period symbol between this and the key.

The line,

```
this.currentSpeed += mph;
```

assigns the parameter mph to the property key currentSpeed of the instance mycar.

The keyword this references the current instance mycar. Placing a dot between this and currentSpeed, this.currentSpeed is a reference to the property key 'currentSpeed ' of mycar.

> NOTE
>
> The operator "+=" is a shortcut arithmetic operator which combines two operations, addition
> and assignment. Line 9 in js/literalnotation-car.js
> ```
>         this.currentSpeed += mph;
> ```
> is equivalent to two statements
> ```
>         var update = this.currentSpeed + mph;
>         this.currentSpeed = update;
> ```
> It updates currentSpeed with an increase of the amount in mph.

# Verify the Instance

To verify whether `mycar` has been created or not, open `js/literalnotation-car.js` in Scratchpad. Run the script. Then switch to the web console, type `mycar` in the command line bar and press `Enter`.

The following log verifies that `mycar` exists and shows its content inside curly brackets. Notice that two anonymous functions are not written in full; instead, a new notation is displayed for each method key: `mycar.accelerate()` and `mycar.brake()`. This will be explained in the section *"Calling a Method"*.

```
●  Net  ▾  ●  CSS  ▾  ●  JS  ▾  ● Security  ▾  ● Logging  ▾  ● Server  ▾    Clear      🔍 Filter output

 ≫  mycar
 ←  Object { make: "Dodge", model: "Charger", avatar: "chevrolet.png", year: 2010, color: "white",
    safety: 5, currentSpeed: 0, accelerate: mycar.accelerate(), brake: mycar.brake() }

 ≫ |
```

Similiarly, to create a second car instance, `mycar2`, simply use the same structure, except with different values for the property keys.

```
1.  var mycar2 = {
2.      make: 'Ford',
3.      model: 'F150',
4.      Avatar: 'fordf150.png',
5.      year: 2014,
6.      color: 'black',
7.      safety: 5,
8.      currentSpeed: 0,
9.      accelerate: function (mph) {
10.       this.currentSpeed += mph;
11.     },
12.     brake: function () {
13.       this.currentSpeed = 0;
14.     }
15. };
```

Noticeably, the structure of these two car instances is exactly the same because they are of the same object type, `car`, even though each defines a concrete car.

Think about creating `100` car instances in a program. Would literal notation be effective? Probably not, because we need to write a statement for each car instance such that the total statements will be `100`. Luckily, most programming languages have features to eliminate tedious code repetition. *Constructor notation* with the keyword `new`, presents such a solution, introduced in the next section *"Declaring an Object"*.

It is worth mentioning that literal notation is the underlying structure in a web data format, *JavaScript Object Notation*, abbreviated to JSON (pronounced "Jason"). Derived from JavaScript, JSON has become very popular in web applications and social web sites.

## Workout 4-1

(Use `js/literalnotation-car.js` as an example) Write a script that creates an instance of college class. A college class is modeled by eight properties and one method.

The property keys are `department`, `courseNumber`, `title`, `year`, `semester`, `credit`, `capacity` and `enrollment`. The key values for the instance are specified below:

```
department: 'CS'
courseNumber: '340'
title: 'Introduction to Web Programming'
year: 2016
semester: 'fall'
credit: 3
capacity: 15
enrollment: 10
```

The method key is `seatsAvailable`. `seatsAvailable` calculates the number of seats which is currently available in a class by subtracting the `enrollment` value from the `capacity value`.

# Declaring an Object

If a program requires many instances of the same object type, *constructor notation* can be more efficient than *literal notation*.

## Constructor Notation with the Keyword new

In programming, a *constructor* is a factory which assembles new instances of a product. The constructor requires values for properties of the new instance. The properties should be declared as parameters of the constructor. To create a new instance, the keyword new invokes the constructor.

A constructor is a function with parameters carrying the properties values into a new instance to be created. The constructor declares *an abstract object* which is a factory for producing concrete instances.

We apply constructor notation to the example discussed in the previous section.

Example 4.2

---

`File Listing`

       js/constructornotation-car.js

The script generates the same result as `js/literalnotation.js` except that it creates two more car instances.

```
1.   // Declare a constructor Car
2.   function Car(make, model, avatar, year, color, safety, currentSpeed) {
3.       this.make = make;
4.       this.model = model;
5.       this.avatar = avatar;
6.       this.year = year;
7.       this.color = color;
8.       this.safety = safety;
9.       this.currentSpeed = currentSpeed;
10.      this.accelerate = function (mph) {
11.          this.currentSpeed += mph;
12.      };
13.      this.brake = function () {
14.          this.currentSpeed = 0;
15.      };
16.  }
17.  // Instantiate four new instances by applying the keyword new to the constructor Car
18.  var car1 = new Car('Dodge', 'Charger', 'dodge.png', 2010, 'white', 5, 0);
19.  var car2 = new Car('Ford', 'F150', 'fordf150.png', 2014, 'black', 5, 0);
20.  var car3 = new Car('Chevrolet', 'Cruze', 'chevrolet.png', 0, 'red', 5, 0);
21.  var car4 = new Car('Ford', 'Edge', 'ford.png', 2015, 'yellow', 5, 0);
```

## Declare a Constructor

Lines 2 through 16 in `js/constructornotation-car.js` declares a constructor. The name of the constructor is
`Car`.

> By convention, an object type name should be a noun or a noun phrase with the first letter of each word capitalized.

The object property keys contain names of the constructor parameters, `make`, `model`, `avatar`, `year`, `color`, `safety`
and `currentSpeed`. During the creation of a new car instance, the constructor needs the caller to pass zero or more
values to the parameters. If any values have been received by the constructor, they are assigned into the paired
parameters. Then the constructor assigns each parameter to its paired property key.

> A programmer often names the contructor parameters the same as the object property keys.

Different from the colons in *literal notation*, constructor notation uses assignment statements to assign a value or a
method to a key.

Lines 3 through 9 assign each constructor parameter to the paired property key that is designed for `Car`.

## Store the Constructor into a Function Expression

Recall the function expression in Chapter 3, we can also assign the constructor to a variable. The constructor in a
function expression is declared as below. Nothing was changed except that the function name after the
keyword `function` was removed.

```
var Car = function (make, model, year, color, safety, currentSpeed) {
    this.make = make;
    this.model = model;
    this.year = year;
    this.color = color;
    this.safety = safety;
    this.currentSpeed = currentSpeed;
    this.accelerate = function (mph) {
        this.currentSpeed += mph;
    };
    this.brake = function () {
        this.currentSpeed = 0;
    };
};
```

## Instantiate New Instances

How does a program call the constructor to create a new instance? See lines 18 through 21
of `js/constructornotation-car.js`.

Lines 18 and 19

```
var car1 = new Car('Dodge', 'Charger', 'dodge.png', 2010, 'white', 5, 0);

var car2 = new Car('Ford', 'F150', 'fordf150.png', 2014, 'black', 5, 0);
```

create two new cars and stores them into car1 and car2.

Each car is instantiated with the keyword new, followed by a function call to the constructor Car with seven argument values. These arguments will substitute the parameters of the constructor Car.

## Undefined Keys

In the cases where some property values are unknown until a later time, even though it will not incur syntax errors by only providing some or even none of arguments in the function call, for example,

```
var car3 = new Car('Chevrolet');

var car4 = new Car();
```

However, leaving a property key uninitialized will set the key to undefined, meaning the key has not been assigned a value. Possibly, an undefined key causes problems if it is used not very careful for calculations.

Thus, for the properties that are unknown during the creation time, assign an empty string " to the property of type string; for the property of type number, set a special number to mark the unitialized status and assigne this number to the key. Say, assign a zero to the key 'year' if the year of a car instance is unknown yet.

```
var car3 = new Car('Chevrolet', 'Cruze', 'chevrolet.png', 0, 'red', 5, 0);
```

A program can always update the key value for any previously uninitialized keys by an assignment statement. This is to be introduced in the next section "Accesing a Property".

## Verify the Instances

To verify four instances, car1, car2, car3 and car4, open js/constructornotation-car.js in Scratchpad. Run the script. Then switch to the web console, type each instance name in the command line bar and press Enter.

The following log shows the content in the display pane after running four commands.

```
●  Net  ▼ ●  CSS  ▼ ●  JS  ▼ ●  Security ▼ ◉ Logging ▼ ●  Server  ▼    Clear    🔍 Filter output

≫  car1
←  Object { make: "Dodge", model: "Charger", avatar: "dodge.png", year: 2010, color: "white",
   safety: 5, currentSpeed: 0, accelerate: Car/this.accelerate(), brake: Car/this.brake() }

≫  car2
←  Object { make: "Ford", model: "F150", avatar: "fordf150.png", year: 2014, color: "black",
   safety: 5, currentSpeed: 0, accelerate: Car/this.accelerate(), brake: Car/this.brake() }

≫  car3
←  Object { make: "Chevrolet", model: "Cruze", avatar: "chevrolet.png", year: 0, color: "red",
   safety: 5, currentSpeed: 0, accelerate: Car/this.accelerate(), brake: Car/this.brake() }

≫  car4
←  Object { make: "Ford", model: "Edge", avatar: "ford.png", year: 2015, color: "yellow", safety:
   5, currentSpeed: 0, accelerate: Car/this.accelerate(), brake: Car/this.brake() }

≫ |
```

Two method values are denoted by `Car/this.accelerate()` and `Car/this.brake()`. Recall that when `mycar` with literal notation is logged, the method values are `mycar.accelerate()` and `mycar.brake()`. Since an instance is created by a constructor, the instance does not own any method and it inherits all methods from the constructor. Thus, the constructor name prefixes both method values for indicating ownership.

## Workout 4-2

(Use `js/constructornotation-car.js` as an example.) Write a script which declares a constructor and instantiate a new instance.

The requirements are described below:

1. The constructor `Course` has eight properties and one method.

2. Eight property keys are named `department`, `courseNumber`, `title`, `year`, `semester`, `credit`, `capacity` and `enrollment`.

3. The method key is `seatsAvailable`. `seatsAvailable` calculates the number of seats which is available in a class by subtracting `enrollment` from `capacity`.

4. Use the constructor `Course` to instantiate a new course which has the following specific key values:

   ```
   department: 'CS'
   courseNumber: '340'
   title: 'Introduction to Web Programming'
   year: 2016
   semester: 'fall'
   credit: 3
   capacity: 15
   enrollment: 10
   ```

# Accessing a Property

There are two ways of accessing a property in an object: dot accessor and array notation.

## Use Dot Accessor

To access a key in an object or an instance, place a *dot* between object name and the key.

Syntax

```
instanceName.key
```

For instance, `car3.model` is a reference to the key `model` in the instance `car3`. Assuming that after `car3` has been constructed, the key `safety` of `car3` needs an update. The statement below will write the new value into the key `safety`.

```
car3.safety = 4;
```

The following two statements will update two keys for `car4`:

```
car4.make = "Tesla;
car4.model = 'Roadster';
```

## Use Array Notation

An alternative to the dot accessor is *array notation*.

Syntax

```
instanceName[key]
```

`key` is a string that is a property key of an object or an instance.

> **NOTE**
>
> When using array notation to access a property key in an object, the key is treated as a string and must be enclosed with quotes. In the accessor, `car3['make']`, make is quoted.

For instance, the expression, `car3['make']`, is an alternative to `car3.model`.

No matter whether an object is created by literal notation or constructor notation, we can always use either *dot accessor* or *array notation* to access its keys.

# Calling a Method

To invoke a method for an object instance, use a dot symbol to connect the instance name and a function call to the method.

## Syntax

```
instanceName.methodName([argument1, argument2, …]);
```

For example,

```
mycar.accelerate(20);

mycar.brake();
```

## Example 4.3

### File Listing

js/constructornotation-car-method.js

```javascript
1.    // Declare a constructor Car
2.    function Car(make, model, avatar, year, color, safety, currentSpeed) {
3.      this.make = make;
4.      this.model = model;
5.      this.avatar = avatar;
6.      this.year = year;
7.      this.color = color;
8.      this.safety = safety;
9.      this.currentSpeed = currentSpeed;
10.     this.accelerate = function (mph) {
11.       this.currentSpeed += mph;
12.     };
13.     this.brake = function () {
14.       this.currentSpeed = 0;
15.     };
16.   }
17.   // Instantiate four new instances by applying the keyword new to the constructor Car
18.   var car1 = new Car('Dodge', 'Charger', 'dodge.png', 2010, 'white', 5, 0);
19.   var car2 = new Car('Ford', 'F150', 'fordf150.png', 2014, 'black', 5, 0);
20.   var car3 = new Car('Chevrolet', 'Cruze', 'chevrolet.png', 0, 'red', 5, 0);
21.   var car4 = new Car('Ford', 'Edge', 'ford.png', 2015, 'yellow', 5, 0);
22.   // Diaplay the current speed of mycar
23.   window.alert('The current speed of car1 is ' + car1.currentSpeed);
24.   // Prompt the user for a mph (If not a number, speed will become NaN.)
25.   var mph = parseInt(window.prompt('Enter an integer for acceleration rate:'));
26.   // Make a call to the method accelerate with mph as the argument
27.   car1.accelerate(mph);
28.   // Display the speed after calling accelerate
29.   window.alert('After calling accelerate, the speed is ' + car1.currentSpeed);
30.   window.alert('Stop the car now.');
31.   // Make a call to the method brake
32.   car1.brake();
33.   // Display the speed after calling brake
```

```
34.    window.alert('After calling brake, The speed of car1 is ' + car1.currentSpeed);
```

js/constructorlnotation-car-method.js

Open `js/contructornotation-car-method.js` in Scratchpad. Run the script.

You should see four alert boxes and one prompt window popping up one after the other.

```
The current speed of car1 is 0.
Enter an integer for acceleration rate:
After calling accelerate, the speed is [the number you have entered].
Stop the car now
After calling brake, the speed is 0.
```

The *dot accessor* is used to access a method. The statement

```
Car1.accelerate(mph);
```

passes the `mph` value as an argument to the parameter `mph` and calls the method `accelerate` for the instance `car1`. After execution, the `currentSpeed` of `car1` is increased by the amount of `mph`.

Another method call

```
car1.brake();
```

stops `car1` by setting the `currentSpeed` to zero.

## Workout 4-3

(Use `js/constructornotation-car-method.js` as an example.) Write a script which declares a constructor `Course`, instantiate a new instance `course1` and call an object method `seatAvailable`.

The requirements are described below:

1. The constructor `Course` has eight properties and one method.

2. Eight property keys are named `department`, `courseNumber`, `title`, `year`, `semester`, `credit`, `capacity` and `enrollment`.

3. The method key is `seatsAvailable`. `seatsAvailable` calculates the number of seats which is available in a class by subtracting `enrollment` from `capacity`.

4. Use the constructor `Course` to instantiate a new course `course1` which has the following specific key values:

```
department: 'CS'
courseNumber: '442'
title: 'Database Systems'
year: 2016
semester: 'fall'
```

```
credit: 3
capacity: 15
enrollment: 10
```

5.  Call the method `seatsAvailable` to find the number of seats currently available. Print the result in an alert box.

# JavaScript Object Notation

As mentioned before, literal notation is used in a popular web data format, *JavaScript Object Notation*, abbreviated to JSON (pronounced "Jason"). JSON is not covered in this book, except JSON.stringify. The purpose of JSON.stringify is to convert a value to JSON string.

Apply the method JSON.stringify to an object, it will create a string that contains all of the defined properties in JSON notation.

## Example 4.4

The following script gives an example of convert an instance to a JSON string.

**File Listing**

js/json-stringify.js

```
1.  // Declare a constructor Car
2.  function Car(make, model, avatar, year, color, safety, currentSpeed) {
3.      this.make = make;
4.      this.model = model;
5.      this.avatar = avatar;
6.      this.year = year;
7.      this.color = color;
8.      this.safety = safety;
9.      this.currentSpeed = currentSpeed;
10.     this.accelerate = function (mph) {
11.         this.currentSpeed += mph;
12.     };
13.     this.brake = function () {
14.         this.currentSpeed = 0;
15.     };
16. }
17.
18. // Instantiate four new instances by applying the keyword new to the constructor Car
19. var car1 = new Car('Dodge', 'Charger', 'dodge.png', 2010, 'white', 5, 0);
20. var car2 = new Car('Ford', 'F150', 'fordf150.png', 2014, 'black', 5, 0);
21. var car3 = new Car('Chevrolet', 'Cruze', 'chevrolet.png', 0, 'red', 5, 0);
22. var car4 = new Car('Ford', 'Edge', 'ford.png', 2015, 'yellow', 5, 0);
23. // Declare an array lists
24. var lists = [];
25.
26. // Convert each instance to a JSON string and log the string
27. lists[0] = JSON.stringify(car1);
28. console.log(lists[0]);
29. lists[1] = JSON.stringify(car2);
30. console.log(lists[1]);
31. lists[2] = JSON.stringify(car3);
32. console.log(lists[2]);
33. lists[3] = JSON.stringify(car4);
34. console.log(lists[3]);
```

The expression

```
JSON.stringify(car1)
```

will return a JSON string consisting of seven key/value pairs in car1. Logging the expression in the web console by

```
console.log(JSON.stringify(car1))
```

the output in the display pane is

```
{"make":"Dodge","model":"Charger","avatar":"dodge.png","year":2010,"color":"white","safety":5,"
currentSpeed":0}
```

To select some properties to display, add a string array as the 2$^{nd}$ argument in JSON.stringify. Use the array to specify the property keys to be converted in the resulting string.

The following statement will return a JSON string having two key/value pairs for two properties, make and safety. The undefined key without a previous assignment will not be included in the resulting string.

```
JSON.stringify(car1, ['make', 'safety']);
```

will return a JSON string having two key/value pairs for make and safety because both are defined in car1.


## Workout 4-4

Use js/json-stringify.js as an example. Write a script to

- Use *constructor notation* to create an abstract object. You determine the object to be modeled.

- The object must have at least 3 properties and 2 methods.

- Use the keyword new to create two instances.

- For each instance, call each method once.

- At the end of the script, print each instance in the console.

# Storing Instances in an Array

How does a program manage multiple instances? Array, as covered in Chapter 2, provides the simplest solution. Each array item holds an object instance. The following example stores four car instances in an array. Use the same instances as in `js/constructornotation-car-method.js` and `js/json-stringify.js`.

## Example 4.5

---

**File Listing**

      js/object-array.js

In this example, we declare an array `cars` at line 2. At lines 6 through 9, store each new car instance into an array element,

```
1.    // Declare two arrays
2.    var cars = [];
3.    var lists = [];

4.    // Instantiate four new instances by applying the keyword new to the constructor Car
5.    cars[0] = new Car('Dodge', 'Charger', 'dodge.png', 2010, 'white', 5, 0);
6.    cars[1] = new Car('Ford', 'F150', 'fordf150.png', 2014, 'black', 5, 0);
7.    cars[2] = new Car('Chevrolet', 'Cruze', 'chevrolet.png', 0, 'red', 5, 0);
8.    cars[3] = new Car('Ford', 'Edge', 'ford.png', 2015, 'yellow', 5, 0);

9.    // Convert each instance to a JSON string and log the string
10.   lists[0]=JSON.stringify(cars[0]);
11.   console.log(lists[0]);
12.   lists[1] = JSON.stringify(cars[1]);
13.   console.log(lists[1]);
14.   lists[2] = JSON.stringify(cars[2]);
15.   console.log(lists[2]);
16.   lists[3] = JSON.stringify(cars[3]);
17.   console.log(lists[3]);

18.   // Declare a constructor Car
19.   function Car(make, model, avatar, year, color, safety, currentSpeed) {
20.       this.make = make;
21.       this.model = model;
22.       this.avatar = avatar;
23.       this.year = year;
24.       this.color = color;
25.       this.safety = safety;
26.       this.currentSpeed = currentSpeed;
27.       this.accelerate = function (mph) {
28.           this.currentSpeed += mph;
29.       };
30.       this.brake = function () {
31.           this.currentSpeed = 0;
32.       };
33.   }
```

js/object-array.js

# Perform Same Operations for Each Instance

Read the eight statements in lines 10 through 17 of js/object-array.js. It is easy to find every two consecutive lines performs the same operations for each car instance, except that the array index value varies from 0 to 3 for both arrays, cars and lists,

1. In the first step, apply JSON.stringify to a car instanc and assign the returned JSON string to lists.

2. In the second step, log the lists item in the console.

Recall that in Chapter 3, the method, Array.forEach(callback), repeats the same callback function over every array item in js/ex-8.js.

## Example 4.6

### File Listing

        js/object-array-forEach.js

Replace the last eight script lines in js/object-array.js with Array.forEach(callback), we have

```
cars.forEach(function (element,index) {
   lists[index] = JSON.stringify(element);
   console.log(lists[index]);
});
```

> **NOTE**
>
> In the callback function, element and index are two parameters. element represents the current array item; index is the index value of element.
>
> The forEach method processes array items in cars one after the other. index starts from 0 and increments after each iteration. In each iteration, the value of element is replaced with cars[index].

The revised script is stored in js/object-array-forEach.js.

```
1.    // Declare two arrays
2.    var cars = [];
3.    var lists = [];

4.    // Declare a constructor Car
5.    function Car(make, model, avatar, year, color, safety, currentSpeed) {
6.        this.make = make;
7.        this.model = model;
8.        this.avatar = avatar;
9.        this.year = year;
10.       this.color = color;
11.       this.safety = safety;
12.       this.currentSpeed = currentSpeed;
13.       this.accelerate = function (mph) {
14.           this.currentSpeed += mph;
15.       };
```

```
16.        this.brake = function () {
17.            this.currentSpeed = 0;
18.        };
19.    }

20.    // Instantiate four new instances by applying the keyword new to the constructor Car
21.    cars[0] = new Car('Dodge', 'Charger', 'dodge.png', 2010, 'red', 5, 0);
22.    cars[1] = new Car('Ford', 'F150', 'ford.png', 2014, 'black', 5, 0);
23.    cars[2] = new Car('Chevrolet');
24.    cars[3] = new Car('Kia', 'Optima');

25.    // Run a callback for each cars item
26.    cars.forEach(function (element,index) {
27.      lists[index] = JSON.stringify(element);
28.      console.log(lists[index]);
29.    });
```

js/object-array-forEach.js

# Chapter 5    CASE STUDY – *CARS*

Depending on data structure that are used to store objects, techniques of processing objects are different. In this chapter, we learn how to retrieve JavaScript objects and display them on a web page.

We will illustrate, in a case study, how JavaScript generates HTML source content for printing object instances on a web page.

## Table of Contents

# Compose HTML Source and CSS Style

Before start scripting in JavaScript, we first design and test style sheets in a static HTML sample page. The following example gives a sample static page that prints a car with custom style.

## Example 5.1

This case includes two following files.

---

### File Listing

        `carSample.html, css/car.css, img/dodge.png`

---

Load `carSample.html` in a browser. The page will display specifications of a car alike the following picture.

The specifics data is distributed into several thematic sections and divisons. Each section or division associates with a style selector for a custom look and feel. The HTML structure of page layout is illustrated in the following tree diagram.

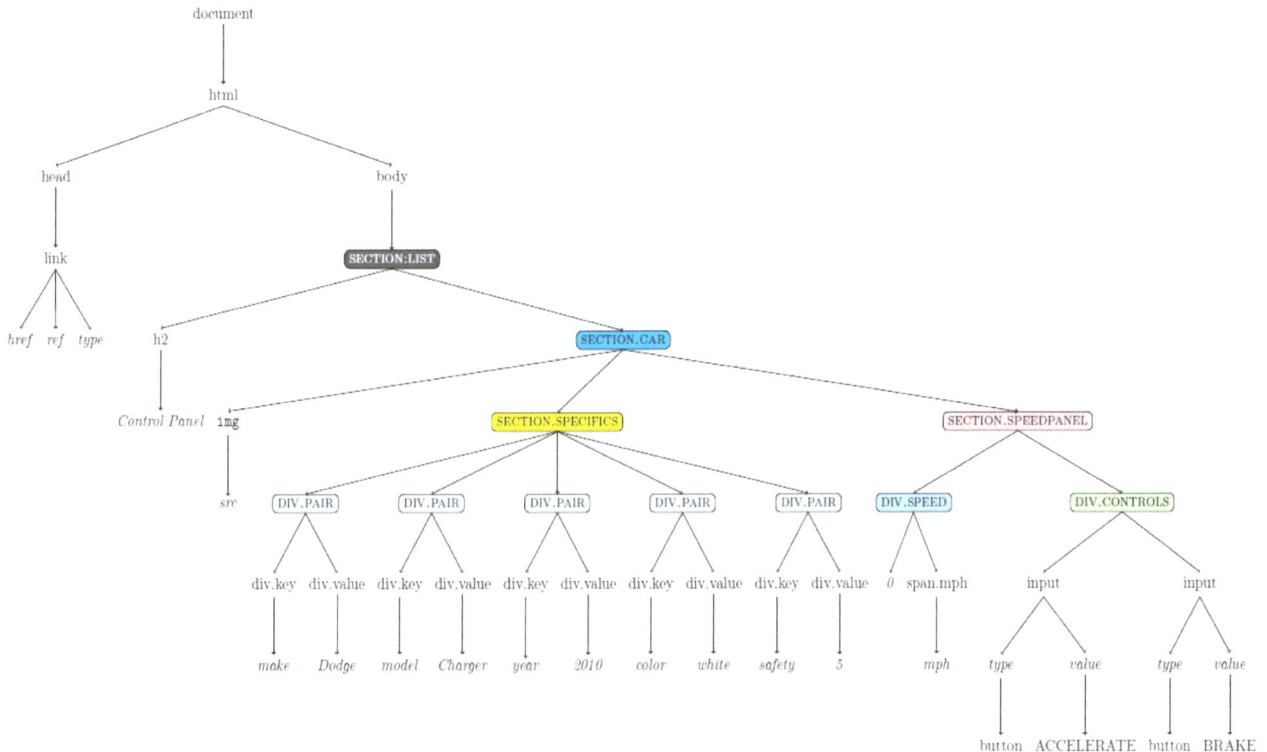

The top node `document` represents the entire HTML page. Starting with the root node `document`, the tree grows from top to bottom. Each tree node represents an HTML element. The leave nodes at the bottom are simple text and values which cannot be further broken down into smaller components.

The topmost section with the `id` value 'list', section#list, encloses all of the sections `section.car` with the `class` name 'car'; this sample page only displays one car section.

In each car section, there are three nodes:

1)  `img`: An `img` element shows a metaphor image

2)  `section.specifics`: A section with the `class` name 'specifics' displays five key/value pairs for `make`, `model`, `year`, `color` and `safety`

3)  `section.controls`: A section having the `class` name 'controls' includes two input buttons for trigger the methods 'accelerate' and 'brake'

The HTML and CSS source to implement the tree are listed below.

In the tree diagram and both sources, the same highlighting colors are used for the tree nodes and the related HTML statement lines as well as the associated CSS selectors.

```
1.    <!DOCTYPE html>
2.    <html lang="en">
3.        <head>
4.            <title>A sample HTML page displaying a car</title>
5.            <meta charset="UTF-8">
```

```
  6.                <meta name="viewport" content="width=device-width, initial-scale=1.0">
  7.                <link href="css/car.css" rel="stylesheet" type="text/css"/>
  8.         </head>
  9.         <body>
 10.            <section id='list'>
 11.            <h2>Control Panel </h2>
 12.                    <section class='car'>
 13.
 14.                        <img src="img/dodge.png">
 15.
 16.                        <!-- subsection specifics -->
 17.                        <section class='specifics'>
 18.                            <div class='pair'>
 19.                                <div class='key'>make:</div>
 20.                                <div class='value'>Dodge</div>
 21.                            </div>
 22.                            <div class='pair'>
 23.                                <div class='key'>model:</div>
 24.                                <div class='value'>Charger</div>
 25.                            </div>
 26.                            <div class='pair'>
 27.                                <div class='key'>year:</div>
 28.                                <div class='value'>2010</div>
 29.                            </div>
 30.                            <div class='pair'>
 31.                                <div class='key'>color:</div>
 32.                                <div class='value'>white</div>
 33.                            </div>
 34.                            <div class='pair'>
 35.                                <div class='key'>safety:</div>
 36.                                <div class='value'>5</div>
 37.                            </div>
 38.                        </section>
 39.
 40.                        <!-- subsection speedpanel -->
 41.                        <section class='speedpanel'>Current Speed
 42.                            <!-- division speed -->
 43.                            <div class='speed'>
 44.                                0<span class='mph'>mph</span>
 45.                            </div>
 46.                            <!-- division control buttons -->
 47.                            <div class="controls">
 48.                                <input type='button' value='ACCELERATE'>
 49.                                <input class='red' type='button' value='BRAKE'>
 50.                            </div>
 51.                        </section>
 52.
 53.                    </section>
 54.            </section>
 55.         </body>
 56.     </html>
```

```
1.    @import url(https://fonts.googleapis.com/css?family=Oswald);
2.    body {
3.        background-color: #f1f1f1;
4.        font-family: 'Oswald', 'Futura', sans-serif;
5.    }
6.    section#list {
7.        position: absolute;
8.        margin: auto;
9.        top: 0;
10.       right: 0;
11.       bottom: 0;
12.       left: 0;
13.   }
14.   section.car {
15.       display: inline-block;
16.       background-color: #f1f1f1;
17.       border: 5px #FFFFFF solid;
18.       margin-right: 5px;
19.       padding: 15px;
20.       font-size: 120%;
21.       color: #666666;
22.       text-align: center;
23.   }
24.   img {
25.       border: 2px white dotted;
26.       height: 130px; width:180px;
27.       box-shadow: 2px 5px 5px #699297;
28.   }
29.   section.specifics {
30.       background-color: #fdfdfd;
31.       padding: 0px;
32.   }
33.   .specifics .pair {
34.       display: block;
35.   }
36.   .pair .key {
37.       display: inline-block;
38.       font-variant: small-caps;
39.       text-align: right;
40.       width: 40%;
41.   }
42.   .pair .value {
43.       display: inline-block;
44.       text-align: left;
45.       width: 40%;
46.       padding-left: 10px;
47.   }
48.   section.speedpanel {
49.       border: 2px white double;
50.       padding: 10px;
51.       font-size: 120%;
52.   }
53.   .speed {
54.       display: block;
55.       font-size: 200%;
```

```
56.        color: #ff692e;
57.    }
58.    .mph {
59.        font-size: 50%;
60.        margin-left: 10px;
61.    }
62.    .controls {
63.    }
64.    input {
65.        display: block;
66.        width: 150px;
67.        height: 50px;
68.        padding: 0;
69.        font-size: 80%;
70.        color: #ffffff;
71.        background-color: #c6c6c6;
72.        border: 2px #ffffff solid;
73.        margin-bottom: 5px;
74.    }
75.    input:hover{
76.        background-color: #9a9a9a;
77.    }
78.    input.red {
79.        background-color: #ffc6af;
80.        border: 2px #c6c6c6 solid;
81.    }
82.    input.red:hover{
83.        background-color: #ff692e;
84.    }
```

css/car.css

In order to display a second car without using JavaScript, we need to make a copy of the entire HTML source of section#car, and manually replace the src value of the img element and five property values in five div elements having the class name 'value'.

This repetition can be automated in JavaScript. JavaScript views HTML source in strings and updates page content with the HTML strings.

# Compose HTML Strings

In a code editor, open carSample.html. Copy the entire HTML source in the element section#car, excluding the comment lines, into a string. Remove all whitespace characters. The resulting string is

```
<section class='car'><img src="img/dodge.png"><section class='specifics'><div class='pair'><div
class='key'>make:</div><div class='value'>Dodge</div></div><div class='pair'><div
class='key'>model:</div><div class='value'>Charger</div></div><div class='pair'><div
class='key'>year:</div><div class='value'>2010</div></div><div class='pair'><div
class='key'>color:</div><div class='value'>white</div></div><div class='pair'><div
class='key'>safety:</div><div class='value'>5</div></div></section><section
class='speedpanel'>Current Speed <div class='speed'> 0<span class='mph'>mph</span></div><div
```

```
class='controls'><input type='button' value='ACCELERATE'><input class='red' type='button'
value='BRAKE'></div></section></section>
```

To display a new car, eight highlighted parts in the string need to be replaced with new values. In JavaScript, these specific values can be substituted by an expression which accesses a property of an object instance.

Assuming cars are stored in an array and `element` is the common name to access each car, the following substitutions can be made to the highlighted parts.

- `Dodge.png -> element.avatar`

- `Dodge -> element.make`

- `Charger -> element.model`

- `2010 -> element.year`

- `White -> element.color`

- `5 -> element.safety`

- `0 -> element.currentSpeed`

These expressions are in JavaScript and they must be contained in a JavaScript script or block. The JavaScript interpreter needs to evaluate these expressions and combines the evaluation result into the `HTML` string.

Let us now comment on quotation marks as parts of the `HTML` string. By default, JavaScript interprets quotation marks, either double or single, as the opening or closing syntax symbols for a string. If quotation marks are part of a string, they need to be prefixed by a backslash \.

> If quotation marks are part of a string, they need to be prefixed by a backslash \.
>
> The backslash is referred to as an escape character

Optionally, we can split the long string into multiple substrings; each is assigned to a variable just for readability. In the end, we join all the substrings.

We assume that the following four variables are given.

- `cars`: an array that stores all the cars

- `index`: the key of an item in `cars`

- `objectHTML`: an array storing the `HTML` string for all the cars

- `element`: representing `cars[index]`

The following is a code block that generates the `HTML` string to display `cars[index]` by joining all substrings into `objectHTML[index]`. The variable declaration code are skipped in the block.

```
1.    begin = '<section class=\'car\'>';
2.    avatar = '<img src=\'img/' + element.avatar + '\'>';
3.    specifics = '<section class=\'specifics\'>';
4.    make = '<div class=\'pair\'><div class=\'key\'>make:</div><div class=\'value\'>' +
      element.make + '</div></div>';
```

```
5.    model = '<div class=\'pair\'><div class=\'key\'>model:</div><div class=\'value\'>' +
      element.model + '</div></div>';
6.    year = '<div class=\'pair\'><div class=\'key\'>year:</div><div class=\'value\'>' +
      element.year + '</div></div>';
7.    color = '<div class=\'pair\'><div class=\'key\'>color:</div><div class=\'value\'>' +
      element.color + '</div></div>';
8.    safety = '<div class=\'pair\'><div class=\'key\'>safety:</div><div class=\'value\'>' +
      element.safety + '</div></section>';
9.    speedpanel = '<section class=\'speedpanel\'>Current Speed';
10.   speed = '<div class=\'speed\'>' + element.currentSpeed + '<span class=\'mph\'>mph</span></div>
      '
11.   controls = '<div class=\'controls\'><input type=\'button\' value=\'ACCELERATE\'><input
      class=\'red\' type=\'button\' value=\'BRAKE\'></div>';
12.   end = '</div></section></section>'
13.   objectHTML[index] = begin + avatar + specifics + make + model + year + color + safety +
      speedpanel + speed + controls + end;
```

The parts highlighted in white are expressions whose values vary with `element`. The last line in the code block joins all the separate HTML substrings into a single one and stores the string into `objectHTML[index]`.

To run the code block for each `cars` item, apply `Array.forEach` to `cars` with the code block being the callback function. The statement

```
cars.forEach(function (element, index) {
    [The code block]
});
```

will populate `objectHTML` with new items. Each item is the HTML string for the `cars` item having the same `index`.

# Print HTML Strings

After generating the HTML strings in `objectHTML`, we can print every HTML string on the web page by doing the following steps:

Step 1.   Get a reference to the element 'section#list' which is designed as the area for the `cars`

```
var listArea = document.getElementById('list');
```

Step 2.   Read the current HTML content in 'section#list'

```
var content = listArea.innerHTML;
```

Step 3.   Loop over `objectHTML` to append all HTML strings to `content`

```
objectHTML.forEach(function (element, index) {
    content = content + element;
});
```

Step 4.   Write content to innerHTML of 'section#list'

```
listArea.innerHTML = content;
```

# Formulate Code

## Case 1.1 Cars

Based on *Example 5.1*, this case provides the complete code for displaying all the four cars on a web page. The case files are stored in the subfolder `case1`.

**File Listing**

        cars.html,
        css/car.css,
        js/cars.js, js/listCars.js,
        img/dodge.png, img/fordf150.png, img/chevrolet.png, img/ford.png

`cars.html` is the main web page linking to the following three files:

→ `css/car.css`: style sheets (the same as in *Example 5.1*)

→ `js/cars.js`: four car instances by using constructor notation

→ `js/listCars.js`: the script which composes HTML strings and print them on the main page.

We separate the JavaScript code into two scripts, `js/cars.js` and `js/listCars.js` because this will separate the data source from data processing. So a change to either part will not affect the other.

*Separation of concerns is a common programming practice for minimizing code coupling.*

To see the resulting page, load `cars.html` in a browser. The page should be alike the picture below.

**Control Panel**

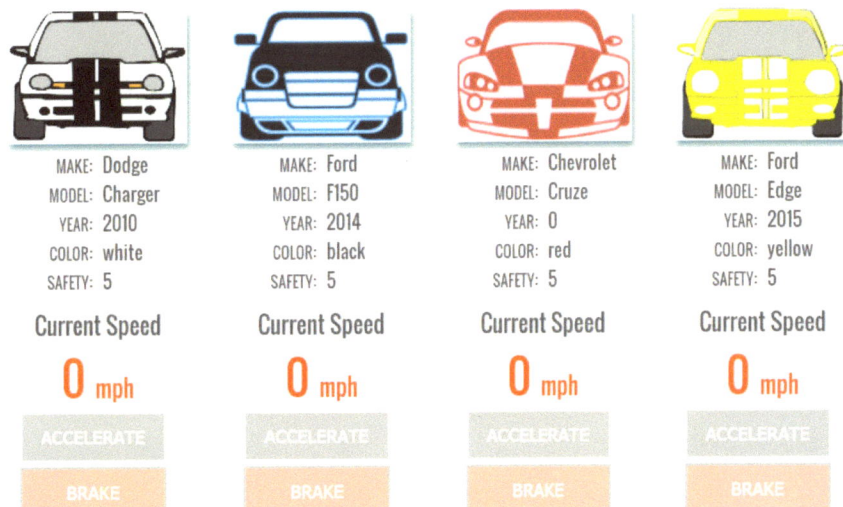

| | | | |
|---|---|---|---|
| MAKE: Dodge | MAKE: Ford | MAKE: Chevrolet | MAKE: Ford |
| MODEL: Charger | MODEL: F150 | MODEL: Cruze | MODEL: Edge |
| YEAR: 2010 | YEAR: 2014 | YEAR: 0 | YEAR: 2015 |
| COLOR: white | COLOR: black | COLOR: red | COLOR: yellow |
| SAFETY: 5 | SAFETY: 5 | SAFETY: 5 | SAFETY: 5 |
| **Current Speed** | **Current Speed** | **Current Speed** | **Current Speed** |
| 0 mph | 0 mph | 0 mph | 0 mph |
| ACCELERATE | ACCELERATE | ACCELERATE | ACCELERATE |
| BRAKE | BRAKE | BRAKE | BRAKE |

Read the source in `cars.html`.

```
1.    <!DOCTYPE html>
2.    <html lang="en">
3.        <head>
4.            <meta content="text/html; charset=utf-8" http-equiv="Content-Type">
5.            <title>Displaying JavaScript Objects - Car</title>
6.            <link rel="stylesheet" href="css/car.css">
7.        </head>
8.
9.        <body>
10.           <section id="list">
11.               <h1>Control Panel</h1>
12.           </section>
13.           <script src="js/cars.js"></script>
14.           <script src="js/listCars.js"></script>
15.       </body>
16.   </html>
```

The original page only contains the element 'section#list' with a heading. Two script statements will retrieve the linked scripts. The interpreter will run the script and insert cars to 'section#list'.

## Question:

In the source of cars.html, can we move the statement in line 14 to somewhere above the statement in line 13? Will the web page be affected by this order change? You can find it out yourself by switching these two script statements and reload cars.html.

The following is the source of js/listCars.js. There is an additional part 'Part 4' that will be discussed in the next section 'Activate Input Buttons'.

```
1.    // +++++++++++++++++++++++++++
2.    // Part 1: Declare variables
3.    // +++++++++++++++++++++++++++
4.    var begin = '';
5.    var avatar = '';
6.    var specifics = '';
7.    var make = '';
8.    var model = '';
9.    var year = '';
10.   var color = '';
11.   var safety = '';
12.   var speedpanel = '';
13.   var speed = '';
14.   var controls = '';
15.   var end = '';
16.   // Declare an array; each item stores the HTML source that displays a car on the web page.
17.   var objectHTML = [];
18.
19.   // +++++++++++++++++++++++++++
20.   // Part 2: Compose HTML source
21.   // +++++++++++++++++++++++++++
22.   // Iterate over cars. Compose the HTML source that displays a car on the web page.
23.   cars.forEach(function (element, index) {
24.       begin = '<section class=\'car\'>';
25.       avatar = '<img src=\'img/' + element.avatar + '\'>';
```

```
26.        specifics = '<section class=\'specifics\'>';
27.        make = '<div class=\'pair\'><div class=\'key\'>make:</div><div class=\'value\'>' +
           element.make + '</div></div>';
28.        model = '<div class=\'pair\'><div class=\'key\'>model:</div><div class=\'value\'>' +
           element.model + '</div></div>';
29.        year = '<div class=\'pair\'><div class=\'key\'>year:</div><div class=\'value\'>' +
           element.year + '</div></div>';
30.        color = '<div class=\'pair\'><div class=\'key\'>color:</div><div class=\'value\'>' +
           element.color + '</div></div>';
31.        safety = '<div class=\'pair\'><div class=\'key\'>safety:</div><div class=\'value\'>' +
           element.safety + '</div></section>';
32.        speedpanel = '<section class=\'speedpanel\'>Current Speed';
33.        speed = '<div class=\'speed\'>' + element.currentSpeed + '<span
           class=\'mph\'>mph</span></div> '
34.        controls = '<div class=\'controls\'><input type=\'button\' value=\'ACCELERATE\'><input
           class=\'red\' type=\'button\' value=\'BRAKE\'></div>';
35.        end = '</div></section></section>'
36.        objectHTML[index] = begin + avatar + specifics + make + model + year + color + safety +
           speedpanel + speed + controls + end;
37.    });
38.
39.    // +++++++++++++++++++++++++++++++++++++++++
40.    // Part 3: Display each car on the page
41.    // +++++++++++++++++++++++++++++++++++++++++
42.    // Get a reference to the element whose id value is list.
43.    var listArea = document.getElementById('list');
44.    // Read the current innerHTML value into content
45.    var content = listArea.innerHTML;
46.
47.    // Loop over objectHTML to append each item to content
48.    objectHTML.forEach(function (element, index) {
49.        content = content + element;
50.    });
51.
52.    // Set the innerHTML value of listArea to content
53.    listArea.innerHTML = content;
54.
55.    // +++++++++++++++++++++++++++++++++++++++++++++++++++++++++++
56.    // Part 4: Attach click event with two input buttons of cars[0]
57.    // +++++++++++++++++++++++++++++++++++++++++++++++++++++++++++
58.    // Get a reference collection of all elements with tag 'input'
59.    var inputs = document.getElementsByTagName('input');
60.    // Get a referecne collection of all elements with the class name 'speed'
61.    var speeds = document.getElementsByClassName('speed');
62.
63.    function btnAccelerate() {// button action for cars[0]
64.        var mph = parseInt(window.prompt('Enter an integer for acceleration rate:'));
65.        if (mph) {
66.            cars[0].accelerate(mph);
67.        }
68.        speeds[0].innerHTML = cars[0].currentSpeed + '<span class=\'mph\'>mph</span>';
69.    }
70.
71.    function btnBrake() { //button action for cars[0]
72.        if (window.confirm("Stop?")) {
```

```
73.            cars[0].brake();
74.        }
75.        speeds[0].innerHTML = cars[0].currentSpeed + '<span class=\'mph\'>mph</span>';
76.    }
77.
78.    // Define a click event for the 1st input element with a callback btnAccelerate
79.    inputs[0].addEventListener('click', btnAccelerate);
80.    // Define a click event for the 2nd input element with a callback btnBrake
81.    inputs[1].addEventListener('click', btnBrake);
```

*js/listCars.js*

# Activate Input Buttons

In the script `js/listCars.js`, an additional function has been implemented to activate two input buttons for the first car `cars[0]`.

On the page of `cars.html`, press the button ACCELERATE. Enter an integer in the prompt window. The current speed will be increased by the number that has been entered. If the button BRAKE is pressed at any time, the current speed is reset to zero. Right now this function is only enabled for the first car.

In later chapters, after the relevant techniques have been covered, we will be able to set up all the cars to respond to button clicks.

The implementing code is in part 4 of `js/listCars.js` at lines 58 through 81. The following part will give a brief introduction of the relevant code.

## Get input buttons

There are eight input buttons on the page. Line 59

```
var inputs = document.getElementsByTagName('input');
```

gets a reference collection for all the elements with HTML tag `'input'`. As `inputs` is a collection of references, use array notation to access individual references in the collection.

Thus, the first two input buttons ACCELERATE and BRAKE can be referenced by array notations `inputs[0]` and `inputs[1]`.

## Get elements with class name `speed`

To update the speed number on the page, we need to get the reference of the element that holds the speed number. The `div` elements with the class name `'speed'` are the divisions where the current speed value is printed.

Line 61

```
var speeds = document.getElementsByClassName('speed');
```

will get a referecne collection of all elements with the class name `'speed'`.

If the current speed value needs an update for a car, write the new speed into the associated `div` element. `speeds[0]` is a reference to the speed area in the first car, `speeds[1]` is for the second car and so on.

The following table shows the array notations to access each car, both buttons and speed division on the page.

| cars[0] | cars[1] | cars[2] | cars[3] |
|---|---|---|---|
| speeds[0] | speeds[1] | speeds[2] | speeds[3] |
| ACCELERATE inputs[0] | ACCELERATE inputs[2] | ACCELERATE inputs[4] | ACCELERATE inputs[6] |
| BRAKE inputs[1] | BRAKE inputs[3] | BRAKE inputs[5] | BRAKE inputs[7] |

## Register an event with **ACCELERATE** button

At line 79,

```
inputs[0].addEventListener('click', btnAccelerate);
```

the method `addEventListener` registers a listener with ACCELERATE for the event type `'click'` that triggers a callback function, `btnAccelerate`. The callback `btnAccelerate` is triggered only once when user clicks the element `inputs[0]`, which is ACCELERATE in the first car.

Details of the relevant techniques with events will be covered in later chapters.

The callback function `btnAccelerate` is declared specifically for the first car `cars[0]`. The purpose of the callback is to prompt the user for acceleration rate and increase the car speed by that rate; at the same time, the current speed number on the page is udpated.

```
function btnAccelerate() {// button action for cars[0]
    var mph = parseInt(window.prompt('Enter an integer for acceleration rate:'));
    if (mph) {// if mph is valid and true, increase speed
        cars[0].accelerate(mph);
    }
    speeds[0].innerHTML = cars[0].currentSpeed + '<span class=\'mph\'>mph</span>';
}
```

Note that the keyword `if`, which will be introduced in Chapter 7.

## Register a **click** event with **BRAKE** button

To register a click event with the BRAKE button, we follow the same idea as the ACCELERATE button.

Line 81,

```
inputs[1].addEventListener('click', btnBrake);
```

the method `addEventListener` registers a listener with BRAKE for the event type `'click'` that triggers a callback function, `btnBrake`.

```
function btnBrake() { //button action for cars[0]
    if (window.confirm("Stop?")) {// if user presses OK button in the confirmation window
```

```
            cars[0].brake();
        }
        speeds[0].innerHTML = cars[0].currentSpeed + '<span class=\'mph\'>mph</span>';
    }
```

To activate buttons for other cars, by the skills that have been introduced so far, we have to duplicate this part for each car instance and replace the array index value from 0 to 1, 2, and 3, respectively in each copy.

## Workout 5-1

(Refer to js/constructornotation-car-method.js, js/object-array.js and *Case 1.1*.) Write an application that is made of four following programs.

1) A JavaScript file 'courses.js' which declares a constructor Course, instantiate five instances and store them in an array courses.

2) An HTML file 'courses.html' which creates a main page where all courses are displayed.

3) A JavaScript file 'listCourses.js' that prints each course from 'courses.js' on the main page. Course properties are printed in key/value pairs and each object method is represented in an input button.

4) A CSS file 'courses.css' that creates sheets for customize the look and feel of the main page.

The specific data requirements are described below:

1. The constructor Course has eight properties and one method.

2. Eight property keys are named department, courseNumber, title, year, semester, credit, capacity and enrollment.

3. The method key is seatsAvailable. seatsAvailable calculates the number of seats which is available in a class by subtracting enrollment from capacity.

4. Use the constructor Course to instantiate five course instances. A course sample is given below.

```
        department: 'CS'
        courseNumber: '442'
        title: 'Database Systems'
        year: 2016
        semester: 'fall'
        credit: 3
        capacity: 15
        enrollment: 10
```

For the web page and its apperance, there is no specific requirement. Either you can use the same styles as in *Case 1.1*, or you are free to design page layout and styles as long as the required contents are all present on the web page.

# Chapter 6    CASE STUDY – ROLES AT THE SCENE

In this chapter, we create a running case that will be continually augmented through the rest of the book. The name of this case is *Roles at the Scene*. Here, animal roles are modeled by JavaScript objects and two animals will be instantiated and placed in a scene area on a web page. This running case helps you review and practice the topics that have been covered in previous chapters.

## Table of Contents

## Case 2.1 Roles at the Scene

Locate the subfolder *case2* in the book source directory. Download the following files for this case.

### File Listing

```
scene.html,
css/scene.css,
js/Role.js, js/playRoles.js,
img/dogface.png, img/cat.png
```

Open `scene.html` in the browser. The page should be similar to the screenshot below. Reload the page and the cat's location may differ.

Keep `scene.html` open in the browser. Right click anywhere on the page. Choose View Page Source if using Firefox. A new browser tab will open to display the source of `scene.html`, the same as the code box below.

```
1.  <!DOCTYPE html>
2.  <html lang="en">
3.      <head>
4.          <title>Case 2.1 Chapter 6 Objects</title>
5.          <meta charset="UTF-8">
6.          <meta name="viewport" content="width=device-width, initial-scale=1.0">
7.          <link rel="stylesheet" href="css/scene.css">
8.      </head>
```

```
9.
10.    <body>
11.        <h1>Case 2.1 - Roles at the Scene</h1>
12.        <section id='scene'></section>
13.
14.        <script src="js/Role.js"></script>
15.        <script src="js/playRoles.js"></script>
16.    </body>
17.
18. </html>
```

scene.html

Line 7 links the web page with an external style file css/scene.js.

In scene.html, the scene is simulated by a section element whose id value is 'scene'. The look and size of the scene area is determined by the id selector 'section#scene', which is marked as light pink segment in the following code of css/scene.css.

```
1.    @import url(https://fonts.googleapis.com/css?family=Oswald);
2.    body {
3.        background-color: dimgrey;
4.        font-family: 'Oswald', 'Futura', sans-serif;
5.        text-align: center;
6.    }
7.    h1 {
8.        color: #fff;
9.        letter-spacing: 0.5em;
10.    }
11.    section#scene {
12.        margin: 0 auto;
13.        width: 530px;
14.        height:700px;
15.        background-color: #ffffff;
16.        border: darkolivegreen 15px dotted;
17.        border-radius: 10px;
18.    }
19.    div.role {
20.        position: relative;
21.        visibility: hidden;
22.        width: 50px;
23.        height: 50px;
24.        background-size: contain;
25.        background-repeat: no-repeat;
26.        padding: 0px;
27.        margin: 0px;
28.    }
29.    div#control {
30.        margin: 0 auto;
31.        width: 500px;
32.    }
33.    input {
34.        width: 200px;
35.        font-size: 1.5em;
36.        height: 50px;
```

```
37.        font-family: 'Oswald', 'Futura', sans-serif;
38.        color: darkolivegreen
39.    }
```

css/scene.css

As highlighted in gray blue, the `class` selector, `div.role`, is declared to customize the common looks that are shared among cat, dog and any other animal roles that are to be inserted into the scene.

The last two style sheets `div#control` and `input` are not needed currently and will be used in later development of this case.

## Inspect Page Elements

Line 12 of `scene.html`

```
<section id='scene'></section>
```

is the element `'section#scene'` without any inner content. The scene area should be empty, but two animals are seen on the page. Where are they from? The linked JavaScript script `js/playRoles.js` in line 15 created them and placed them into the scene. Though the browser always re-renders a page element if a JavaScript statement requests for updating the element, the View Page Source function only shows the original HTML page source, not including the content from JavaScript.

In order to view the updated HTML source after running JavaScript, in the browser tab of `scene.html`, open the *Inspector* tool by pressing Ctrl+Shift+c. The *Inspector* window will appear alike the picture below, with two panes showing HTML source and Rules.

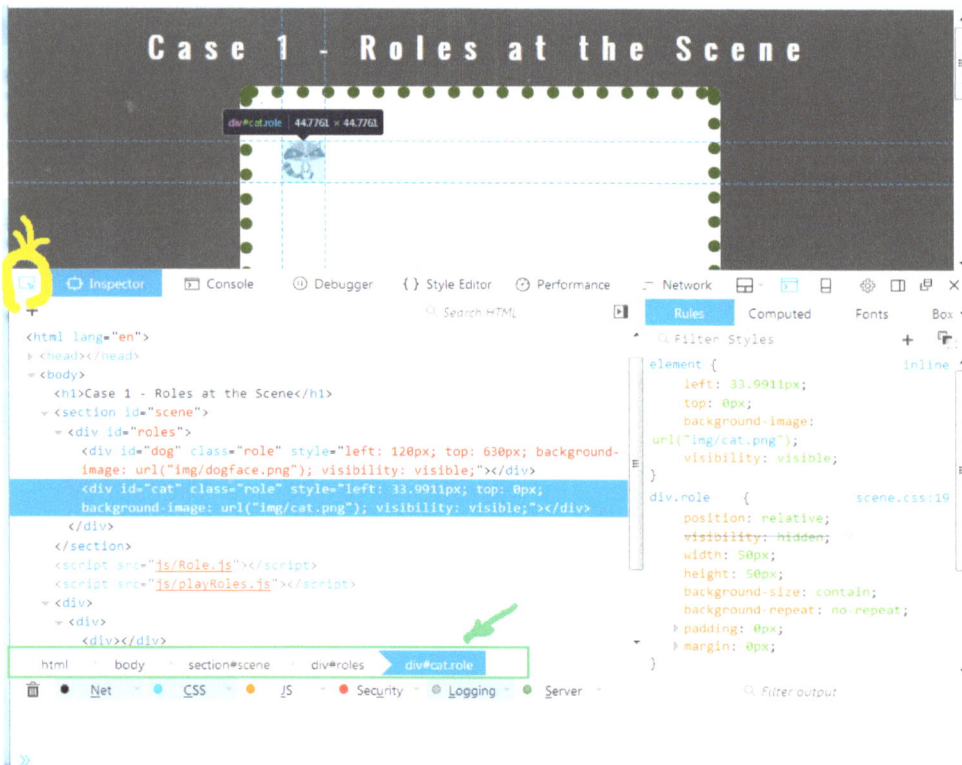

To inspect an element on the page, for instance, cat, click the leftmost tool icon "Pick an element from the page". Move the mouse cursor to the page and hover on the cat to select. The following results will appear:

1) On the page, a grid in dotted blue line will outline the cat with a black bar showing its selector div#cat.role and dimension of 44.761 by 44.761.

2) On the Inspector window,

- In the left pane, the HTML source of the selected element is highlighted in blue It shows that the cat element has three attributes: style, class and id.

  ```
  <div style="left: 33.9911px; top: 0px; background-image: url('img/cat.png');
  visibility: visible;" class="role" id="cat"></div>
  ```

- Under the Rules tab of the right pane, all style rules that the element cat has, including inline, external and inherited styles, are listed.

  a. In the first group, there is an item 'element' containing all inline rules within the style property of the element div#cat.role. It specifies the left and top positions, background image and visibility.

  ```
  element {
      left: 33.9911px;
      top: 0px;
      background-image: url('img/cat.png');
      visibility: visible;
  }
  ```

  b. In the second group, there is an external id selector div.role from css/scene.css. Noticeably, the rule

  ~~visibility: hidden;~~

  is crosslined. This means this rule has been removed or modified for the cat element; so the cat is not hidden on the page.

  c. The last group "*Inherited from body*" contains all rules that are inherited from the body element or more parent elements of the cat, if there are more.

Besides inspecting elements, the Inspector tool supports many other functions, such as editing HTML, inserting new node, deleting the node and so on. These functions are beyond the scope of this book.

By comparing the actual HTML source in the web browser, as shown below, with the original HTML source from scene.html, we know the original page has been augmented by three new elements: div#roles, div#dog.role and div#cat.role.

```
<section id="scene">
  <div id="roles">
      <div style="left: 120px; top: 630px; background-image: url('img/dogface.png');
      visibility: visible;" class="role" id="dog"></div>
      <div style="left: 33.9911px; top: 0px; background-image: url('img/cat.png');
      visibility: visible;" class="role" id="cat"></div>
  </div>
```

```
</section>
```

In the following, we will go through the JavaScript code which implements instantiating role instances as well as positioning them.

# Declare Constructor Role

To instantiate animal role instances, a contructor, **Role**, is defined in `js/Role.js`.

```
1.    var Role = function (ref, avatar, left, top, showup) {
2.        this.ref = ref;
3.        this.avatar = avatar;
4.        this.left = left + 'px';
5.        this.top = top + 'px';
6.        this.showup = showup;
7.
8.        this.setup = function() {
9.            this.ref.style.left = this.left;
10.           this.ref.style.top = this.top;
11.           this.ref.style.backgroundImage ="url(" + avatar + ")";
12.           this.ref.style.visibility = this.showup;
13.       };
14.
15.       this.setVisibility = function(showup) {
16.           this.showup = showup;
17.           this.ref.style.visibility = showup;
18.       };
19.
20.       this.setPosition = function(left, top) {
21.           this.left = left + 'px';
22.           this.top = top + 'px';
23.           this.ref.style.left = this.left;
24.           this.ref.style.top = this.top;
25.       };
26.   };
```

js/Role.js

The constructor Role is created as a function expression. The object **Role** has eight keys. Five keys in light orange are properties. Three keys in sky blue are methods; each of them is declared as a function expression.

## Role properties

We can customize a **Role** instance by specifying values for each of the following keys.

1. ref:     a reference to the div element which contains the role

2. avatar: a string which is a resource address pointing to an image to be set as background for the role

3. left:    a number that is the horizontal distance to the left edge to be assigned to the left CSS property

4. top:    a number that is the vertical distance to the top edge to be assigned to the top CSS property

5.  `showup`: a string which has two valid values, `'hidden'` and `'visible'`", to control the CSS property `'visibility'` of the role

The key `ref` is a reference that needs to be returned from calling the method `document.getElementById`.

The key `'showup'` is used to set up the CSS property `'visibility'`. To hide an HTML element, assign the `'visibility'` attribute to `'hidden'`; or `'visible'` for showing the element.

The keys `'left'` and `'top'` determine the left and top positions of a role instance at the scene.

> Be aware that the CSS properties 'left' and 'top' only take a string of two components: a number postfixed with a length unit.

The length unit can take px, em or %.

```
left: 100px;  // px: pixel
left: 2em;    // em: point size of the current typeface
left: 20%;    // %: percentages of height of the containing (parent) element
```

Joining a number `120` and a string `'px'`, the expression

```
120 + 'px'
```

produces a string `'120px'`. This explains the statements at lines 4, 5, 21 and 22 in `js/Role.js`.

## Use the constructor

Assuming a `div` element with the `id` value `'cat'` has been added to the page, the following sample statement will instantiate a `Role` instance that is associated with the element:

```
var cat = new Role(document.getElementById('cat'), 'img/cat.png', 0, 0, 'hidden');
```

## Role methods

Besides these five properties, **Role** supports the following three methods.

1.  The **setup** method initializes the `Role` instance for its left and top positions, avatar and visibility. The key value of `avatar` is assigned to the JavaScript attribute `'backgroundImage'` which is equivalent to the CSS property `background-image`. The key value of `showup` is assigned to the JavaScript attribute `'visibility'` that is equivalent to the CSS property `visibility`.

2.  The **setVisibility** method either hides or shows the role according to the parameter `showup`.

3.  The **setPosition** method moves the role to a new position that is determined by the parameters `left` and `top`.

## Access CSS properties in JavaScript

All of the CSS properties are accessible in JavaScript by the expression with the following syntax.

Syntax

```
reference.style.attributename
```

Assign a value to the expression above changes the look of the referenced element in term of the attribute `attributename`.

> Be aware that CSS and JavaScript use different names for the style properties.
>
> To change a CSS style property in JavaScript, we need to find its equivalent name in JavaScript.

To look up CSS and JavaScript names, either refer to

→ Book Appendix A. *Common CSS Properties and Their Equivalent Names in JavaScript*

Or visit the following two web links

→ To find a list of CSS style properties, visit https://developer.mozilla.org/en-US/docs/Web/CSS/Reference

→ To find the equivalent JavaScript attribute names. Visit https://developer.mozilla.org/en-US/docs/Web/CSS/CSS_Properties_Reference.

## Manage Role Instances

Next we will view another script, `js/playRoles.js`, which manages instances and the web page.

The following is `js/playRoles.js` that is organized in three parts.

```
1.   // +++++++++++++++++++++++++++++++++++
2.   // Part 1: Declare global variables
3.   // +++++++++++++++++++++++++++++++++++
4.   var bottom; // Height of game area
5.   var right; // Width of game area
6.   var xini; // Initial left position
7.   // Declare an array for role names
8.   var roleNames = [];
9.   // Declare an array for role avatar images
10.  var roleAvatars = [];
11.  // Declare an array for role instances
12.  var roles = [];
13.  // Declare an array, prex, to store the left position of each role
14.  // which is the horizontal distance to the left wall.
15.  var prex = [];
16.  // Declare an array, prey, to store the top position of each role
17.  // which is the vertical distance to the top wall
18.  var prey = [];
19.  // Get a reference to div scene
20.  var scene = document.getElementById('scene');
21.
22.  // +++++++++++++++++++++++++++++++++++
23.  // Part 2: Implement a specific case
```

```
24.    // +++++++++++++++++++++++++++++++++
25.    roleNames = ['dog', 'cat'];
26.    roleAvatars = ['img/dogface.png', 'img/cat.png'];
27.
28.    // Set size of scene: bottom,right,xini
29.    setArea(630, 220, 120);
30.    // Set the initial positions, left and top, for role[0]
31.    prex[0] = xini;
32.    prey[0] = bottom;
33.    // Set the initial positions, left and top, for role[1]
34.    prex[1] = Math.random() * xini;  // a random horizontal distance between 0(inclusive) and
       xini(exclusive)
35.    prey[1] = 0;
36.    // Call functions
37.    insertHTMLelements();
38.    createRoles();
39.    placeRoles();
40.
41.    // +++++++++++++++++++++++++++++++++
42.    // Part 3: Function declarations
43.    // +++++++++++++++++++++++++++++++++
44.    function setArea(vbottom, vright, vxini) {
45.        bottom = vbottom; // Height of game area
46.        right = vright; // Width of game area
47.        xini = vxini; // Initial left position
48.    }
49.
50.    function insertHTMLelements() {
51.        // Read the current HTML content in scene
52.        var content = '<div id=\'roles\'>';
53.        // Compose the HTML string that creates a div element for each new animal.
54.        // Append them to content
55.        roleNames.forEach(function (element, index) {
56.            content = content + '<div class=\'role\' id=\'' + element + '\'></div>';
57.        });
58.        // Update scene
59.        scene.innerHTML = content + '</div>';
60.    }
61.
62.    function createRoles() {// Create a role instance for each name in roleNames
63.        roleNames.forEach(function (element, index) {
64.          roles[index] = new Role(document.getElementById(element), roleAvatars[index], 0, 0,
         'hidden');
65.        });
66.    }
67.
68.    function placeRoles() {// Place each role in the scene
69.        roles.forEach(function (element, index) {
70.            element.setup();
71.            element.setPosition(prex[index], prey[index]);
72.            element.setVisibility('visible');
73.        });
74.    }
```

All global variables are declared in part 1. There are nine global variables.

All function declarations are in part 3. There are four functions.

- `setArea(vbottom, vright, vxini)`: set size of the scene

- `insertHTMLelements()`: Compose the HTML string that creates a `div` element for each new animal. Append all the elements to the target container.

- `createRoles()`: Create a `role` instance for each name in `roleNames`

- `placeRoles()`: Place each instance in the scene

By using variables in part 1 and functions in part 3, we can make different scenes. The statements in part 2 implements a specific scene that has two instances, dog and cat.

```
1.      // +++++++++++++++++++++++++++++++++++
2.      // Part 2: Implement a specific case
3.      // +++++++++++++++++++++++++++++++++++
4.      // Give names
5.      roleNames = ['dog', 'cat'];
6.      // Give resource files for avatar
7.      roleAvatars = ['img/dogface.png', 'img/cat.png'];
8.      // Set size of scene: bottom, right, xini
9.      setArea(630, 220, 120);
10.     // Set the initial left and top for role[0]
11.     prex[0] = xini;
12.     prey[0] = bottom; // at the bottom
13.     // Set the initial left and top for role[1]
14.     prex[1] = Math.random() * xini;  // a random horizontal distance between
                0(inclusive) and xini(exclusive)
15.     prey[1] = 0; // top
16.     // Call functions
17.     insertHTMLelements();
18.     createRoles();
19.     placeRoles();
```

## Initialize data

In the code box above, the function call `setArea(630, 220, 120)`, at line 9, assigns values to `bottom`, `right` and `xini`, creating a game area in a rectangular of `220` by `630`. Change these values for a different dimension.

Next, set initial positions in `prex` and `prey` for both roles.

The first role instance will be positioned by `prex[0]` an `prey[0]`. The second role instance is determined by `prex[1]` an `prey[1]`. The following code sets the position for both roles. Change these values for different positions.

```
    // Set the initial position for role[0]
```

```
    prex[0] = xini;
    prey[0] = bottom;
    // Set the initial position for role[1]
    prex[1] = Math.random() * xini;
    prey[1] = 0;
```

## Call functions

After initializing the required data for both roles, start calling functions for inserting HTML elements, instantiating roles and configuring roles.

Step 1.   insertHTMLelements();

insertHTMLelements adds a div element for each name in rolesName. Use the name as the id value of the element for identification purpose in document.getElementById.

Step 2.   createRoles();

createRoles instantiates a new instance for each name in rolesName. The first instance, roles[0], is associated with the div element 'dog'. The second instance, roles[1], is associated with the div element 'cat'.

The number of new instances depends on how many names in rolesName. The initial visibility is hidden for both roles. The initial left and top values are all zero.

As the initial visibility is hidden, the role elements are invisible on the page. The next step is to adjust the position and turn on the visibility for each role instance.

Step 3.   placeRoles();

The function placeRoles invokes three Role methods for each roles item in the following order:

- The first call to Role.setup method sets two CSS properties, visibility and background-image.

- The second call to Role.setPosition method will reposition the associated div element by two arguments prex and prey.

- The last call to the Role.setVisibility method will make the associated div element visible.

## Workout 6-1

Based on *Case 2.1*, add a new **Role** instance to the scene. To do so, you need to modify the files of *Case 2.1*.

Make a new folder c6w1 and three subfolders css, js and img.

Copy all the files listed below to the folder

```
scene.html,
css/scene.css,
js/Role.js, js/playRoles.js,
img/dogface.png, img/cat.png, img/ostrich.png
```

Find an avatar for the new `Role` instance. You can use "`ostrich.png`" or free to use other image. Copy the avatar to the subfolder `img`.

In `scene.html`, include the text 'Workout 6-1' in the text content of both `<title>` element and `<h1>` element.

Modify `playRoles.js` according to the following instructions.

- Give the new instance a name. Add the name to `roleNames`

- Add the avatar file name to `roleAvatars`

- Initialize the left and top positions for the new role. `prex[2]` and `prey[2]` determine the position for the new instance.

  `xini` (which is `120`) makes a separating line which splits the game area vertically into two parts.

  - To place the instance on the left part of the game area,

    ```
    prex[2] = Math.random()*xini;
    ```

  - To place the instance on the right part of the game area,

    ```
    prex[2] = xini + Math.random()*100;
    ```

  - To place the instance on the right half of the game area,

    ```
    prex[2] = 220 + Math.random()*200;
    ```

  For `prey[2]`, you can either generate a random value less than `530` or just specify a value less than `530`.

  For example, the following statements set the left position to `300` and the top position to `Math.round(bottom/2)`.

    ```
    prex[2] = 300;
    prey[2] = Math.round(bottom/2);
    ```

A sample page look is provided below.

# Workout 4-6 Roles at the Scene

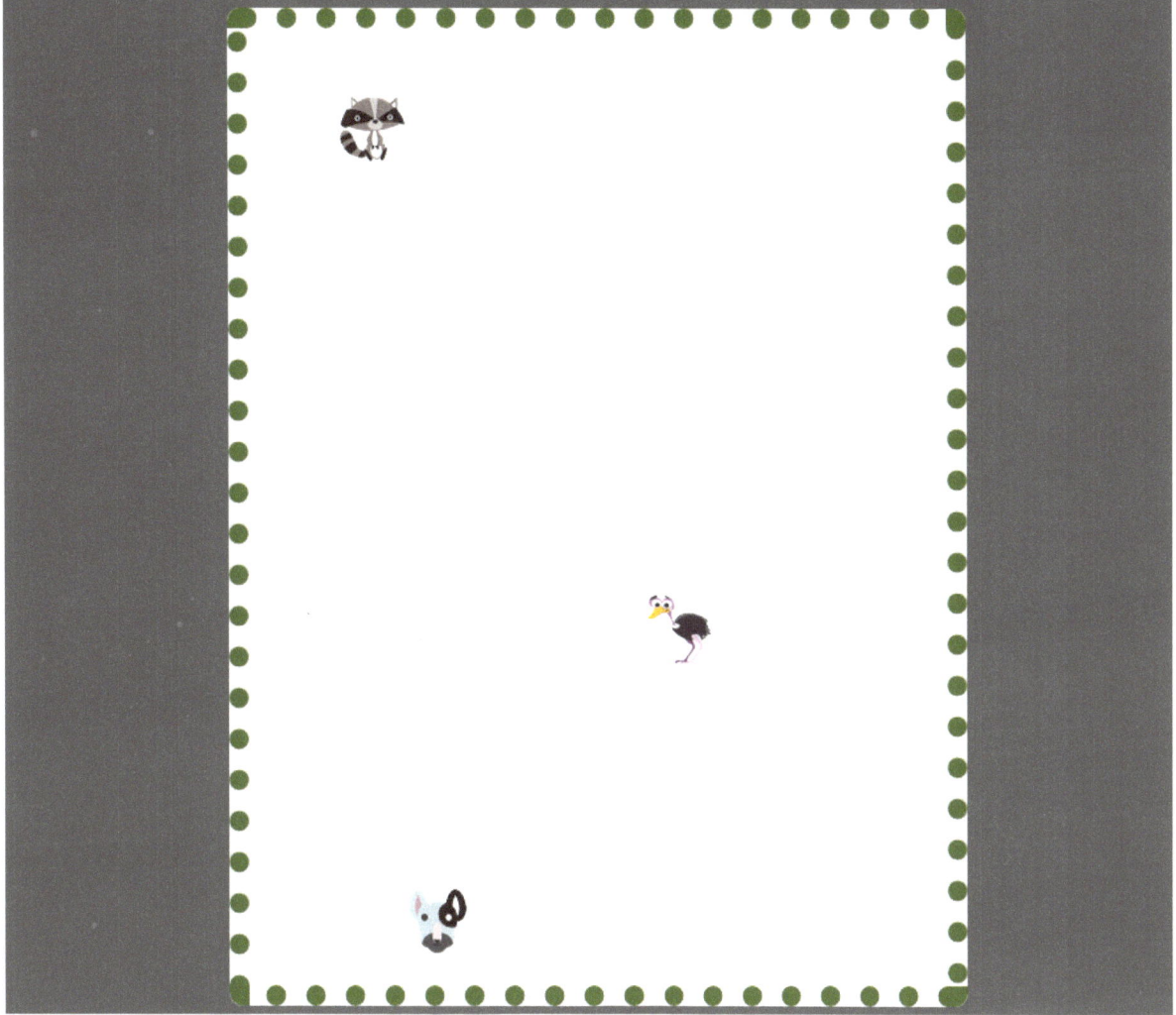

# Chapter 7    Making Decisions

Recall *Case 2.1 "Roles at the Scene"* from the last chapter: two animal roles, dog and cat, are placed at the scene area. They stay quiet and no other event takes place at the scene. What about creating new behaviors and abilities for these animals? Can we command them to run up, down, left or right?

To do so, we firstly need to learn a programming structure for decision making. Three decision or selection structures will be introduced in this chapter: `if`, `if else` and `switch`.

Objects develop with various endings. A story in a computer program usually consists of critical moments where characters must select one from multiple directions to move forward. A decision structure supports multiple alternatives in a computer program.

## Table of Contents

# Selection

In a two-dimensional space, a point or an object can move freely in 360 degrees. Now assume that the dog at the scene can take four directions (up, down, left and right) and the dog understands four standard commands that are represented by four case-sensitive strings: Run up, Run down, Run left and Run right. After receiving a message, the dog compares the message with standard commands. If there is a match, the dog will follow the matched command and run toward that direction. This scenario is visualized in the activity diagram below. An activity diagram is also referred to as a flow chart in programming.

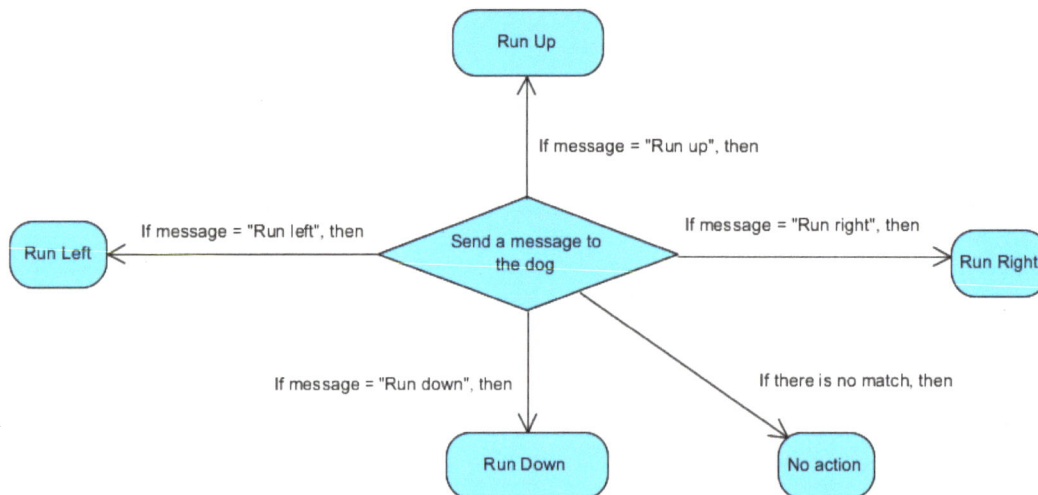

In the diagram above, the diamond shape box is a decision node. After sending the dog a message, this decision node makes four equal-to comparisons that are marked above the lines from the diamond. Each line checks if the message is equal to one standard command. If a comparison finds equality, the dog will run to the corresponding direction. If no equality is found after going through all of the comparisons, the dog takes no action. Five lines out of the decision node lead to five possible actions that the dog is able to take.

The decision process is scripted in the following example.

## Example 7.1

File Listing
        js/if-1.js

```
1.    var commands = [
2.       'Run up',
3.       'Run down',
4.       'Run left',
5.       'Run right'
6.    ];
7.    var message = window.prompt('Enter your message:');
8.    if (message === commands[0]) {
9.       window.confirm('You entered ' + commands[0] + '.');
10.   }
11.   if (message === commands[1]) {
12.      window.confirm('You entered ' + commands[1] + '.');
```

```
13.   }
14.   if (message === commands[2]) {
15.      window.confirm('You entered ' + commands[2] + '.');
16.   }
17.   if (message === commands[3]) {
18.      window.confirm('You entered ' + commands[3] + '.');
19.   }
```

js/if-1.js

Run the script in a Scratchpad window. A dialog pops up and waits for you to enter a message. Enter 'Run up' and press OK. A confirmation will show 'You entered Run up.'

Run the script again by entering 'Run down', 'Run left' and 'Run right', respectively. If you enter a message not matching any of these four standard commands, the script does nothing.

> **NOTE**
>
> window.prompt(message) displays a dialog with an optional message prompting the user to input text. The method returns a string containing the text entered by the user or NaN (Not A Number) if the user clicks OK button without entering anything. The optional parameter, message, displays a text to the user. There are also many other methods for the user to enter data into a web page.

Four commands are stored in the array commands. The decision process is implemented by four if statements. Each if statement runs in two steps: evaluating a condition and taking conditional actions according to the evaluation result.

For example, the following if statement in js/if-1.js,

```
if (message == commands[0]) {
   window.confirm('You entered ' + commands[0] + '.');
}
```

begins with the keyword if, followed by two components:

- The first part highlighted in yellow, enclosed by parentheses, evaluates an equal-to expression to a Boolean, true or false.

- The second part is a code block enclosed by curly brackets which will only be executed if the condition in the 1st part is true.

In order to use if structure, we need to understand comparison expressions.

# Comparison Expression

A condition must be examined prior to making a selection. A condition is often specified in a comparison expression.

## Binary Comparison

A binary comparison makes a condition which usually compares two values, formatted in three parts: $1^{st}$ value, comparison operator and $2^{nd}$ value. The structure is shown as below.

Syntax

```
operand1 [comparison operator] operand2
```

A comparison expression returns a `Boolean`. If the condition holds, the expression returns `true` and `false` otherwise.

We use comparison operators to build conditions. Eight comparison operators are listed in the following table with examples.

| Expression | Condition | Examples and the evaluation results | |
|---|---|---|---|
| v1 == v2 | Compares two values to see if they are the same, i.e., if v1 is equal to v2.<br>=== is preferred to ==. | 'Run up' == 'Run up' | true |
| | | 'run up' == 'Run up' | false |
| | | '3' == 3 | true |
| | | 3 == 3 | true |
| v1 != v2 | Compares two values to see if they are not the same, i.e., if v1 is not equal to v2.<br>!== is preferred to !=. | 'Run up' != 'Run up' | false |
| | | 'run up' != 'Run up' | true |
| | | '3' != 3 | false |
| | | 3 != 5 | true |
| v1 === v2 | Compares two values to check that **both the data type and value are the same**, i.e., if v1 is strictly equal to v2. | 'Run up' === 'Run up' | true |
| | | '3' === '3' | true |
| | | '3' === 3 | false |
| | | 'hello' === 'Hello' | false |
| v1 !== v2 | Compares two values to check that **both the data type and value are not the same**, i.e., if v1 is strictly not equal to v2. | 'Run up' !== 'Run up' | false |
| | | '3' !== '5' | true |
| | | '3' !== 3 | true |
| | | 3 !== 5 | true |
| v1 > v2 | Checks if v1 is greater than v2. | 2 > 1 | true |
| | | 2 > 5 | false |
| | | 2 > '3' | false |
| | | 2 > '1' | true |
| | | 'a' > 'b' | false |
| v1 < v2 | Checks if v1 is less than v2. | 2 < 1 | false |
| | | 2 < 5 | true |
| | | 2 < '3' | true |
| | | 2 < '1' | false |
| | | 'a' < 'b' | true |
| v1 >= v2 | Checks if v1 is greater than or equal to v2. | 2 >= 2 | true |
| | | 5 >= 2 | true |
| | | 2 >= '3' | false |
| | | '1' >= 2 | false |

| v1 <= v2 | Checks if v1 is less than or equal to v2. | 2 <= 1 | false |
|---|---|---|---|
| | | 2 <= 2 | true |
| | | 2 <= '3' | true |
| | | 2 <= '2' | true |

## Example 7.2

### File Listing

if-2.html, css/if-2.css, js/if-2.js

Load if-2.html in the browser. The web page links to css/if-2.css and js/if-2.js. The page prompts the user to enter a score and tells the user whether he has passed the level or not.

```
1.    var pass = 60;
2.    var input = window.prompt("Enter your score [0-100]: ");
3.    var score = parseFloat(input);
4.    var hasPassed = (score >= pass);
5.    var place = document.getElementById('answer');
6.    place.textContent = "Level Passed: " + hasPassed;
```

*js/if-2.js*

## Convert string to floating point number

Because the prompt method returns user input in a string, the statement at line 3 of js/if-2.js

```
var score = parseFloat(input);
```

calls parseFloat to parse the user input to a floating point number, which is the valid type for comparing to another number 60.

parseFloat parses a string to a floating point number. To see how parseFloat works, open the web console and in the command line bar, run the following expressions to see the returned value from each.

```
parseFloat('85.6')
parseFloat('a85.6')
parseFloat('85a.6')
parseFloat('.85.6a')
parseFloat('-.85.6a')
```

When reading an input from a prompt window which is generated by window.prompt(message), if the input is expect to be a numeric value, use this method to convert the string input into a a floating point number. The conversion adheres to the following rules:

- The first character should be a digit, a sign (+ or -) or a decimal point (.) ,

- The sign (+ or -) must be the first character if it exists.

- The sign (+ or -), the decimal point (.) or an exponent (e-) can only appear once. The 2nd occurrence is considered as invalid character.

- After the first character, the succeeding characters can be digits (0-9) or an exponent (e-).

- A digit must follow an exponent (e-).

- If the first character is invalid, parseFloat returns NaN; otherwise, it continues parsing until encountering a character violating a rule, it returns the value up to that point and ignores that character and all succeeding characters.

## Grouping operator

The statement

```
var hasPassed = (score >= pass);
```

evaluates the expression (`score >= pass`) and assigns the evaluation result, either `true` or `false`, to the variable `hasPassed`.

The comparison expression is grouped by parentheses for indicating the operator >= precedes assignment = operator.

A grouping operator () is used to group the expression `score >= pass` that overrides the normal operator precedence. Removing the grouping will not give any error because comparison operator has higher priority than assignment operator. However, using grouping operators can make it easy to read.

Operator precedence determines the order in which operators are evaluated.

Operators with higher precedence are evaluated first.

Using grouping operators can override the normal operator prededence.

The last two statements

```
var place = document.getElementById('answer');
place.textContent = "Level Passed: " + hasPassed;
```

write the value of `hasPassed` into the HTML element with the `id` value `'answer'` on the web page.

## Workout 7-1

Suppose you are given the following variable declaration statements

```
var score = 85;
var pass = 60;
var message = 'Run down';
var orders = ['Run up', 'Run down'];
```

Evaluate the following expressions.

```
1.  (score == true)
2.  (score != true)
3.  (score > pass)
4.  (score >= pass)
5.  (score <  pass)
6.  (score == pass)
7.  (score === pass)
8.  (score != pass)
9.  (message === orders[0])
10. (message === orders[1])
11. (message !== orders[0])
12. (message !== orders[1])
```

Hint:

To test these expressions, you can follow these steps:

1) Open a new browser window.

2) Open the web console.

3) Open a Scratchpad window. Type all the variable declaration statements in the window. Run the script.

4) Then switch to the web console. In the command line bar, enter each comparison expression. Press Enter and you will see the evaluation result in the display pane.

# Unary Operand

A condition can also be made of a single operand without any comparison operator. In a conditional statement, such as the previously discussed `if` statements, we can check existence of a variable or an object, only using its name (identifier).

## Example 7.3

---

`File Listing`

      `js/if-3.js`

---

Let the following variable declarations be given:

```
var artist1;
var artist2 = undefined;
var artist3 = null;
var artist4 = '';
var artist5 = 'Van Gogh';
```

- `artist1` is declared while uninitialized.

- `artist2` is given the value `undefined`.

- `artist3` is set to `null`.

- `artist4` is assigned with an empty string.

- `artist5` is set to 'Van Gogh'.

Refer to Chapter 2 section "*Know Data Types*" for `null` and `undefined`, two special values in JavaScript.

The following five `if` statements check existence of these five artists by using unary operator. If an artist exists for being `true`, the unary expression is evaluated to `true` and the `alert` statement in curly brackets will display the result.

```
1.    if (artist1) {
2.       window.alert('artist1 is true.');
3.    }
4.    if (artist2) {
5.       window.alert('artist2 is true.');
6.    }
7.    if (artist3) {
8.       window.alert('artist3 is true.');
9.    }
10.   if (artist4) {
11.      window.alert('artist4 is true.');
12.   }
13.   if (artist5) {
14.      window.alert('artist5 is true.');
15.   }
```

The script is stored in `js/if-3.js`.

Run the script in a Scratchpad window. Only the alert from the last `if` statement appears for the reason that only `artist5` is evaluated to `true`. This implies that only `artist5` exists.

To understand the result, read the following part for the relevant rules in JavaScript.

# Evaluation Rules with Special Values

The following rules are applied in JavaScript when special values are used in a comparison.

1. `null`, `undefined` and an empty string `""` are all evaluated to `false`.

2. `null` and `undefined` types are *strictly* equal to themselves and to each other.

3. A nonzero value is evaluated to `true`.

4. zero (`0`) is evaluated to `false`.

5. An empty string is evaluated to `false`.

6. A nonempty string is evaluated to `true`.

## Workout 7-2

Find the evaluation result for each value in the left column of the table below. Write down the result, either `true` or `false`, to the right column. A method is recommended below the table.

| Comparison Expression | Result |
|---|---|
| 1 | |
| 0 | |
| null | |
| undefined | |
| NaN | |
| "" | |
| "hello" | |
| (0 == undefined) | |
| (null === undefined) | |
| (null == false) | |
| (0 == false) | |
| ('hello' == true) | |
| (0 == null) | |
| (0 == NaN) | |
| (undefined == false) | |
| (null == true) | |

In Scratchpad, enter the following script:

```
var myvalue = [placeholder];
if (myvalue) {
    alert(myvalue + ' is true.');
} else {
    alert(myvalue + ' is false.');
}
```

In each run, replace *[placeholder]* with an expression from the left column of the table. Run the script and an alert will display whether the value is evaluated to true or false.

# if Statement

The syntax for if statement is shown below.

Syntax

```
if (condition) {
    //Statements executed when condition is evaluated to true
}
```

The code block in curly brackets is executed only if condition is evaluated to true.

On a web page, we can use unary operand to check whether an HTML element exists or not. Recall that document.getElementById scans HTML elements on a web page; if an HTML element has the matching id, the getElementById method returns a reference to the first matching element and null otherwise.

The following is an example which examines existence of HTML elements by using if statements.

## Square, Circle and Triangle

Example 7.4

File Listing
        if-4.html, css/if-4.css, js/if-4.js

In this example, the web page contains two div elements with the id values 'square' and 'circle', respectively. The corresponding id selectors, #square and #circle, are declared in css/if-4.css to render an element in the shape of either a square or a circle. Each element associates with a class name which configures color setting for the element.

```
1.    <!DOCTYPE html>
2.    <html>
3.       <head>
4.          <meta charset="UTF-8">
5.          <title> Square and Circle: Checking Existence of HTML Elements</title>
6.          <link href="css/if-4.css" rel="stylesheet" type="text/css"/>
7.       </head>
8.       <body>
9.          <section id='shapes'>
10.             <div id="square" class="yellow"></div>
11.             <div id="circle" class="white"></div>
12.          </section>
13.          <script src="js/if-4.js"></script>
14.       </body>
15.    </html>
```

if-4.html

In the stylesheets, `css/if-4.css`, two `id` selectors are specified for making `square` and `circle`. Two class selectors, `.yellow` and `.white`, give two color options.

```
1.    @import url(http://fonts.googleapis.com/css?family=Wellfleet);
2.    body {
3.        background-color: #523620;
4.        color: #fff;
5.        font-family: 'Wellfleet', times, serif;
6.        font-size: 150%;
7.    }
8.    div {
9.        width: 150px;
10.       height: 150px;
11.       margin-left: 20px;
12.       float: left;
13.       text-align: center;
14.   }
15.   #square {
16.   }
17.   #circle {
18.       border-radius: 150px;
19.   }
20.   .yellow{
21.       background-color: #fecc6f;
22.   }
23.   .white{
24.       background-color: #fff;
25.       color: #000;
26.   }
```

css/if-4.css

The main page links to a script `js/if-4.js` at line 13

```
<script src="js/if-4.js"></script>
```

which checks whether there is a square or a triangle or both. The actions by the script are illustrated below in an activity diagram.

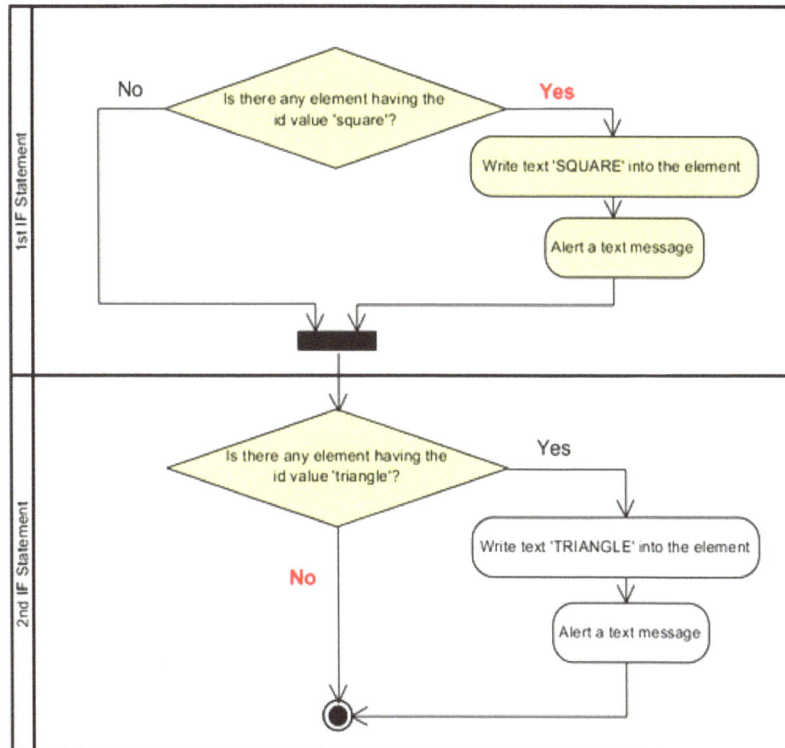

In the 1<sup>st</sup> if statement block, the diamond shape displays the condition for checking any HTML element has the id value 'square'. The method call, document.getElementById('square'), can implement this condition. This condition will generate two possible selections:

Branch 1.    (Yes) If there is at least one square, it returns a *not null* reference. Then the block with the 'Yes' branch is chosen to be executed next. The block writes the text "SQAURE" into the square element and alert a message to the user.

Branch 2.    (No) If there is no square, it returns null and the block with the 'No' branch is executed next. As the block is empty, the program does nothing if there is no square.

The 2<sup>nd</sup> if statement does exactly the same things except for triangles.

The script in js/if-4.js implements the activity diagram.

```
1.    // Get a reference to the first element with the id value 'square'
2.    var squareHandler = document.getElementById('square');
3.    if (squareHandler) {// If the reference is not null
4.        squareHandler.textContent = "SQUARE";
5.        window.alert("There is a square.");
6.    }
7.    // Get a reference to the first element with the id value 'triangle'
8.    var triangleHandler = document.getElementById('triangle');
9.    if (triangleHandler) {// If the refence is not null
10.       triangleHandler.textContent = "triangle";
11.       window.alert("There is a triangle.");
12.   }
```

Based on the web page in if-4.html, because none of the HTML elements on the page has the id value 'triangle', triangleHandler is null and the condition in the second if statement is evaluated to false. The block in the 2<sup>nd</sup> if statement will not be executed.

Thus, in the diagram, only the activities in yellow will be performed.

Now load the page if-4.html in a web browser window. The browser firstly shows an alert *"There is a square."* Close the alert and the brower writes the text SQUARE to the square element.

In the end, the page has the view alike the picture below.

## Workout 7-3

Based on *Example 7.4* with the files `if-4.html`, `css/if-4.css` and `js/if-4.js`, make a new web page.

Do the following modification steps:

1. Copy `css/if-4.css` to a new file `css/c7w3.css`

2. Copy `js/if-4.js` to a new file `js/c7w3.js`

3. Copy `if-4.html` to a new file `c7w3.html`

4. In `css/c7w3.css`, add a new `id` selector `#triangle` which can make a red up-pointing triangle.

   ```
   #triangle {
       width: 0;
       height: 0;
       border-left: 90px solid transparent;
       border-right: 90px solid transparent;
       border-bottom: 150px solid red;
   }
   ```

   Reference – Make a shape in a single HTML element. https://css-tricks.com/examples/ShapesOfCSS/

5. In `c7w3.html`,

   a. Update the `src` attribute for the statement

      `<script src="js/if-4.js" type="text/javascript"></script>`

      Replace `if-4.js` with `c7w3.js`.

   b. Update the `href` attribute for the statement

      `<link href="css/if-4.css" rel="stylesheet" type="text/css"/>`

      Replace `if-4.css` with `c7w3.css`

   c. Add a new `div` that has the `id` value 'triangle' by the statement:

      `<div id="triangle"></div>`

6. In `js/c7w3.js`, write a new `if` statement block which discovers circle(s) and write the text `'CIRCLE'` to the circle element if there is at least one circle.

7. Test the page: Load `c7w3.html` in a web browser window. Each shape should be marked with the associated text. The expected result is shown below.

# Customizing the Sort Method

Previously in Chapter 2 "*Sorting an Array*", we have shown how to sort an array by the sort method with the Array object. As *Example 2.8* indicates, the default comparing is Unicode codepoint based and it is not suitable for sorting numbers.

To compare array items by special comparing criteria, we must provide the criteria in a function. The function name is passed as an argument to the callback parameter in the sort method. The syntax is shown below.

Syntax

```
arrayName.sort([comparingFunction]);
```

comparingFunction is a callback function which defines how two array items are compared. The callback can either be declared in a function or embedded as an IIFE.

## Callback Function

To declare a comparing function and pass its name as callback to Array.sort, the comparing function must follow a specific format, given below.

Syntax – Comparing Function

```
function compare(a, b) {
    [// statements for processing a and b if any]
    if (a is less than b by certain ordering criterion) {
        return -1;
    }
    if (a is greater than b by the ordering criterion) {
        return 1;
    }
    if (a is equal to b by the ordering criterion) {
        return 0;
    }
}
```

In compare(a,b), a and b are two items to be compared. The sort mehod determines the position of a and b by the integer returned from compare(a, b). There are three possible cases.

- If compare(a, b) returns -1, place a before b;

- If compare(a, b) returns 1, place a after b;

- If compare(a, b) returns 0, keep a and b in their current position.

This comparing function will sort the numbers in ascending order.

With the comparing function, the `Array.sort` method becomes very flexible in adapting to different sorting circumstances.

In *Example 2.8*, the `sort` method without a comparing function will sort the array `[20, -2, 100, 35]` to the order as `[-2, 100, 20, 35]`. For numbers, the correct order should be `[-2, 20, 35, 100]`. The followng example shows how to define a comparing function for sorting the numbers in ascending order.

## Example 7.5

File Listing

js/array-sort.js

In Scratchpad, run the script `js/array-sort.js`.

```
1.    var numbers = [20, -2, 100, 35];
2.    // Declare a comparing function
3.    function compare(a, b) {
4.        if (a > b) {
5.          return 1;
6.        }
7.        if (a < b) {
8.          return -1;
9.        }
10.       if (a === b) {
11.         return 0;
12.       }
13.   }
14.   // Call Array.sort with compare as callback
15.   numbers.sort(compare);
16.   // Log the sorted array
17.   console.log(numbers);
```

js/array-sort.js

The correct sorting result should be shown in the web console as `"Array [ -2, 20, 35, 100 ]"`.

## Anonymous Callback

Alternatively, callback can be anonymous inside `Arrary.sort`. See the following script for using an anonymous comparing function.

## Example 7.6

File Listing

js/array-sort-anonymous.js

```
1.    var numbers = [20, -2, 100, 35];
2.    // Call Array.sort with an anonymous callback
3.    numbers.sort(function (a, b) {
4.        if (a > b) {
5.          return 1;
```

```
6.        }
7.        if (a < b) {
8.          return -1;
9.        }
10.       if (a === b) {
11.         return 0;
12.       }
13.    });
14.    console.log(numbers); // Log the sorted array
```

js/array-sort-anonymous.js

# Sort in Descending Order

The previous callback `compare` sorts numerical values in ascending order.

Question: what would be the comparing function for sorting numbers in descending order?

This can simply be done by switching the return statements between greater than and less than statements. By this change, the greater number will be placed before the smaller number.

## Example 7.7

### File Listing

js/array-sort-descending.js

Run the script below. The output in the web console will show the result "Array [ 100, 35, 20, -2 ]".

```
1.    var numbers = [20, -2, 100, 35];
2.    // Declare a comparing function
3.    function compare(a, b) {
4.      if (a > b) {
5.        return -1;
6.      }
7.      if (a < b) {
8.        return 1;
9.      }
10.     if (a === b) {
11.       return 0;
12.     }
13.   }
14.   // Call Array.sort with passing compare as callback
15.   numbers.sort(compare);
16.   // Log the sorted array
17.   console.log(numbers);
```

js/array-sort-descending.js

## Workout 7-4

Write a script to

1.  Prompt user three times; each time asking the user to input a number,

2.  Store three input numbers in an array,

3.  Sort the numbers in ascending order,

4.  Print the sorted array in the web console.

# Sort Array of Objects

So far, we have discussed sorting an array of primitive types for strings or numbers. To sort an array of objects, such as car instances, we may need to derive new values from a and b in the comparing function.

## Example 7.8

---

```
File Listing
        js/array-sort-objects.js
```

Given an object array cars as declared in js/cars.js of *Case 1.1*,

```
cars[0] = new Car('Dodge', 'Charger', 'dodge.png', 2010, 'white', 5, 0);

cars[1] = new Car('Ford', 'F150', 'fordf150.png', 2014, 'black', 5, 0);

cars[2] = new Car('Chevrolet', 'Cruze', 'chevrolet.png', 0, 'red', 5, 0);

cars[3] = new Car('Ford', 'Edge', 'ford.png', 2015, 'yellow', 5, 0);
```

As a car contains multiple property keys, cars can be sorted by any key in ascending or descending order. The following method call shows an anonymous comparing function that sorts the cars by the key make in ascending order.

```
cars.sort(function(a, b) {
    var makeA = a.make.toLowerCase(); // read the key make and convert it to lowercase
    var makeB = b.make.toLowerCase();
    if (makeA < makeB) {
      return -1;
    }
    if (makeA > makeB) {
      return 1;
    }
    if (makeA === makeB) {
      return 0;
    }
});
```

The two blue-highlighted statements

```
    var makeA = a.make.toLowerCase();

    var makeB = b.make.toLowerCase();
```

extract the key value of make for both items a and b and convert the key values to lowercase. makeA and makeB become two strings to be compared in the following if statements.

In a Scratchpad window, open the script js/array-sort-objects.js.

```
1.    // Declare an array
2.    var cars = [];
3.
4.    // Instantiate four new instances by applying the keyword new to the constructor Car
5.    cars.push(new Car('Dodge', 'Charger', 'dodge.png', 2010, 'white', 5, 0));
6.    cars.push(new Car('Ford', 'F150', 'fordf150.png', 2014, 'black', 5, 0));
7.    cars.push(new Car('Chevrolet', 'Cruze', 'chevrolet.png', 0, 'red', 5, 0));
8.    cars.push(new Car('Ford', 'Edge', 'ford.png', 2015, 'yellow', 5, 0));
9.
10.   // Before sorting, log cars
11.   console.log("Before sorting:");
12.   cars.forEach(function (element, index){
13.     console.log(JSON.stringify(element));
14.   });
15.
16.   // Sort cars by the key 'make' in ascending order
17.   cars.sort(function (a, b) {
18.       var makeA = a.make.toLowerCase(); // read the key make and convert it to lowercase
19.       var makeB = b.make.toLowerCase();
20.       if (makeA < makeB) {
21.         return - 1;
22.       }
23.       if (makeA > makeB) {
24.         return 1;
25.       }
26.       if (makeA = makeB) {
27.         return 0;
28.       }
29.   });
30.
31.   // After sorting, log sorted cars
32.   console.log("After sorting:");
33.   cars.forEach(function (element, index){
34.       console.log(JSON.stringify(element));
35.   });
36.
37.   // Declare a constructor Car
38.   function Car(make, model, avatar, year, color, safety, currentSpeed) {
39.       this.make = make;
40.       this.model = model;
41.       this.avatar = avatar;
42.       this.year = year;
43.       this.color = color;
44.       this.safety = safety;
45.       this.currentSpeed = currentSpeed;
```

```
46.        this.accelerate = function (mph) {
47.          this.currentSpeed += mph;
48.        };
49.        this.brake = function () {
50.          this.currentSpeed = 0;
51.        };
52.    }
```

js/array-sort-objects.js

Opne the web console. Run the script. The output in the console should be alike below.

```
Before sorting:
{"make":"Dodge","model":"Charger","avatar":"dodge.png","year":2010,"color":"white","safety":5,"currentSpeed":0}
{"make":"Ford","model":"F150","avatar":"fordf150.png","year":2014,"color":"black","safety":5,"currentSpeed":0}
{"make":"Chevrolet","model":"Cruze","avatar":"chevrolet.png","year":0,"color":"red","safety":5,"currentSpeed":0}
{"make":"Ford","model":"Edge","avatar":"ford.png","year":2015,"color":"yellow","safety":5,"currentSpeed":0}
After sorting:
{"make":"Chevrolet","model":"Cruze","avatar":"chevrolet.png","year":0,"color":"red","safety":5,"currentSpeed":0}
{"make":"Dodge","model":"Charger","avatar":"dodge.png","year":2010,"color":"white","safety":5,"currentSpeed":0}
{"make":"Ford","model":"F150","avatar":"fordf150.png","year":2014,"color":"black","safety":5,"currentSpeed":0}
{"make":"Ford","model":"Edge","avatar":"ford.png","year":2015,"color":"yellow","safety":5,"currentSpeed":0}
```

## Workout 7-5

Modify *Example 7.8* to sort the car instances in cars by the key year in descending order.

# Roles at the Scene Revisited

In Chapter 6, we initiated a case *Roles at the Scene* in *Case 2.1*. In *Example 7.1*, we discussed about commanding animal roles. In this chapter, we will continue working with this case by augmenting it with more functions.

Before getting started, locate the following script files in the subfolder `case2`.

---

```
File Listing - Case 2.1
        scene.html,
        css/scene.css,
        js/Role.js, js/playRoles.js,
        img/dogface.png, img/cat.png
```

---

## Case 2.2

We will update *Case 2.1* to *Case 2.2* by applying `if` statements to move roles around. The same as *Example 7.1*, a `Role` instance is expected to understand a command from the user and run towards the correct direction.

The final script files for *Case 2.2* is listed below.

---

```
File Listing - Case 2.2
        scene-1.html,
        css/scene.css,
        js/Role-1.js, js/playRoles-1.js,
        img/dogface.png, img/cat.png
```

---

In the following, we will present details about this update.

## 1. Add a new property speed for Role

Normally, a role can have a moving speed. In `js/Role.js`, we add a new property key `speed` to `Role`. For each new Role instance, a numerical value is required for `speed`. The larger the value of `speed`, the further the role can move in one step.

## 2. Create a new method `Role.move(direction)`

Next, we enable `Role` with capability of moving. To do so, in the constructor `Role`, we create a new method `move(direction)`. `Role.move` is designed to take a given direction and move a role instance toward the direction.

The direction is identified by four integers `0` through `3` going clockwise with `0` representing up. The direction will be passed as an argument into `Role.move`.

Add `Role.move` to the constructor. The new constructor is stored in `js/Role-1.js`, which is listed below with the new code highlighted.

---

```
1.    var Role = function (ref, avatar, left, top, showup, speed) {
2.        this.ref = ref;
3.       this.avatar = avatar;
```

---

```
4.        this.left = left + 'px';
5.        this.top = top + 'px';
6.        this.showup = showup;
7.        this.speed = speed;
8.
9.        this.setup = function () {
10.           this.ref.style.left = this.left;
11.           this.ref.style.top = this.top;
12.           this.ref.style.backgroundImage = "url(" + avatar + ")";
13.           this.ref.style.visibility = this.showup;
14.       };
15.
16.       this.setVisibility = function (showup) {
17.           this.showup = showup;
18.           this.ref.style.visibility = showup;
19.       };
20.
21.       this.setPosition = function (left, top) {
22.           this.left = left + 'px';
23.           this.top = top + 'px';
24.           this.ref.style.left = this.left;
25.           this.ref.style.top = this.top;
26.       };
27.
28.       this.move = function (direction) {
29.           // Read the current position
30.           var left = parseFloat(this.left);
31.           var top = parseFloat(this.top);
32.           var speed = this.speed;
33.           // Update the position according to direction and speed
34.           if (direction === 0) {//up
35.               top = top - this.speed;
36.           }
37.           if (direction === 1) {//Left
38.               left = left + speed;
39.           }
40.           if (direction === 2) {//down
41.               top = top + speed;
42.           }
43.           if (direction === 3) {//right
44.               left = left - speed;
45.           }
46.           // Move the role to the new position
47.           this.setPosition(left, top);
48.       };
49.
50. };
```

js/Role-1.js

The lines highlighted in blue is the new method `Role.move`, which does the following three steps.

Step 1.   The first two statements, at lines 30 and 31, retrieve the current position and store the position in two function-scope variables `top` and `left`. The value of the key `left` and `top` is of type string. Recall that `parseFloat` parses the numerical part from the string.

NOTE

The CSS property `left` and `top` store position data in strings. Load `scene.html` in a browser. In the web console, run two following expressions one by one in the command line bar:

• `document.getElementById('dog').style.top`
• `parseFloat(document.getElementById('dog').style.top)`

The first one returns a string "625px". The second one returns a number 625.
In order to use position date for calculations, apply `parseFloat` to parse the numerical part from string values that are returned from reading CSS position properties.

Step 2.   Line 32 stores value of the key `speed` to a local variable `speed`.

Step 3.   According to the parameter `direction`, the succeeding four `if` statements update either `top` or `left`. If an equality condition holds, the associated `if` statement will calculate new `top` or `left` by value of `speed`.

Step 4.   In the end, line 47 calls the method `Role.setPosition` to relocate the `Role` instance to the new position and update the keys `left` and `top` as well.

## 3. Create a new array `speed`

After adding the property `speed` to the object **Role**, there are six parameters in total in the **Role** constructor. From now on, for each new instance, a speed value needs to be included in the argument list for each instantiation.

Recall that in the main script `js/playRoles.js` of *Case 2.1*, we have declared five arrays for storing the following data:

→ `roleNames[]`: role names

→ `roleAvatars[]`: avatars

→ `roles[]`: Role instances

→ `prex[]`: left positions

→ `prey[]`: top positions

Now we need to declare a new array `speed` to store speed values. The following statements will declare such an array and assign 5 to the `dog` and 3 to the `cat`.

```
var speed = [];
speed = [5, 3];
```

## 4. Update instantiation statements

Also, the instantiation statements need to be modified to accommodate the new key speed. In the main script, js/playRoles.js, locate the function createRoles, append a speed value to the argument list in the new statement.

```
function createRoles() {// Create a role instance for each name in roleNames
    roleNames.forEach(function (element, index) {
      roles[index] = new Role(document.getElementById(element), roleAvatars[index], 0, 0,
'hidden', speed[index]);
  });
}
```

## 5. Create a new function moveRole

After augmenting the Role object, now we can start to add new functions in the main script js/playRoles.js which enables the user to command the animal roles to move around. For this purpose, we will create a function moveRole.

The new function requires an input parameter that is an integer, being used as the array index to retrieve the target Role instance from the array roles. The function takes a command from the user and move the target instance to the direction by its speed value.

The including steps in moveRole are listed below.

1. Receive the argument index

2. Declare a local variable direction and set it to null

3. Prompt the user to enter an integer and stores the command to the variable input

4. Call the parseInt method to convert the string input to an integer. Store the resulting integer to direction

5. Call Role.move(direction) for roles[index] with the argument direction

For the steps above, the matching method declaration is shown below.

```
function moveRole(index) {
    var direction = null;
    var input = window.prompt("Command " + roleNames[index].toUpperCase() + ": \n Four standard
commands denoted by 0, 1, 2 and 3: \n 0. Run up \n 1. Run right \n 2. Run down \n 3. Run left.
\n Enter an integer [0, 3] for your command: ");
    direction = parseInt(input);
    roles[index].move(direction);
};
```

NOTE

The string "\n" makes a new line in the prompt window.

To print the instance name in the prompt text, the expression roleNames[index].toUpperCase() returns the name in the index-th item from the array roleNames.

The JavaScript method String.toUpperCase() converts a string to upper case. For instance, the expression

```
"javascript".toUpperCase()
```

returns a new string "JAVASCRIPT".

Given

```
var roleNames = ['dog', 'cat'];
```

roleNames[0].toUpperCase() returns "DOG".

roleNames[1].toUpperCase() returns "CAT".

If the user input is out of the range [0, 3], then none of if statements has the condition evaluated to true and the top and left values will not be updated. As the position remains the same, the setPosition method will just place the role at the same position again.

## 6. Call moveRole for a role instance

With the new function moveRole, we are able to command a role instance. For instance, in order to move the dog that is stored in roles[0] in the main script, call moveRole with the argument value 0. The function call is

```
moveRole(0);
```

To move the cat, set the argument value to 1 in calling moveRole

```
moveRole(1);
```

The new main script is stored in js/playRoles-1.js. The new code is highlighted in green.

```
1.    // +++++++++++++++++++++++++++++++++++
2.    // Part 1: Declare Global variables
3.    // +++++++++++++++++++++++++++++++++++
4.    var bottom; // Height of game area
5.    var right; // Width of game area
6.    var xini; // Initial left position
7.    // Declare an array for role names
8.    var roleNames = [];
9.    // Declare an array for role avatar images
10.   var roleAvatars = [];
11.   // Declare an array for speed
12.   var speed = [];
13.   // Declare an array for role instances
14.   var roles = [];
15.   // Declare an array, prex, to store the left position of each role
16.   // which is the horizontal distance to the left wall.
17.   var prex = [];
```

```
18.    // Declare an array, prey, to store the top position of each role
19.    // which is the vertical distance to the top wall
20.    var prey = [];
21.    // Get a reference to div scene
22.    var scene = document.getElementById('scene');
23.
24.
25.    // +++++++++++++++++++++++++++++++++++
26.    // Part 2: Implement a specific case
27.    // +++++++++++++++++++++++++++++++++++
28.    // Give names
29.    roleNames = ['dog', 'cat'];
30.    // Give resource files for avatar
31.    roleAvatars = ['img/dogface.png', 'img/cat.png'];
32.    // Assign each role with a speed
33.    speed = [5, 3];
34.
35.    // Set size of scene: bottom,right,xini
36.    setArea(630, 220, 120);
37.    // Set the initial left and top for role[0]
38.    prex[0] = xini;
39.    prey[0] = bottom; // bottom
40.    // Set the initial left and top for role[1]
41.    prex[1] = Math.random() * xini;   // a random horizontal distance between 0(inclusive) and
         xini(exclusive)
42.    prey[1] = 0; // top
43.    // Call functions
44.    insertHTMLelements();
45.    createRoles();
46.    placeRoles();
47.    // Command roles[0]
48.    moveRole(0);
49.    // Command roles[1]
50.    moveRole(1);
51.
52.
53.    // +++++++++++++++++++++++++++++++++++
54.    // Part 3: Function Declarations
55.    // +++++++++++++++++++++++++++++++++++
56.    function setArea(vbottom, vright, vxini) {
57.        bottom = vbottom; // Height of game area
58.        right = vright; // Width of game area
59.        xini = vxini; // Initial left position
60.    }
61.
62.    function insertHTMLelements() {
63.        // Read the current HTML content in scene
64.        var content = '<div id=\'roles\'>';
65.        // Compose the HTML string that creates a div element each new animal
66.        // Append them to content
67.        roleNames.forEach(function (element, index) {
68.            content = content + '<div class=\'role\' id=\'' + element + '\'></div>';
69.        });
70.        // Update scene
71.        scene.innerHTML = content + '</div>';
```

```
72.    }
73.
74.    function createRoles() {// Create a role instance for each name in roleNames
75.        roleNames.forEach(function (element, index) {
76.            roles[index] = new Role(document.getElementById(element), roleAvatars[index], 0, 0,
       'hidden', speed[index]);
77.        });
78.    }
79.
80.    function placeRoles() {// Place each role in the scene
81.        roles.forEach(function (element, index) {
82.            element.setup();
83.            element.setPosition(prex[index], prey[index]);
84.            element.setVisibility('visible');
85.        });
86.    }
87.
88.    function moveRole(index) {// Command a role to move around
89.        var direction = null;
90.        var input = window.prompt("Command " + roleNames[index].toUpperCase() + ": \n Four
       standard commands denoted by 0, 1, 2 and 3: \n 0. Run up \n 1. Run right \n 2. Run down \n
       3. Run left. \n Enter an integer [0,3] as your command: ");
91.        direction = parseInt(input);
92.        roles[index].move(direction);
93.    }
```

js/playRoles-1.js

## 7. Test the case

The complete file set for *Case 2.1* is in the subfolder `case2`.

```
File Listing
        scene-1.html,
        css/scene.css,
        js/Role-1.js, js/playRoles-1.js
        img/dogface.png, img/cat.png
```

Load `scene-1.html` in a web browser window. The first prompt window shows up.

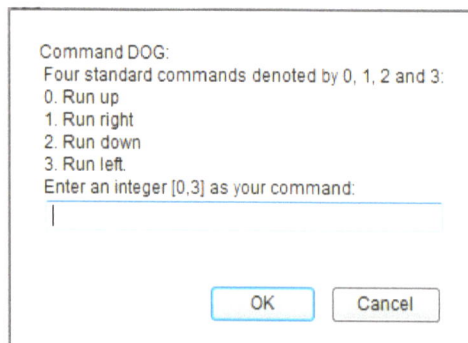

In the text field, you can enter an integer between 0 an 3. After entering the integer, press OK. You should observe the dog making one movement in the direction that matches the integer that you has entered.

After the dog has moved, the second prompt window pops up for commanding the cat.

Command CAT:
Four standard commands denoted by 0, 1, 2 and 3:
0. Run up
1. Run right
2. Run down
3. Run left.
Enter an integer [0,3] as your command:

☐ Prevent this page from creating additional dialogs

OK        Cancel

Currently, the function only supports a one-time command. Each time the page is loaded or refreshed, the current program only allows us to send the command to each animal one time. Reload the page for multiple commands. In order to continuously send commands, we need a special programming structure, which will be introduced in Chapter 8.

# switch Statement

Different programmers write different programs to compute and generate the same results. Some programs have better performance than others. Many factors determine the performance of a computer program. One of the factors is the execution time. Usually, but not always, a script may possibly run faster with fewer statements.

Think about speeding up the method Role.move(direction) in js/Role-1.js of *Case 2.2* in term of the execution time. The logic flow in Role.move(direction) can be visualized by the following activity diagram.

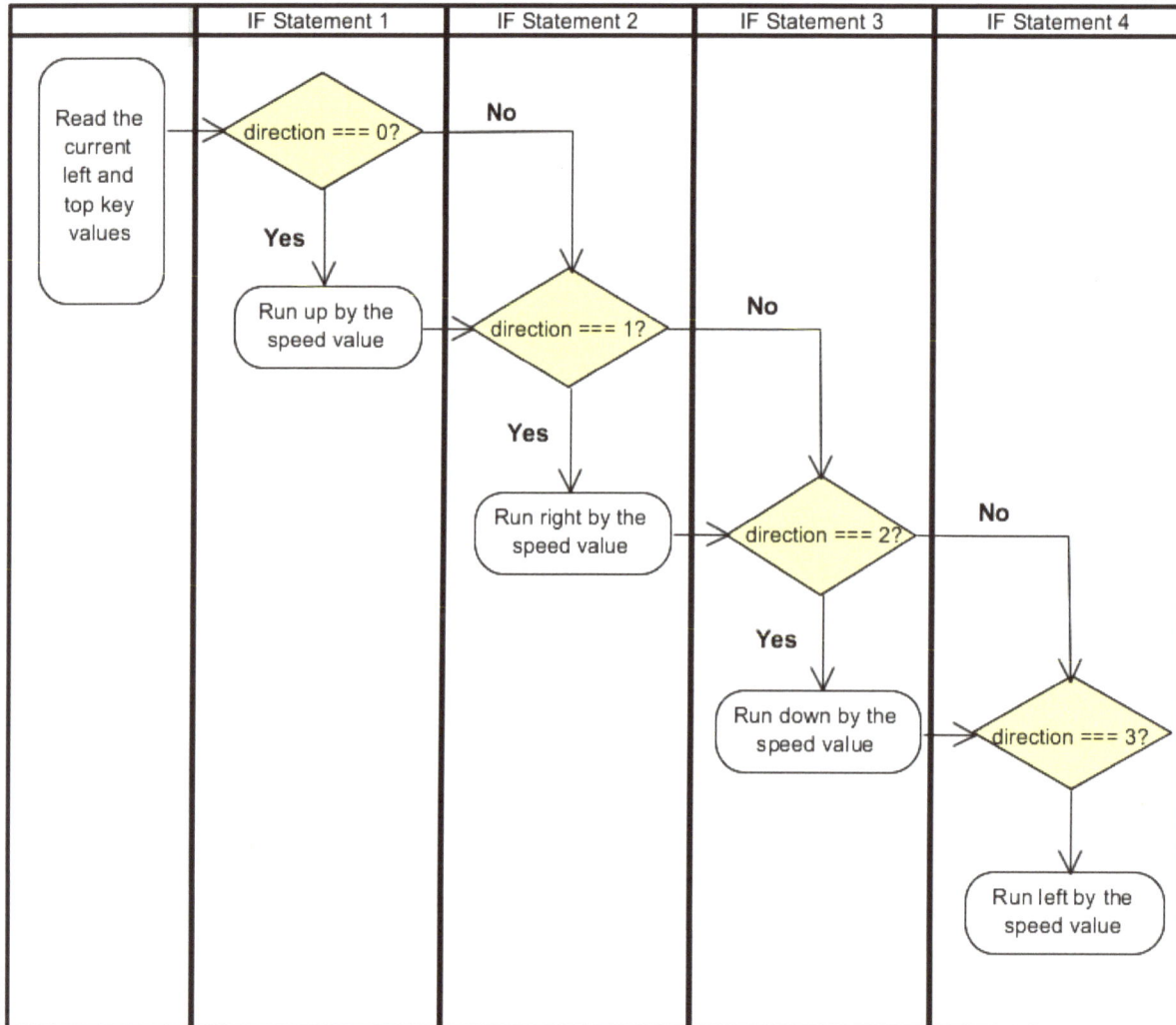

The JavaScript interpreter will execute from left to right, all five columns, one after the other. Each part will take a certain amount of execution time.

The actual execution time is determined by the user input. We can measure the execution time by counting evaluations and code blocks to be executed.

There are five run cases for the user input being equal to 0, 1, 2, 3 and all other values. In the following table, we count the evaluated conditions and the code blocks executed in each case.

| User Input | Conditions to be Evaluated | Number of Evaluations | Number of Code Blocks |
|---|---|---|---|
| 0 | `direction === 0, direction === 1, direction === 2, direction === 3` | 4 | 1 |
| 1 | `direction === 0, direction === 1, direction === 2, direction === 3` | 4 | 1 |
| 2 | `direction === 0, direction === 1, direction === 2, direction === 3` | 4 | 1 |
| 3 | `direction === 0, direction === 1, direction === 2, direction === 3` | 4 | 1 |
| others | `direction === 0, direction === 1, direction === 2, direction === 3` | 4 | 0 |

The table shows that no matter what the user input is, the interpreter always has to go through every condition and make the evaluation. The execution time is 5 for the first four cases, except that it becomes 4 for the last case because no condition is evaluated to true and therefore no block is executed.

However, because all the four conditons are mutually exclusive, if a condition has already been evaluated to `true`, it implies that all the following conditions are `false`. It is a waste of time to execute the following `if` statements. In order to speed up the script, we can replace the four `if` statements with a **switch case** statement.

By the name 'switch case', during each run, the switch can only make one connection to open one case and all the other cases are closed.

The `switch` statement evaluates an expression, matches the expression's value to a **case clause**, and executes the statement block associated with that case. The syntax of `switch` statement is shown below.

Syntax

```
switch (expression) {
  case value1:
    [//Statements executed when the result of expression matches value1]
    [break;]

  case value2:
    [//Statements executed when the result of expression matches value2]
    [break;]

  ...

  case valueN:
    [//Statements executed when the result of expression matches valueN]
    [break;]

  default:
    [//Statements executed when none of the case values match the value of
     the expression]
    [break;]
}
```

There are a few things that we should know when using `switch case` statement.

- The values following the keyword **case** can be an integer or a string.

- The **break** statement is optional.

a. When **break** is encountered in a case clause, the script breaks out of `switch` and executes the statement following `switch`.

b. If the **break** statement is omitted in a case clause, instead of exiting from the `switch`, the execution flow will fall into the next case clause and execute it.

- The **default** clause is optional for default operations if none of the case clauses matchs.

c. If placing the **default** clause after all of the **case** clause(s), we can specify the default operations when none of the `case values` match the evaluation result of `expression`.

# switch Statement Using Integers

## Revisiting the Case: *Roles at the Scene*

We will apply the switch statement to the latest version of *Roles at the Scene* in *Case 2.2*.

Locate the following files from *Case 2.2*.

```
File Listing - Case 2.2

       scene-1.html,

       css/scene.css,

       js/Role-1.js, js/playRoles-1.js,

       img/dogface.png, img/cat.png
```

## Case 2.3

*Case 2.3* will do the same things as *Case 2.2* except for the decision structure with the method Role.move in the main script js/Role-1.js.

Recall that direction is an integer. Use direction as the expression in the switch. The four if statements can be replaced with four case clauses. The new structure is shown below.

```
1.          switch (direction) {
2.              case 0:
3.                  top = top - speed;
4.                  break;
5.              case 1:
6.                  left = left + speed;
7.                  break;
8.              case 2:
9.                  top = top + speed;
10.                 break;
11.             case 3:
12.                 left = left - speed;
13.                 break;
14.             default:
15.                 window.alert("Wrong command!");
16.         }
```

In the switch statement, there are four normal cases and one default case. The default case processes any invalid direction and displays a reminer to the user.

Looking at the table below, this structure replacement can reduce the total number of evaluations in three cases when input is 0, 1 and 2. When there are more than three cases, a switch case statement may speed up the program.

| User Input | Conditions to be Evaluated | Number of Evaluations | Number of Code Blocks |
|---|---|---|---|
| 0 | direction === 0, | 1 | 1 |
| 1 | direction === 0, direction === 1 | 2 | 1 |
| 2 | direction === 0, direction === 1, direction === 2 | 3 | 1 |

| 3 | direction === 0, direction === 1, direction === 2, direction === 3 | 4 | 1 |
| others | direction === 0, direction === 1, direction === 2, direction === 3 | 4 | 0 |

The final set of files for *Case 2.3* are listed below.

---

**File Listing - Case 2.3**

        scene-1-switch.html,

        css/scene.css,

        js/Role-1-switch.js, js/playRoles-1.js,

        img/dogface.png, img/cat.png

To test the new version, load `scene-1-switch.html` in a web browser window. It should allow us control both animals in the same way as *Case 2.2*.

# `switch` Statement Using Strings

As mentioned previously, the expression part following the keyword `switch` also can return a string.

Let us look back to *Example 7.4* with the files `if-4.html`, `css/if-4.css` and `js/if-4.js`. We will start a new example which is based on *Example 7.4*. It adds two more shapes to the web page: a white square and a yellow circle. The program will be revised to write a text above the shape that the user has chosen.

## Example 7.9

---

`File Listing`

switch-1.html, css/switch-1.css, js/switch-1.js

---

Open switch-1.html in a web browser window. A prompt window pops up to ask you for an integer between 1 and 4. Enter 2 and press OK. A new text 'Selected' will be written above the 2$^{nd}$ shape. The result is shown below.

Reload the page and you can enter a different integer. The text will be written to the shape at the position that you have entered.

If you don't enter any value and press OK, the page will display "You didn't select any shape."

If you enter an integer out of the range [1, 4], the page will display "You didn't select any shape."

The following part will discuss the scripts in *Example 7.9*.

## Define new `class` selector

In order to distinguish four shapes, we make a new `class` selector `.shape`. The rule set in `.shape` contains all the common styles for shapes.

Additionally, for each distinct shape, keep the previous four `class` selectors in *Example 7.4*: `.square`, `.circle`, `.yellow` and `.white`. The new style file is shown below as in `css/switch-1.css`.

```
1.    @import url(https://fonts.googleapis.com/css?family=Wellfleet);
2.    body {
3.        background-color: #523620;
4.        color: #fff;
5.        font-family: 'Wellfleet', times, serif;
6.        font-size: 150%;
7.    }
8.    .shape {
9.        display: block;
10.       width: 100px;
11.       height: 100px;
```

```
12.        padding: 10px;
13.        margin-left: 20px;
14.        float: left;
15.        text-align: center;
16.    }
17.    .square {
18.    }
19.    .circle {
20.        border-radius: 150px;
21.    }
22.    .yellow{
23.        background-color: #fecc6f;
24.    }
25.    .white{
26.        background-color: #fff;
27.        color: #000;
28.    }
```

css/switch-1.css

> NOTE
>
> Typically, an id selector is usually applied only to one element while a class selector can be assigned to multiple elements.
>
> We can apply multiple class selectors to an HTML element. For instance, `<div class="shape square yellow"></div>`. Three class selectors are applied to the div element. Multiple class names are separated by a space.

Typically, an **id** selector is usually applied only to one element while a **class** selector can be assigned to multiple elements.

## Apply class selectors

To make a yellow square with a div element, assign two class selectors .square and .yellow, to the attribute class of the div element. The following four lines

```
<div class="shape square yellow"></div>
<div class="shape circle white"></div>
<div class="shape square white"></div>
<div class="shape circle yellow"></div>
```

will create four distinct shapes; each has a specific color and shape. The result is displayed in the picture below.

*We can apply multiple class selectors to an HTML element.*

*Multiple class names are separated by a space.*

## Retrieve all elements with given `class` names

As mentioned earlier in the book, before processing an HTML element, we must get a reference to the element. In previous chapters, we have used the method `document.getElementById` for getting *a reference to the first element* by its `id` value.

The same as `id` values, `class` names can also be used to identify HTML elements. By using `class` names, the method `document.getElementsByClassName` returns *an HTML collection of elements* that contains all the elements with the given `class` names.

*An HTML collection is an array-like object. Collection items can be accessed by using array notation.*

Note that the reference is returned in an array-like collection *even though there is only one matching element*. We must use array notation to access the reference(s) in the collection.

For instance, according to the page `switch-1.html`,

- To get a collection of references to all the yellow square shapes, pass the string `'shape square yellow'` as the argument to the method `document.getElementsByClassName`. The statement is

  ```
  var reference =  document.getElementsByClassName('shape square yellow');
  ```

→ As the page only has one `div` element having the class name `'shape square yellow'`, the element is the only one and the first one in `reference`. However, we must use array notation to access individual references in the returned collection even though there is only one matching element. To access the first reference in the collection, use the expression

  ```
  reference[0]
  ```

- To retrieve all the yellow elements, call `document.getElementsByClassName` with the argument value `'yellow'`. Because there are two yellow shapes on the page, the following statement

  ```
  var yellow = document.getElementsByClassName('yellow');
  ```

  returns a collection of two references pointing to the yellow square and the yellow circle on the page.

→     To access the reference to the first yellow element, use `yellow[0]` and `yellow[1]` for the second yellow element.

■     To retrieve all the shapes on the page, the following statement will do.

```
var shapes = document.getElementsByClassName('shape');
```

→     To access the 1[st] shape, use the notation `shapes[0]`

→     To access the 2[nd] shape, use the notation `shapes[1]`

→     To access the 3[rd] shape, use the notation `shapes[2]`

→     To access the 4[th] shape, use the notation `shapes[3]`

## Use string expression in `switch`

In *Example 7.9*, the following statement is used to return a reference collection to all the shapes on the page.

```
var shapes = document.getElementsByClassName('shape');
```

To access each shape from the collection `shapes`, use array notation: `shapes[0]`, `shapes[1]`, `shapes[2]` and `shapes[3]`.

After getting the reference to each shape on the page, prompt the user to select a shape by entering an integer in the range [1, 4].

```
var select = window.prompt("To select a shape, enter an integer [1,4]:\n");
```

What is the data type of `select`? Keep in mind that `window.prompt` returns user input in a string. We can use the input string in `switch` statement. Now, we are ready for writing a `switch case` statement that can switch to one of five cases according to the user input.

## Write `switch` statement

The following switch case statement will write the text `'selected'` into the selected shape.

```
1.    switch (select) {
2.      case '1':
3.          shapes[0].textContent = "selected";
4.          break;
5.      case '2':
6.          shapes[1].textContent = "selected";
7.          break;
8.      case '3':
9.          shapes[2].textContent = "selected";
10.         break;
11.     case '4':
```

```
12.          shapes[3].textContent = "selected";
13.          break;
14.    default:
15.          window.alert("You did not select any one.");
16. }
```

Pay attention to the values following the keyword case. '1', '2', '3' and '4' are enclosed by quotation marks because they are strings.

> Removing the quotation marks with the strings after each keyword case will make the script always stop at the last default case because no case is written for the integer type.

## Workout 7-6

Based on *Example 7.9* in the file set

switch-1.html, css/switch-1.css, js/switch-1.js,

Make a new web page by doing the following modification steps.

1. Copy css/switch-1.css to a new file css/c7w6.css

2. Copy js/switch-1.js to a new file js/c7w6.js

3. Copy switch-1.html to a new file c7w6.html

4. In css/c7w6.css,

    a. Add a new class selector .triangle which can make an up-pointing triangle in coral pink.

```
.triangle {
    width: 0px;
    height: 0px;
    padding: 0px;
    border-left: 80px solid transparent;
    border-right: 80px solid transparent;
    border-bottom: 120px solid #F88379;
}
```

    b. Add a new class selector .bluegreen which makes a new background color.

```
.bluegreen{
    background-color: #07A666;
}
```

    c. Add a new class selector .tri-bluegreen which makes a bottom border in bluegreen.

```
.tri-bluegreen{
    border-bottom: 120px solid #07A666;
}
```

5.  In `c7w6.html`,

    a.  Update the `src` attribute in the statement

        ```
        <script src="js/switch-1.js" type="text/javascript"></script>.
        ```

        Replace `switch-1.js` with `c7w6.js`.

    b.  Update the `href` attribute in the statement

        ```
        <link href="css/switch-1.css" rel="stylesheet" type="text/css"/>.
        ```

        Replace `switch-1.css` with `c7w6.css`.

    c.  Add a red triangle by inserting a new `div` element:

        ```
        <div class="shape triangle"></div>
        ```

    d.  Add a bluegreen triangle by inserting a new `div` element

        ```
        <div class="shape triangle tri-bluegreen"></div>
        ```

    e.  After completing step c and step d, the total shapes on the page is 6.

6.  Modify `js/c7w6.js` to

    a.  Prompt the user to select a shape by entering an integer in the range `[1, 6]`.

    b.  Use `switch case` statement to display a customized text in the selected shape.

Test the page:

After completing all the steps above, open `c7w6.html` in a web browser window and test the page. The sample look of the page should be similar to the screenshot below.

Once the browser has loaded the page, a prompt window pops up.

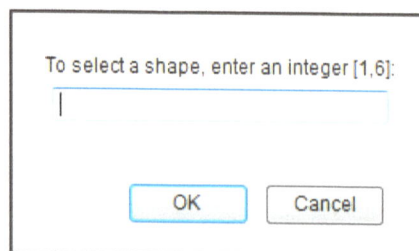

Enter 5 and press `Ok`. A text `'selected'` should appear above the coral triangle.

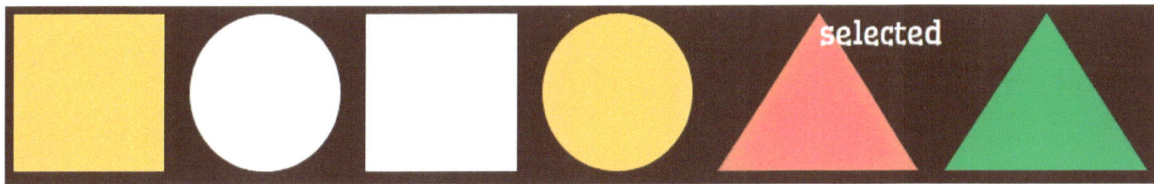

To reselect, reload the page in the browser.

If pressing Cancel in the prompt window or entering an invalid input, the case default should be executed to display an alert saying "You did not select any one."

# Update CSS Properties

## Example 7.10

This example will show you the ability of JavaScript to change the look of HTML elements. You will learn how to access CSS properties of an HTML element and change their values, including setting a picture for background and changing background color.

The files set for this example is listed below.

```
File Listing
        switch-2.html
        css/switch-2.css
        js/switch-2.js
        img/ostrich.png, img/crocodile.png
```

To see the expected result from this example, load switch-2.html in a web browser window. In the beginning, the page displays four shapes, as shown below.

Then an alert box says "There are 2 elements in yellow". After pressing OK to close the alert box, the page will turn to the following look.

Now, let us start discussing the relevant scripts.

## Set up web page

Firstly, we need to build a web page containing such four shapes. The scripts for creating the page are provided in switch-2.html and css/switch-2.css.

The page in switch-2.html displays four shapes; two are in yellow and others are in white.

```
1.    <!DOCTYPE html>
2.    <html>
3.        <head>
```

```
4.              <meta charset="UTF-8">
5.              <title>Example 5.6 </title>
6.              <link href="css/switch-2.css" rel="stylesheet" type="text/css"/>
7.          </head>
8.          <body>
9.              <div class="shape square yellow"></div>
10.             <div class="shape circle white"></div>
11.             <div class="shape square white"></div>
12.             <div class="shape circle yellow"></div>
13.             <script src="js/switch-2.js" type="text/javascript"></script>
14.         </body>
15.     </html>
```

switch-2.html

The associated style rules are specified in `css/switch-2.css`.

```
1.    @import url(https://fonts.googleapis.com/css?family=Wellfleet);
2.    body {
3.        background-color: #523620;
4.        color: #fff;
5.        font-family: 'Wellfleet', times, serif;
6.        font-size: 150%;
7.    }
8.    .shape {
9.        display: block;
10.       width: 200px;
11.       height:200px;
12.       padding: 10px;
13.       margin-left:20px;
14.       float: left;
15.       text-align: center;
16.       background-repeat: no-repeat;
17.       background-position: center;
18.    }
19.    .square {
20.    }
21.    .circle {
22.        border-radius: 150px;
23.    }
24.    .yellow{
25.        background-color: #fecc6f;
26.    }
27.    .white{
28.        background-color: #fff;
29.        color: #000;
30.    }
```

css/switch-2.css

Most rules are the same as those in *Example 7.9* except that the `class` selector `.shape` has two new rules.

→ The rule

```
background-repeat: no repeat;
```

prevents the background image from being repeated.

→ The rule

```
background-position: center;
```

centers the background image.

## Update CSS properties

After setting up the initial static page by switch-2.html and css/switch-2.css, we can start to write the script into js/switch-2.js.

After the page has been loaded in the browser, the script should change the CSS properties for two yellow elements.

```
1.    // Get references to yellow elements
2.    var yellows = document.getElementsByClassName('yellow');

3.    // Alert the totalof yellow elements
4.    window.alert("There are " + yellows.length + " elements in yellow.");

5.    // Change the background of the 1st yellow element
6.    yellows[0].style.backgroundImage ="url(\'img/ostrich.png\')";
7.    yellows[0].style.backgroundColor = 'lightblue';

8.    // Change the background of the 2nd yellow element
9.    yellows[1].style.backgroundImage ="url(\'img/crocodile.png\')";
```

js/switch-2.js

Step 1.    Line 2 gets the references to all of the yellow elements and stores the reference collection to the variable yellows.

Step 2.    At line 4, yellows.length returns the total of references in yellows. Alert the total.

Step 3.    Line 6 updates the CSS property 'backgroundImage' for the first yellow element.

```
yellowShapes[0].style.backgroundImage ="url('img/ostrich.png')";
```

Step 4.    Line 7 assigns a new color 'lightblue' to the CSS property 'backgroundColor' for the second yellow element.

```
yellowShapes[0].style.backgroundColor = 'lightblue';
```

# if else Statement

Both if and switch case statements only allow one set of activities when the condition is evaluated to true. If alternative needs to be done for the false case, if else statement would be a choice. The syntax for this new selection structure is shown below.

Syntax

```
if (condition) {
    [code block 1]
}
else {
    [code block 2]
}
```

If the condition is evaluated to true, execute block 1; if the condition is evaluated to false, go to else clause and run block 2.

## Example 7.11

File Listing

       if-else.html, css/if-else.css, js/if-else.js

If there is a square on the page, the script will write the text "SQUARE" to the square. If there is a triangle on the page, the script will write the text "TRIANGLE" to the triangle. The resulting page is similar to the picture below.

The same HTML file as *Example 7.9* is used in this example, named if-else.html.

```
1.    <!DOCTYPE html>
2.    <html>
3.        <head>
4.            <meta charset="UTF-8">
5.            <title>Example 5.7 Square, Circle & Triangle if-else</title>
6.            <link href="css/if-else.css" rel="stylesheet" type="text/css"/>
7.        </head>
8.        <body>
9.            <section id="shapes">
10.           <div id="square" class="yellow"></div>
11.           <div id="circle" class="white"></div>
12.           </section>
13.           <script src="js/if-else.js" type="text/javascript"></script>
14.       </body>
```

```
15. </html>
```

if-else.html

The if statements in *Example 7.9* are printed in the following.

```
1.     // Get a reference to the first element with the id value 'square'
2.     var squareHandler = document.getElementById('square');
3.     if (squareHandler) {// If the reference is not null
4.         squareHandler.textContent = "SQUARE";
5.         window.alert("There is a square.");
6.     }
7.     // Get a reference to the first element with the id value 'triangle'
8.     var triangleHandler = document.getElementById('triangle');
9.     if (triangleHandler) {// If the reference is not null
10.        triangleHandler.textContent = "triangle";
11.        window.alert("There is a triangle.");
12.    }
```

## Add else clause for false case

Imagine that user wants to see a message if the page has neither square nor triangle. To meet this need, simply append else clause to both existing if clauses.

```
if (squareHandler) {
    squareHandler.textContent = "SQUARE";
    window.alert("There is a square.");
}

else {
    window.alert("No square");
}

if (triangleHandler) {
    triangleHandler.textContent = "TRIANGLE";
    window.alert("There is a triangle.");
}

else {
    window.alert("No triangle");
}
```

## Add a shape for false Case

In addition, the user also wants to add a shape if no such shape exists on the page. Before adding a triangle, be sure to prepare the style rules for making a triangle. The style file css/if-else.css has the id selector #triangle that makes a div element in triangle shape.

## *if else* for the square

Add else clause to the first if statement.

The following diagram shows the decision structure of the if else statement for the square. The diamond in yellow is the condition. The boxes on the right in purple are the block with the if (true) clause. The boxes in green on the left are the block with the else (false) clause.

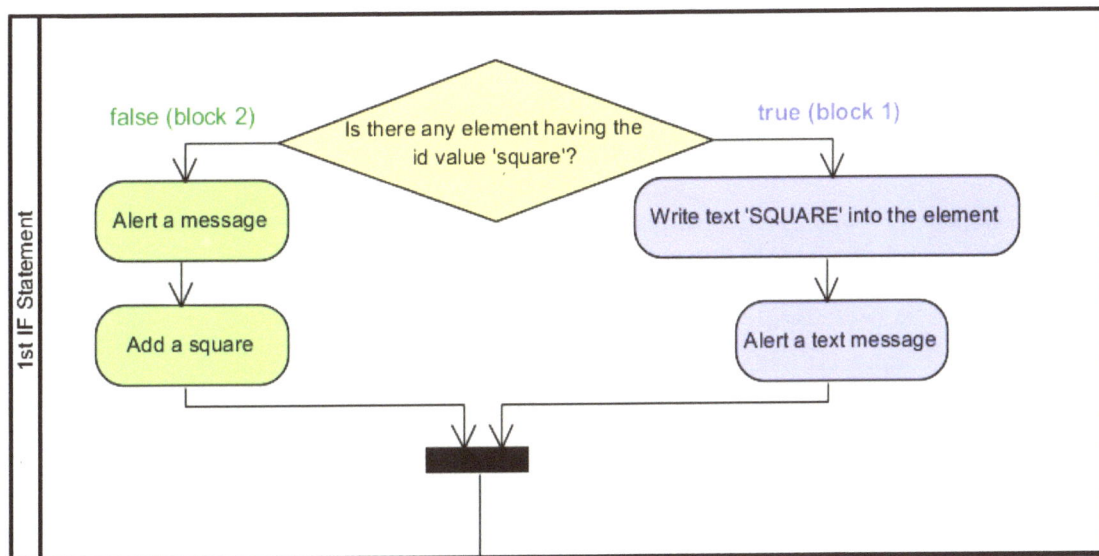

The script that implements this decision structure is as follows.

```
1.    // Get a reference to the element with the id value 'square'
2.   var squareHandler = document.getElementById('square');

3.  // if-else
4.  if (squareHandler) {// If there is a square, do block 1
5.      squareHandler.textContent = "SQUARE";
6.      window.alert("There is a square.");
7.  }
8.  else {// If no square, do block 2
9.      window.alert("There is NO square. Add one now.");
10.     var ref = document.getElementById('shapes');
11.     var square = "<div id=\'square\'></div>";
12.     ref.innerHTML += square;
13. }
```

If squareHandler is false, the block in the else clause will alert a message "There is NO square. Add one now." and add a new div with the id value 'square' to the element section#shapes.

Step 1.    Line 10 gets a reference to the element with the id value "shapes".

Step 2.    Line 11 makes the HTML string, square, that creates a div element having the id value 'square'.

Step 3.    Line 12 appends square to the end of the element ref via its innerHTML property.

## *if-else for the triangle*

Add else clause to the second if statement for triangle.

The decision structure is exactly the same as the previous one for square, except with a few name changes. The if else statement is shown below.

```
1.    // Get a reference to the element with the id value triangle
2.    var triangleHandler = document.getElementById('triangle');
3.    // if-else
4.    if (triangleHandler) {// If there is a triangle, do this block
5.        triangleHandler.textContent = "triangle";
6.        window.alert("There is a triangle.");
7.    }
8.    else {// If no triangle, do this block
9.        window.alert("There is NO triangle. Add one now.");
10.       var ref = document.getElementById('shapes');
11.       var triangle = "<div id=\'triangle\'></div>";
12.       ref.innerHTML += triangle;
13.   }
```

# Conditional Ternary Operator

Both `if` and `if else` statement can be substituted with a shortcut. The shortcut is a conditional operator which takes three operands.

## Syntax

```
condition ? expr1 : expr2
```

The conditional operator returns the value of `expr1` if `condition` is evaluated to `true` and it returns `expr2` otherwise.

## Example 7.12

```
File Listing
        js/conditional-operator.js
```

This example applies conditional ternary operator to do the same thing as *Example 7.2*. The script prompts the user for his test score and tells the user whether he passed a test level or not. You can test this example in a Scratchpad window.

Line 3 in the following script shows a conditional ternary operator.

```
1.    var passscore = 60;
2.    var score = parseFloat(window.prompt("Enter your score ([0, 100]: "));
3.    var pass = (score >= passscore) ? "You passed this level!" : "You  did not pass this level.";
4.    alert(pass);
```

js/conditional-operator.js

The conditional operator is equivalent to the following `if else` statement.

```
var pass = "";
If (score >= passscore) {
    pass = "You passed this level!";
}
else {
    pass = "You did not pass this level";
}
```

# Logical Operators & Composite Comparison Expression

Sometimes a condition is a compound of multiple conditions. The multiple conditions can be connected with logical operators. There are three logical operators: AND, OR and NOT.

Given two conditions in two expressions, expr1 and expr2, the following table shows syntax and evaluation results of applying each logical operator to expr1 and expr2.

Syntax

| Logical AND (&&) | expr1 && expr2 | Returns expr1 if it can be converted to false; otherwise, returns expr2. Thus, when used with Boolean values, && **returns** true **if both operands are** true; **otherwise, returns** false. |
| Logical OR (\|\|) | expr1 \|\| expr2 | Returns expr1 if it can be converted to true; otherwise, returns expr2. Thus, when used with Boolean values, \|\| **returns** true **if either operand is** true; **if both are** false, **returns** false. |
| Logical NOT (!) | !expr1 | Returns false if its single operand can be converted to true; otherwise, returns true. |

In the table below are listed some examples of compound comparison expressions and their evaluation results.

| Compound Expression | Evaluation Result |
|---|---|
| (5 < 2) && (2 >= 3) | false |
| (5 < 2) \|\| (2 >= 3) | false |
| (5 > 2) && (2 >= 3) | false |
| (5 > 2) \|\| (2 >= 3) | true |
| (5 > 2) && (2 <= 3) | true |
| (5 > 2) \|\| (2 >= 3) | false |
| (5 < 2) && (2 <= 3) | false |
| (5 < 2) \|\| (2 <= 3) | true |
| ((5 > 2) && (2 >= 3)) \|\| (1 > 0) | true |
| ((5 > 2) && (2 >= 3)) \|\| (1 < 0) | false |
| !(5 > 2) | false |
| !(5 < 2) | true |
| (5 === 2) && (2 >= 3) | false |
| !(5 < 2) \|\| !(4 === -4) | true |
| ((5 >= 2) && !(2 > 3)) \|\| !(1 === 0) | true |

## Example 7.13

Assuming that `circleHandler` is a reference to a circle and `squareHandler` is a reference to on the page. The following `if else` statement

```
if (circleHandler || squareHandler ) {
    window.alert("We have either one circle or one square or both.");
}
else {
    window.alert("We have neither circle or square.");
}
```

will discover whether there is a circle or a square or both. The condition in the `if` clause is composed of the OR operator which connects two references `circleHandler` and `squareHandler`. If either reference exists, the condition `circleHandler || squareHandler` returns `true`; if neither one exists, it returns `false`.

## Workout 7-7

Evaluate the following expressions that involve logical operators. Hint: Test expressions in the web console.

(a)  `!( 1 < 3)`

(b)  `(4 < 7) && (4 <= 7)`

(c)  `(2 > -3) || (-2 > -3)`

(d)  `!(1 === 1) && !(2 >= 3)`

(e)  `((2 > 3) || (4 > 3)) && !(-1 === 1)`

## Workout 7-8

Revise *Example 7.11* in the following script files:

```
if-else.html
css/if-else.css
js/if-else.js
```

1.  Use the same web page that is scripted by `if-else.html` and `css/if-else.css`.

2.  Modify `js/if-else.js` to apply logical operator AND and `if else` statement. The script should find whether both square and triangle exist on the web page.

    →  `if` Clause: If both shapes exist, alert a message "There are both square and triangle." Write the text `'SQUARE'` to the square and `'TRIANGLE'` to the triangle.

    →  `else` Clause: Otherwise, alert a message saying"There is only square or triangle or neither."

3.  After completing the modifications above, test the web page.
    As the current web page in `if-else.html` contains a square and a circle, `else` clause should be selected

and you should see the alert "There is only square or triangle or neither." If not, edit the script until the page shows the right alert.

4. Modify `if-else.html`.

   In the element `section#shapes`, add a new `div` element with the `id` value `'triangle'`. This can be done by inserting the following line above the closing `</section>` tag.

   ```
   <div id="triangle"></div>
   ```

5. Load the modified `if-else.html` in the browser.

   After the modification in step 4, the page contains a square, a circle and a triangle. So `if` clause will be executed that pops up the alert "There are both square and triangle." The text is written into both shapes.

# Chapter 8    AUTOMATING REPETITIONS WITH LOOP

In chapter 7, we have seen several decision-making structures including `if`, `switch`, `if else` and conditional ternary operator. The decisions render a computer program adaptable to different scenarios by selecting actions from matching branchs. Incorporation of decision structure into a computer program enhances its functionality and augments the program with variety.

This chapter will cover another program structure, loop, which is equally as important as decision structure. Loop offers an easy way to automate repetition of an operation set until a certain prescribed stop condition is satisfied.

In Chapter 3, `Array.forEach` has been elaborated on for automatically repeating the same operations over every array item. As previously shown in *Example 3.8* about displaying star names, `Array.forEach` gives a concise version for `js/ex-4.js` in *Example 3.1*. The script `js/ex-8.js` from *Example 3.8* is shown below.

```
1.    var stars = ["Alpha", "Beta", "Gamma", "Delta", "Epsilon", "Theta", "Chi", "Zeta", "Mu",
      "Eta"];
2.    var lines = [];
3.    stars.forEach(function (element, index){
4.        lines[index] = "<p>The element indexed by " + index + " is " + element + "</p>";
5.    });
6.    var place = document.getElementById("stars");
7.    place.innerHTML = lines[0] + lines[1] + lines[2] + lines[3] + lines[4] + lines[5] + lines[6] +
      lines[7] + lines[8] + lines[9];
```

js/ex-8.js

`stars.forEach` repeats the operation at line 4 for each `stars` item.

However, `forEach` is only limited to `Array` object. For non-array data, JavaScript has generic loop structures, such as `for` loop, `while` loop and `do while` loop. In this chapter, we will discuss these generic loops.

## Table of Content

# for Loop

The for loop structure is implemented in a for statement. A for statement repeats a set of statements until a specified condition is evaluated to false.

## for Statement

The for statement in JavaScript is similar to other programming languages, which is written with the following syntax.

Syntax – for

```
for ([initialExpression]; [condition]; [incrementExpression])
{
   [loop body: a set of statements]
}
```

When a for statement is executed, the following steps occur in order:

Step 1.   The initializing expression initialExpression is executed if there is one. This expression usually initializes one or more loop counters.

> A loop counter is a variable that controls iterations of a loop; often it is an integer justifying its name.
>
> A loop counter is also referred to as an iterator.

Step 2.   The loop condition condition is evaluated. According to the evaluation result, either true or false, one choice will be selected from the following three branches.

- If condition is evaluated to true, the statements in the loop body are executed.

- If condition is evaluated to false, *the loop terminates*.

- If the condition part is omitted entirely, condition is assumed to be true and the statements in the loop body are executed.

> If the condition never turns to false and there is no break statement in the loop body, the loop will repeat infinitely. As a result, the program will never exit the loop.

Step 3.   If there is an update expression incrementExpression, it will update the loop counter in a certain way.

Step 4.   The execution flow returns to step 2.

If we are able to determine maximum count of repetitions prior to execution, for loop is a better choice than while loop and do while loop, which are to be introduced later in this chapter.

## Iterating Over Arrays

The for loop is a generic way to replace `Array.forEach`. In the following, let us replace `Array.foreach` in `js/ex-8.js` of *Example 3.8* with a for statement.

## Example 8.1

---

`FileListing`

> ex-8-forloop.html, css/ex-4.css, js/ex-8-forloop.js, img/star.png

Load `ex-8-forloop.html` in a browser. It should list all the star names on the page.

The following script named `js/ex-8-forloop.js` shows, at lines 8 through 10, a for statement that is a subtitute for `Array.forEach` in `js/ex-8.js`.

```
1.    var stars = ["Alpha", "Beta", "Gamma", "Delta", "Epsilon", "Theta", "Chi", "Zeta", "Mu",
      "Eta"];
2.    // Get a reference to the element 'stars'
3.    var place = document.getElementById("stars");
4.
5.    // Declare newline and initialize it to an empty string
6.    var newline = '';
7.    // for loop
8.    for (var index = 0; index < stars.length; index++) {
9.        newline += "<p>The star indexed by " + index + " is " + stars[index] + ".</p>";
10.   }
11.   // Write newline as the HTML content into the element 'stars'
12.   place.innerHTML = newline;
```

js/ex-8-forloop.js

Comparing the for statement with the `Array.forEach` statement, it is seen that when writing a for statement with an array object, we need to script iteration details, including total of iterations and stop condition. In constrast to this, `Array.forEach` controls the iterations by hiding these details from us. On the other hand, for statement gives programmers more power of controlling the loop, therefore it is more versatile and flexible than `Array.forEach`.

In the following, let us delineate the for statement above.

## Initialize loop

At line 8, after the keyword for, within the parentheses, there are three parts.

→ In the first part, the loop initial conditioin is

    var index = 0

By this condition, index is declared as a loop counter and initially set to zero.

→ In the second part, the condition is

    index < stars.length

stars.length returns 10 which is the size of stars, i.e., the total of items in stars. The condition can be interpreted as "*The loop continues as long as index is less than 10.*"

$\rightarrow$ The third part determines how the counter `index` is updated after each iteration. The counter will increment by one after each iteration.

## Iterations

The loop starts at the initial status when `index` is `0`. During each iteration,

Step 1.  The condition, `index < stars.length`, is evaluated.

Step 2.  If the current `index` is less than `10`, the loop condition is evaluated to `true`, i.e., we have not processed all the items.

o   The statement(s) enclosed in curly brackets is executed:

```
newline += "<p>The star indexed by " + index + " is " + stars[index] + ".</p>";
```

o   Go to Step 4.

Step 3.  If the loop condition is evaluated to `false`, i.e., the current `index` value equals `10` and it indicates that all the array items have been processed. Thus, the loop halts. Go to the next statement, if any, below the `for` statement.

Step 4.  `index` increments by the increment statement `index++`.

Step 5.  Go back to Step 1 for starting a new iteration.

The following table shows how the loop couner `index` varies along with the condition and other variables in each iteration. The iterations are numbered from `1` to `10`.

| #iteration | #1 | #2 | #3 | #4 | #5 | #6 | #7 | #8 | #9 | #10 | |
|---|---|---|---|---|---|---|---|---|---|---|---|
| index | 0 | 1 | 2 | 3 | 4 | 5 | 6 | 7 | 8 | 9 | 10 |
| index < stars.length | true | true | true | true | true | true | true | true | true | true | false |
| Loop body | run | run | run | run | run | run | run | run | run | run | X |
| index++ | 1 | 2 | 3 | 4 | 5 | 6 | 7 | 8 | 9 | 10 | X |
| stars[index] | 'Alpha' | 'Beta' | 'Gamma' | 'Delta' | 'Epsilon' | 'Theta' | 'Chi' | 'Zeta' | 'Mu' | 'Eta' | undefined |

In the table, the increment statement `index++` will increase the loop counter `index` for ten times from `0` until `10`, because only `0` through `9` are valid array indices for `stars`. After the iteration #10, `index` reaches `10`, the condition is evaluated to `false`. Thus, the loop terminates after `10` iterations.

# Inspecting Intermediate Values

Sometimes, in order to debug a program which has not produced desired results, programmers may add a few print statements to observe intermediate values of variables. In the last example *Example 8.1*, if we want to see how the loop develops through each interation, we can add print statements to either print loop-related values in the web console or the page. See the example below.

## Example 8.2

---

```
FileListing
        ex-8-forloop-print.html, css/ex-4.css, js/ex-8-forloop-print.js, img/star.png
```

In js/ex-8-forloop-print.js, add two log statements inside the loop body.

```
for (var index = 0; index < stars.length; index++) {
    console.log("==== Start Iteration #" + (index+1) + " -> loop counter: index = " + index);
    console.log("   stars[index] = " + stars[index]);
    newline += "<p>The star indexed by " + index + " is " + stars[index] + ".</p>";
}
```

Open the web console in a web browser. Load ex-8-forloop-print.html in the browser. The following logs should display in the console.

```
==== Start Iteration #1 -> loop counter: index = 0
   stars[index] = Alpha
==== Start Iteration #2 -> loop counter: index = 1
   stars[index] = Beta
==== Start Iteration #3 -> loop counter: index = 2
   stars[index] = Gamma
==== Start Iteration #4 -> loop counter: index = 3
   stars[index] = Delta
==== Start Iteration #5 -> loop counter: index = 4
   stars[index] = Epsilon
==== Start Iteration #6 -> loop counter: index = 5
   stars[index] = Theta
==== Start Iteration #7 -> loop counter: index = 6
   stars[index] = Chi
==== Start Iteration #8 -> loop counter: index = 7
   stars[index] = Zeta
==== Start Iteration #9 -> loop counter: index = 8
   stars[index] = Mu
==== Start Iteration #10 -> loop counter: index = 9
   stars[index] = Eta
```

# Generating Sequence

Loop is useful to generate a sequence of numbers. The following example shows a for statement that creates, in an array, a sequence of 10 positive odd integers starting with 1. The sequence rule is the difference between every two consecutive values is always 2.

In a browser window, open the web console. In a Scratchpad window, open the script js/for-sequence.js. Click Run. The output log displays how the sequence develops through each iteration. After 10 iterations, the last log shows the final sequence is (1, 3, 5, 7, 9, 11, 13, 15, 17, 19, 21).

## Example 8.3

FileListing

js/for-sequence.js

```
1.    var start = 1; // Set up the first value
2.    var step = 2; // Set up the step
3.    var length = 10; // Set up the sequence length
4.    var sequence = []; // Declare a sequence in an array
5.    sequence.push(start); // push the first value into sequence
6.
7.    for (var i = 0; i < length; i++) {
8.      var next = sequence[i] + step; //Calculate the next value by sequence rule
9.      sequence.push(next); // Push next into sequence
10.     // Print log
11.     console.log('==== Iteration #' + (i + 1) + ' -> sequence: ');
12.     sequence.forEach(function (element) { //Print the current sequence
13.       console.log(element + ',');
14.     });
15.   }
16.
17.   console.log('Loop terminates.');
```

js/for-sequence.js

Each iteraton in the for statement generates the next sequence number next. Line 9 realizes the sequence rule by adding 2 to the last sequence number. Line 10 pushes the new number into the sequence. Lines 12 through 15 are the statements that print the log messages in the web console.

## Workout 8-1

Based on *Case 2.3* with the following script files,

---

```
File Listing - Case 2.3
        scene-1-switch.html,
        css/scene.css,
        js/Role-1-switch.js, js/playRoles-1.js,
        img/dogface.png, img/cat.png
```

---

In js/playRoles-1.js, locate the function declaration of placeRoles. In placeRoles, there is a roles.forEach statement, shown as below.

```
function placeRoles() {// Place each role in the scene
    roles.forEach(function (element, index) {
        element.setup();
        element.setPosition(prex[index], prey[index]);
        element.setVisibility('visible');
    });
}
```

Write a for statement to replace this roles.forEach statement.

## Workout 8-2

Open a browser window. Open a Scratchpad window. Open the web console.
In the Scratchpad window,

Step 1. Enter the following script:

```
var start = 1;
var sum = 0;
for (var i = 0; i < end; i++) {
    sum += i;
}
console.log('sum = ' + sum);
```

Step 2. Run the script. The web console should display the message "sum = 45". Note: If the log message will not show in the console, be sure to turn on the tab [Logging] in the web console.

Step 3. Explain the meaning of this value 45.

Step 4. Modify the script to produce the following logs.

```
==== Iteration #1 -> loop counter: i = 0          Scratchpad/1:5:3
    sum = 0                                        Scratchpad/1:6:3
==== Iteration #2 -> loop counter: i = 1          Scratchpad/1:5:3
    sum = 1                                        Scratchpad/1:6:3
==== Iteration #3 -> loop counter: i = 2          Scratchpad/1:5:3
    sum = 3                                        Scratchpad/1:6:3
==== Iteration #4 -> loop counter: i = 3          Scratchpad/1:5:3
    sum = 6                                        Scratchpad/1:6:3
==== Iteration #5 -> loop counter: i = 4          Scratchpad/1:5:3
    sum = 10                                       Scratchpad/1:6:3
==== Iteration #6 -> loop counter: i = 5          Scratchpad/1:5:3
    sum = 15                                       Scratchpad/1:6:3
==== Iteration #7 -> loop counter: i = 6          Scratchpad/1:5:3
    sum = 21                                       Scratchpad/1:6:3
==== Iteration #8 -> loop counter: i = 7          Scratchpad/1:5:3
    sum = 28                                       Scratchpad/1:6:3
==== Iteration #9 -> loop counter: i = 8          Scratchpad/1:5:3
    sum = 36                                       Scratchpad/1:6:3
==== Iteration #10 -> loop counter: i = 9         Scratchpad/1:5:3
    sum = 45                                       Scratchpad/1:6:3
Loop terminates. sum = 45                         Scratchpad/1:8:1
```

## Workout 8-3

Refer to *Example 8.3*. Write a script that runs in Scratchpad to generate the first 20 elements of the Fibonacci sequence:

1, 1, 2, 3, 5, 8, 13, 21, 34, 55, 89, 144, 233, 377, 610, 987, 1597, 2584

In the Fibonacci sequence, the first two numbers are fixed as 1 and 1, and each subsequent number is the sum of the previous two. Hint: Use for loop.

# while & do while Loop

Often, the number of times a set of operations needs to be repeated is unknown; we only know the repetition should continue until a specific condition is satisfied. In such cases, we can use `while` loop or `do while` loop.

`while` loop is the same as `do while` loop except for their minimum number of iterations. A `do while` loop runs the loop body before evaluating the condition, and operations will be run at least one time. A `while` loop first evaluates the condition and the loop body may not run if the condition is never met.

The following shows a syntax of a `while` statement.

Syntax

```
while (condition) {
    [Loop body in a statement block]
}
```

The `while` statement is structured in such a way that the loop continues as long as `condition` is evaluated to `true`. If `condition` evaluates `false` in the beginning, then *loop body* will never run.

The following is a syntax for a `do while` statement.

Syntax

```
do {
    [Loop body in a statement block]
} while (condition);
```

In the `do while` statement, because the `do` clause is placed before the `while` clause, the statement does the *loop body* before `condition` is evaluated. This means that *loop body* must run at least once no matter whether the initial condition is `true` or `false`. After the first iteration is complete, `condition` is evaluated and its result is used to decide if the next iteration should start or the loop should just terminates.

In cases where the action within *loop body* must execute at least once, a `do while` statement is preferred.

## Counting

The following example uses `while` loop to keep asking the user a question in a prompt window. If the user enters 'y' in the prompt window, count numbers and increment the total by one each time; if the user enters 'n', the loop terminates. Each time after receiving 'y' from the user, the current total is logged to a section 'log' on a web page.

Example 8.4

```
File Listing
       while-1.html, js/while-1.js
```

```
1.    <!DOCTYPE html>
```

```html
2.    <html>
3.        <head>
4.            <title>Using While Loops</title>
5.            <meta charset="UTF-8">
6.            <meta name="viewport" content="width=device-width, initial-scale=1.0">
7.        </head>
8.        <body>
9.            <section id='log'></section>
10.           <script src="js/while-1.js" type="text/javascript"></script>
11.       </body>
12.   </html>
```

while-1.html

```javascript
1.    //continue counting until the user enters 'n'
2.    var total = 0;
3.    var log = document.getElementById('log');
4.    var next = true;
5.    while (next) {
6.        total++;
7.        var logline = "<p>You have counted " + total + " times.</p>";
8.        log.insertAdjacentHTML('beforeend', logline);
9.        var input = window.prompt('Do you want to continue counting? Enter y for yes or n for no:
      ');
10.       next = (input === 'y') ? true : false;
11.   }
12.   var summary = "<p>In summary, you have counted " + total + " times.</p>";
13.   log.insertAdjacentHTML('beforeend', summary);
```

js/while-1.js

In this example, as the user decides when he wants to terminate the loop, the number of iterations is unpredictable. During each iteration, the user will be asked to answer a question "Do you want to continue counting?" The loop continues until the user enters 'n'.

Thus, the answer from the user can constitute the loop condition.

→ Lines 5 through 11 make a while statement.

→ Line 5 states the loop condition be a Boolean variable next.

→ Before the loop starts, line 4 sets the variable next to true as to enable the first iteration.

→ Lines 6 through 8 are the operations to be repeated every time.

→ At the end of each iteration, the code in the yellow part updates the loop condition next.

  – Line 9 prompts the user to answer the question about whether continuing counting or not.

  – The conditional ternary expression at line 10 sets next to true if the user enters 'y' or false for 'n'.

Load while-1.html in a web browser. Enter 'y' to continue counting or 'n' to terminate the counting. If you enter 'n' in the sixth prompt window, the page ends with the following content.

You have counted 1 times.

You have counted 2 times.

You have counted 3 times.

You have counted 4 times.

You have counted 5 times.

In summary, you have counted 5 times.

## Workout 8-4

Create a web page that links to an external script which keeps asking the user if he wants to generate a random number between 1 and 100; if the user says yes, the page displays a random number in an HTML paragraph; otherwise the page quits asking the user and prints a summary for the total number of random numbers that have been generated.

# Looping Through Arrays

*Example 8.1* shows that for loop can iterate over an array. while loop and do while loop can also scan an array for repeating operations.

Below is an example that apply while loop to scan through an array; during each iteration, print the loop counter and its associated array element.

## Example 8.5

**File Listing**

      js/while-2.js

```
1.    var stars = [
2.        'Alpha',
3.        'Beta',
4.        'Gamma',
5.        'Delta',
6.        'Epsilon',
7.        'Theta',
8.        'Chi',
9.        'Zeta',
10.       'Mu',
11.       'Eta'
12.    ];
13.    var i = 0; // Set up loop counter
14.    while (stars[i]) { // If stars[i] is defined, run statements in loop body
15.        console.log('loop counter i = ' + i + ', ' + 'stars[' + i + '] = ' + stars[i]);
16.        i++; // Increment loop counter
17.    }
18.    console.log('Now the while loop ends. The loop counter i = ' + i + '. stars[' + i + '] = ' +
           stars[i]);
```

In the while statement, the variable i is a loop counter and stars[i] is the loop condition. As long as stars[i] is defined that will be evaluated to true, the loop continues.

Open the web console. Run js/while-2.js in Scratchpad. The output in the web console is shown below.

```
loop counter i = 0, stars[0] = Alpha                              Scratchpad/4:16:3
loop counter i = 1, stars[1] = Beta                               Scratchpad/4:16:3
loop counter i = 2, stars[2] = Gamma                              Scratchpad/4:16:3
loop counter i = 3, stars[3] = Delta                              Scratchpad/4:16:3
loop counter i = 4, stars[4] = Epsilon                            Scratchpad/4:16:3
loop counter i = 5, stars[5] = Theta                              Scratchpad/4:16:3
loop counter i = 6, stars[6] = Chi                                Scratchpad/4:16:3
loop counter i = 7, stars[7] = Zeta                               Scratchpad/4:16:3
loop counter i = 8, stars[8] = Mu                                 Scratchpad/4:16:3
loop counter i = 9, stars[9] = Eta                                Scratchpad/4:16:3
Now the while loop ends. The loop counter i = 10. stars[10] = undefined    Scratchpad/4:19:1
```

The loop ends immediately after the counter i turns to 10 which falsefies the loop condition because stars[10] is undefined which evaluates to false.

## Workout 8-5

Create a web page ex-while-1.html that links to an external script js/ex-while-1.js.

1. Place an HTML section element in ex-while-1.html. Assign the section with the id value 'list'.

2. Link the web page to js/ex-while-1.js

3. In js/ex-while-1.js,

   a. Declare an array **A**. Initialize the array with 5 numeric elements.

   b. Write a while statement to iterate over the array and write new paragraphs to the section 'list'.

      i.   Set the loop counter **k**. Initialize **k** to 0.

      ii.  **A[k]** is the loop condition. Terminate the loop when **A[k]** is undefined.

      iii. In each iteration,

           → Write a new paragraph to the section 'list'. The paragraph displays the array element indexed by the current loop counter.

           → Increment the loop counter **k** by one.

# Validating User Input

Recall *Example 1.1* in Chapter 1 that prompts the user for an integer between 1 and 3 and open the box at the position by the integer. The relevant files are listed below where ex-0.html is the main page.

---

`File Listing`

        ex-0.html,

        css/ex-0.css,

        js/ex-0.js,

        img/nespresso.jpg, img/kinderegg.jpg, img/capsule.jpg

---

Load ex-0.html in a web browser. In the prompt window, enter an invalid symbol that is not 1 or 2 or 3. The script will respond to the user by displaying a new prompt window, alerting the user for the invalid input and reminding the user for a new input. The same alert will be repeated until a valid input has been entered.

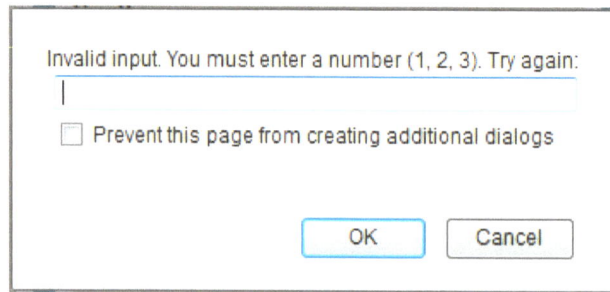

```
Invalid input. You must enter a number (1, 2, 3). Try again:
|
☐ Prevent this page from creating additional dialogs

                                    OK            Cancel
```

This is one of the applications where while loop prevents the program flow from proceeding until receiving a valid input. The loop condition is responsible for validating the user input.

Let us look into the while statement in js/ex-0.js.

```
1.    // Search HTML elements with the tag 'li'
2.    var items = document.getElementsByTagName('li');
3.    // Prompt user for an integer between 1 and 3
4.    var input = window.prompt('There are 3 boxes on the page. To open a box, enter a number (1, 2,
      3): ');
5.    // Repeat prompting until the user enters a valid value
6.    while ( Number.isNaN(parseInt(input)) || (parseInt(input) > 3 || parseInt(input) < 1) )
7.    {
8.      input = window.prompt('Invalid input. You must enter a number (1, 2, 3). Try again: ');
9.    }
10.   // Locate the selected li element and apply a class selector
11.   var select = parseInt(input) - 1;
12.   items[select].innerHTML = 'Open...';
13.   // Use String.concat to join 'b' and the integer in select
14.   var name = 'b'.concat(select);
15.   // Set the class attribute to the value in name: b0 or b1 or b2
16.   items[select].setAttribute('class', name);
```

js/ex-0.js

In the script above, lines 6 through 9 make a `while` statement that will keep looping until receiving a valid input from the user.

The action in the loop body produces a prompt window and reads user input into a variable `input`. If `input` is `1` or `2` or `3`, the loop condition should evaluate to `false` and the loop terminates. For any other values, the loop condition should evaluate to `true`, continuing the loop to the next iteration for a new input.

Thus, the most challenging problem is building such a loop condition. The script box above has already shown us an answer:

```
Number.isNaN(parseInt(input))
||
( parseInt(input) > 3 || parseInt(input) < 1 )
```

This conditional expression is compound as it connects two sub-expressions with a comparison operator OR, denoted by `||`. The expression will return `true` for *invalid* input and false for *valid* input.

The expression to the left of OR identifies non-numeric input and the expression to the right of OR examines any integer out of the right range `[1,3]`.

> The OR operator returns `true` as long as either operand evaluates `true`.

The first sub-expression in the green part calls `Number.isNaN` method on `parseInt(input)`.

→ If `parseInt(input)` returns `NaN`, `Number.isNaN` will return `true`. As the first operand in the OR operator is `true`, the rest part of the expression will be neglected. The entire expression is evaluated to `true`. The loop continues.

→ If `parseInt(input)` returns an integer, `Number.isNaN` returns `false`. Then the second sub-expression in blue needs to be evaluated to decide if the integer is within the right range `[1,3]`.

```
parseInt(input) > 3 || parseInt(input) < 1
```

- If `parseInt(input)` is an integer greater than 3 or less than 1, the blue part will return `true`. Then the whole expression returns `true`. The loop continues.

- If `parseInt(input)` is an integer between 1 and 3, the blue part will return `false`. Then the whole expression returns `false`. The loop terminates and the program flows to the next statement below the `while` statement.

The following part is a brief introduction of three methods that are used in `js/ex-0.js`.

## String.concat

At line 14 of `js/ex-0.js`, the method `String.concat` is an alternative to the operator `+` for joining one or more strings into a new string. The syntax of using the method is

### Syntax

```
str.concat(string2[, string3, ..., stringN])
```

Open the web console. Enter the two following statements in the command line bar one after the other:

```
var hello = 'Hello ';
hello.concat('world', '!'));
```

The echo after entering the 2nd statement is the new string "Hello world!" this was produced from concatenating three strings: 'Hello', 'world' and '!'.

## Element.setAttribute

Line 16 of js/ex-0.js

```
items[select].setAttribute('class', name);
```

calls the method `Element.setAttribute` to add a new attribute `'class'` to the target element and assign `name` to the new attribute.

The syntax of calling the `setAttribute` method over a target element is shown below.

### Syntax

```
target.setAttribute(attributeName, value);
```

The method will assign `value` to the attribute named `"attributeName"`. If the target element has no such attribute, the method will add the attribute and assign the value as well.

At line 14, the variable `name` is generated by

```
var name = 'b'.concat(select);
```

and it may take three possible values, 'b0', 'b1' and 'b2'. Recall that these three values are names of three `class` selectors in the style file `css/ex-0.css`. Each `class` selector sets a background image.

```
.b0 {
    background-image: url(../img/nespresso.jpg);
}
.b1 {
    background-image: url(../img/kinderegg.jpg);
}
.b2 {
    background-image: url(../img/capsule.jpg);
}
```

For instance, if the user enters 1, `input` equals 1 and `select` is 0, then `name` will be 'b0'. The expression `items[select].setAttribute('class', name)` turns to

```
items[0].setAttribute('class', 'b0')
```

So the image `nespresso.jpg` is displayed in the target element `items[0]` which is the first box on the page.

Correspondingly, JavaScript also supports a method `getAttribute` which can read the current value of a specified attribute on an `HTML` element.

## Element.getAttribute

The `getAttribute` method is called over a target element when we want to get the current value of a given attribute. Use the following syntax.

### Syntax

```
target.getAttribute(attributeName);
```

If the given attribute does not exist, the return value will either be `null` or `""` which is the empty string.

If we want to find whether an `HTML` element has the attribute `'class'` and its value, assuming `target` is a reference to the target element, the following statement will read the value of the attribute `'class'` and write the value into a variable `classname`:

```
var classname = target.getAttribute('class');
```

Sometimes, we may need to know if the target element has the attribute `'class'` or not. The following `if` statement will answer this question.

```
if (classname === null || classname === "") {
    console.log("The element currently does not have the attribute 'class'.)
}
```

Now, load `ex-0.html` in a web console. Enter 2 in the prompt window. The page should diplay the image `kinderegg.jpg` in the 2nd box.

Keep `ex-0.html` open in the browser window. Open the web console. Run the following three expressions one by one in order.

```
document.getElementsByTagName('li')[0].getAttribute('class')
document.getElementsByTagName('li')[1].getAttribute('class')
document.getElementsByTagName('li')[2].getAttribute('class')
```

The echo in the display pane should be like

```
>>  document.getElementsByTagName('li')[0].getAttribute('class')
←   null
>>  document.getElementsByTagName('li')[1].getAttribute('class')
←   "b1"
>>  document.getElementsByTagName('li')[2].getAttribute('class')
←   null
```

The result is consistent with the active page which has assigned the value **'b1'** to the attribute `class` of the 2$^{nd}$ `li` element due to the user choice.

## Workout 8-6

Revise *Example 1.1* such that the main page shows 6 boxes and allows users to open one box.

## Workout 8-7

The current main page in *Example 1.1* only allows the user to open one box. Revise *Example 1.1* such that the main page shows 6 boxes and allows users to continue opening a box until all boxes are open.

Hint: To examine if a box is open or not, assuming `boxReference` is a reference to the box element, the expression

```
boxReference.getAttribute('class')
```

will return `null` if the box is not open; if the box is open, it will return the value of the attribute `class`, which is not null.

# HTML input Element & Input Validation

This case provides the user with 12 subpattern options. In the first version *Case 3.1*, the user can custom a subpattern and enter an integer. The custom pattern will be printed on the page with the integer number inside. The case files are stored in the subfolder case3.

### File Listing

```
input.html,
css/input.css,
js/input.js
```

Load the main page input.html in a web browser window. (Note: This case is currently not compatible with Internet Explorer brower.)

On the left side of the page, a control section holds custom options. Basically, the user is required to select a shape from the first button group, a color from the second button group and enters or selects an integer in the spinner for the toal number of shapes. Then click PRINT NOW! to fire the action.

Below, the pictures in the middle and rightmost columns are some sample outputs. The leftmost picture shows a run case when he user clicks the button without providing any number in the spinner; the yellow alert message will appear below the spinner. The actual output in each run depends on user selections.

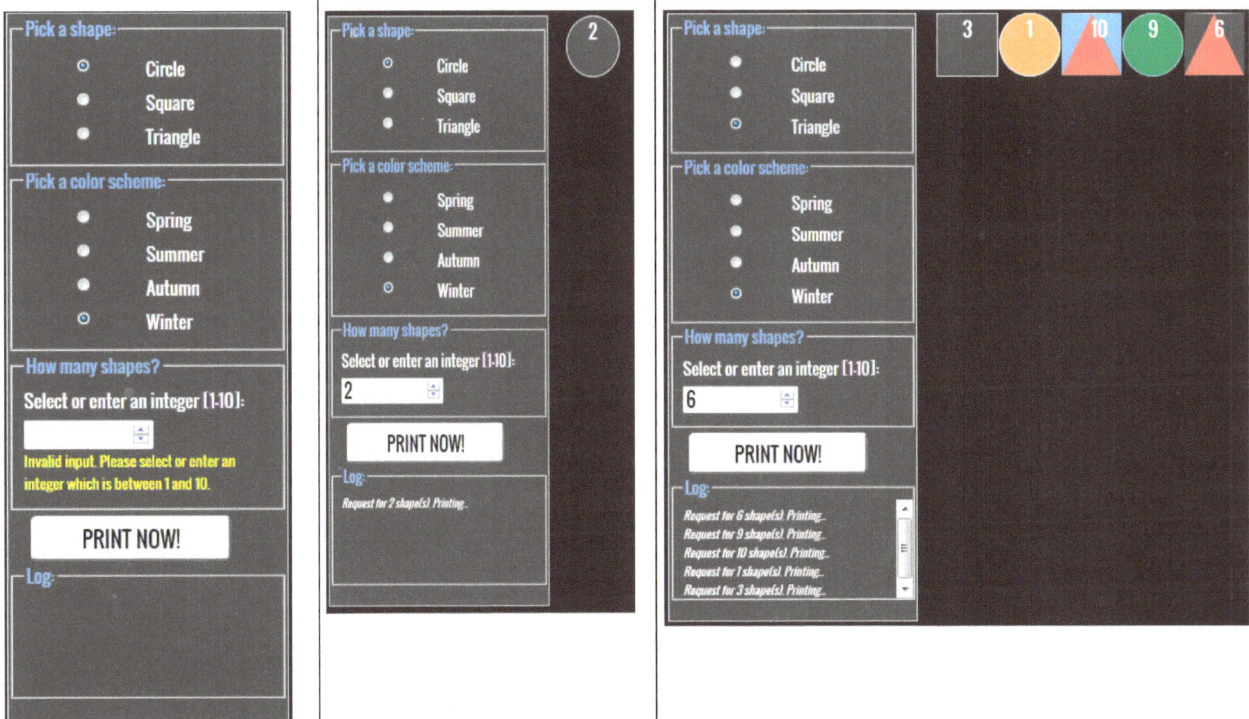

## Layout of the Control Section

The main page, `input.html`, contains two HTML elements `section#control` and `section#theme`.

The `control` section holds five parts; the first three parts are outlined by a `<fieldset>` tag and each part consists of related custom input options. A `<legend>` tag gives each fieldset a title. Below a `button` element PRINT NOW!, the last `<fieldset>` tag creates a log pane.

The `theme` section is originally empty as it is the target place where the JavaScript code will print subpattern shapes. The HTML source is displayed below.

```
1.  <!DOCTYPE html>
2.  <html lang="en">
3.      <head>
4.          <title>HTML Input Elements & Input Validation</title>
5.          <meta charset="UTF-8">
6.          <link href="css/input.css" rel="stylesheet" type="text/css"/>
7.      </head>
8.
9.      <body>
10.         <section id='control' class="winter">
11.             <fieldset>
12.                 <legend>Pick a shape: </legend>
13.                 <input type="radio" name="shape" value="circle" checked />Circle
14.                 <input type="radio" name="shape" value="square" />Square
15.                 <input type="radio" name="shape" value="triangle" />Triangle
16.             </fieldset>
17.             <fieldset>
18.                 <legend>Pick a color scheme: </legend>
19.                 <input type="radio" name="color" value="spring" />Spring
20.                 <input type="radio" name="color" value="summer" />Summer
21.                 <input type="radio" name="color" value="autumn" />Autumn
22.                 <input type="radio" name="color" value="winter" checked />Winter
23.             </fieldset>
24.             <fieldset>
25.                 <legend>How many shapes?</legend>
26.                 <label>Select or enter an integer [1-10]:</label>
27.                 <input type="number" name="shapeTotal" min="1" max="10" />
28.                 <p id='alertSpinner' class='alertmsg'>Invalid input. Please select or enter an
    integer which is between 1 and 10.</p>
29.             </fieldset>
30.             <button name='submit' class='submit'>PRINT NOW!</button>
31.             <fieldset id='log'>
32.                 <legend>Log:</legend>
33.             </fieldset>
34.         </section>
35.
36.         <section id="theme"></section>
37.
38.         <script src="js/input.js" type="text/javascript"></script>
39.     </body>
40. </html>
```

The HTML source in the color blocks above highlights four `fieldset` tags and one `button` tag. The source creates the content in the same look as the left picture below. The right picture shows the look after applying the style rules in `css/input.css`.

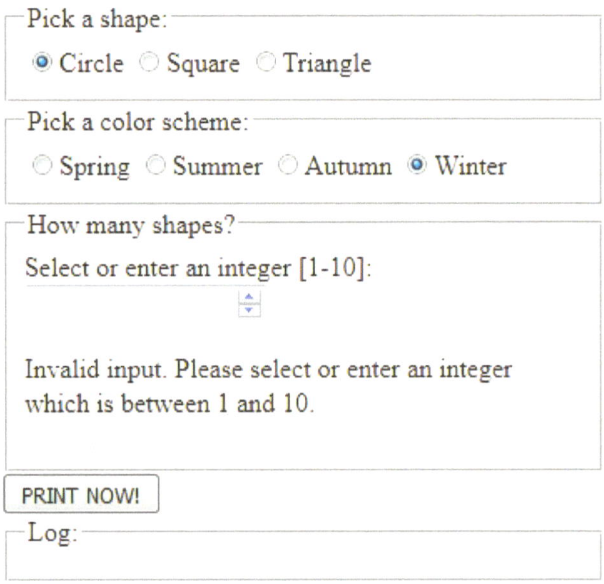

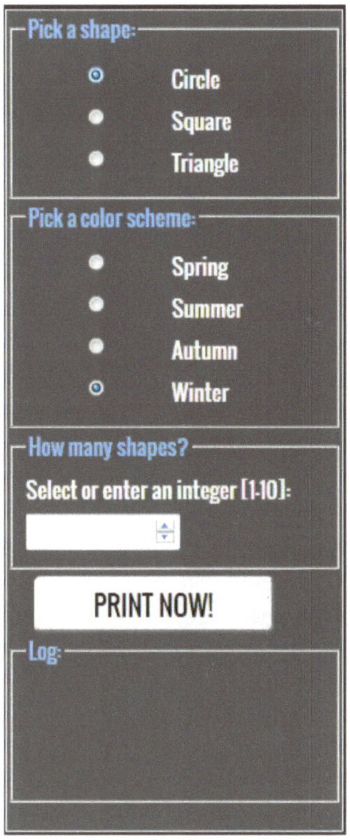

## The CSS Property display & visibility

Comparing two page captures above, the content is almost the same except for a paragraph below the spinner that is visible in the left picture while not visible in the right picture. The paragraph "*Invalid input. Please select or enter an integer which is between 1 and 10.*" is the message that only shows up when the user has not provided a valid input in the spinner or clicked PRINT NOW! without input.

The HTML source of this alert paragraph is at line 28 of `input.html`,

```
<p id='alertSpinner' class='alertmsg'>Invalid input. Please select or enter an integer which is
between 1 and 10.</p>
```

The paragraph has the `id` value `'alertSpinner'` and the `class` name `'alertmsg'`.

CSS is capable of controlling visibility of an element, with two CSS properties, `display` and `visibility`. In `css/input.css`, `.alertmsg` sets a rule for `display`.

Open the style file `css/input.css`.

```
1.    @import url(https://fonts.googleapis.com/css?family=Oswald);
2.    body {
3.        font-family: 'Oswald', 'Futura', sans-serif;
4.        background-color: #403c3b;
5.        color: white;
```

```
 6.     }
 7.     section {
 8.         margin: 0 auto;
 9.         padding-bottom: 20px;
10.         float:left;
11.     }
12.     section#control {
13.         width: 250px;
14.     }
15.     section#theme {
16.         padding-left: 20px;
17.     }
18.     legend {
19.         color: #70b8ff;
20.     }
21.     input, button {
22.         width: 110px; height: 20px;
23.         font-size: 1.2em; font-family: 'Oswald', 'Futura', sans-serif;
24.         margin: 0; margin-top: 5px;
25.     }
26.     input:invalid {
27.         background-color: #f84c53;
28.         border: 2px solid #f84c53;
29.     }
30.     input:out-of-range {
31.         background-color: greenyellow;
32.         border: 2px solid greenyellow;
33.     }
34.     button.submit {
35.         width: 180px;
36.         height: 40px;
37.         border-radius: 5px;
38.         margin-left:20px;
39.     }
40.
41.     .spring {background-color: #009966;     border: 1px #B9D7D9 dotted;}
42.     .summer {background-color: #70b8ff;     border: 1px white solid;}
43.     .autumn {background-color: #ffb87a;     border: 1px white solid;}
44.     .winter {background-color: #666666;     border: 1px white solid;}
45.
46.     div {
47.         width: 60px;
48.         height: 60px;
49.         margin-left:1px;
50.         float: left;
51.         text-align: center;
52.         font-size: 1.2em;
53.     }
54.     .square {
55.     }
56.     .circle {
57.         border-radius: 60px;
58.     }
59.     .triangle {
60.         width: 0px;
```

```
61.        height: 0px;
62.        border-left: 30px solid transparent;
63.        border-right: 30px solid transparent;
64.        border-bottom: 60px solid #F88379;
65.    }
66.    .clear {
67.        clear: both;
68.    }
69.    .alertmsg {
70.        margin: 0px;
71.        color: yellow;
72.        font-size: 0.8em;
73.        display: none;
74.    }
75.    #log {
76.        height: 100px;
77.        overflow: auto;
78.    }
79.    .log {
80.        font-size: 0.7em;
81.        font-style: italic;
82.        margin: 0px;
83.    }
```

*css/input.css*

At line 73, the class selector .alertmsg has a rule to set the property display to none, which hides the paragraph.

> The CSS display property is very important to control page layout and element visibility.

The property display specifies the type of box for an element. The values that display can take are shown in the following.

none    inline    block    list-item    inline-list-item    inline-block    inline-table

table    table-cell    table-column    table-column-group    table-footer-group

table-header-group    table-row    table-row-group    flex    inline-flex    grid

inline-grid    run-in    ruby    ruby-base    ruby-text    ruby-base-container    ruby-

text-container    contents

The default display value is inline. The value 'block' will show an element. The value none will turn of the display of an element as well as all decendent elements. The space that the element(s) take will also be removed from the layout.

> Later in JavaScript, display will be set to 'block' to show the previously hidden alert paragraph.

The visibility property can also be used to hide an element while leaving the space where the element would be. The values are

visible    hidden    collapse    inherit    initial    unset

Setting `visibility` to `hidden` will hide an element while not affecting its decendent elements if their `visibility` is `visible`.

## Workout 8-8

---

`FileListing`

      `c8w8.html, css/c8w8.css`

---

Open `c8w8.html` in a browser window.

Open `css/c8w8.css` in a code editor.

    $\rightarrow$ Remove line 5, the element selector `ul`

       `ul {display:none;}`

       Save the change to the file.

       Reload the page to see how this selector controls the display of `ul` elements and their descendant elements.

    $\rightarrow$ Add the following selector:

       `ul {visibility:hidden;}`

       Save the change to the file.

       Reload the page to see how the CSS property `visibility` controls the display of `ul` elements and their descendant elements.

## HTML `input` Element

To collect user inputs on a web page, we make HTML `input` elements by inserting `<input>` tags. Besides the common attributes with HTML `Element` object, `input` supports some specific attributes including `type` and `value`. Not only is the look of an `input` element determined by its attribute `type`, but also the type of data that it can accept.

In *Appendix C Common Values of the Attribute type for input Element*, common values are listed for the attribute `type`. Two values, `number` and `radio` are used in the main page.

### Create a radio button

To create a radio button to the right of the text 'Square' with the associated value 'square',

  ◯  Square

the HTML source is

```
<input type="radio" value="square" />Square
```

To set the initial status for the button to be checked, add `checked`

```
<input type="radio" value="square" checked />Square
```

### Build a button group

To make the buttons mutually exclusive in a button group, assign the same name to all the participating radio button elements. For example, the following source creates a radio button group 'shape' that consists of three radio buttons. The first button is initially set to be checked. Each button should have unique value in the group scope.

```
<input type="radio" name="shape" value="square" checked />Square
<input type="radio" name="shape" value="square" />Square
<input type="radio" name="shape" value="triangle" />Triangle
```

The browser renders the source above to the following content.

&#9673; Circle &#9675; Square &#9675; Triangle

### Check button status

To examine whether a button is checked or not, assuming `btn` is the reference to the `input` element with `type='radio'`, the following expression

```
btn.checked
```

returns `true` if the button is checked and `false` otherwise.

### Create a spinner input control

The third fieldset has a spinner control.

Enter an integer [1-10]:

A spinner control provides an interface for the user to enter numbers. The `input` element with `type='number'` configures a spinner control. In a spinner control, the user can either enter a number into the text field or click up or down arrow to increment or decrement a number within a specified range. The range is specified with two attributes `max` and `min`. The step between two values is `1` by default. To configure a step other than `1`, use the attribute `step`.

Lines 26 and 27 of `input.html`

```
<label>Select or enter an integer [1-10]:</label>
<input type="number" name="shapeTotal" min="1" max="10" />
```

creates a spinner named 'shapeTotal' in the range of [1, 10] with a text label.

### *Access input elements*

We have previously used the following three methods to access HTML elements

```
document.getElementById
document.getElementsByClassName
document.getElementsByTagName
```

To retrieve input elements with the name value, we can use the method document.getElementsByName.

For example, the following statement will access all the elements with name='shape'.

```
var shapeBTN = document.getElementsByName('shape');
```

As all the buttons in a button group must have the same name value, document.getElementsByName is an easy way to retrieve all the buttons in the same button group. To access each button, use array notation, say, shapeBTN[0] is a reference to the first button, shapeBTN[1] for the second button and so on.

### *Read associated value*

To read the value associated with the input element, use its reference to access the attribute 'value'. Assuming btn is the reference to the input element, btn.value reads its associated value. If the element is a radio button, btn.value returns the attribute 'value'. If the element is a spinner, btn.value will return the current value that the user has entered.

> The attribute 'value' of an HTML element is of a **string** type.
>
> Call parseInt or parseFloat to parse, from a string, an integer or a floating point number.

### Testing:

Load input.html in a web browser window. Open the web console.

In the command bar,

→   Enter

```
document.getElementsByName('shape').
```

The output in the display pane is shown below.

```
>> document.getElementsByName('shape')
← NodeList [ <input>   , <input>   , <input>   ]
```

The first line is the command that has been entered. The second line is the output from running the command. It shows that document.getElementsByName returns a group of references in a special data type NodeList, which has three input elements.

→   Then enter

```
document.getElementsByName('shape')[0].
```

At the end of the last output, the new lines are

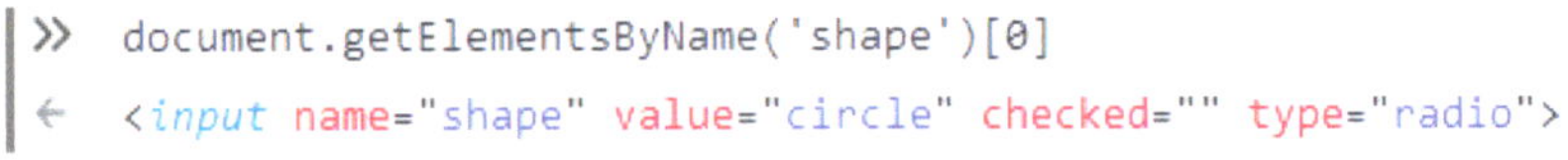

```
>>   document.getElementsByName('shape')[0]
←    <input name="shape" value="circle" checked="" type="radio">
```

The second line shows the partial content in the first button item.

→   To get the current status of the first button, enter

```
document.getElementsByName('shape')[0].checked
```

The output is true.

→   To get the associated value of the first button, enter

```
document.getElementsByName('shape')[0].value
```

The output is "circle".

By now, if you have not cleared the web console output, the outputs in the display pane should be like the capture below.

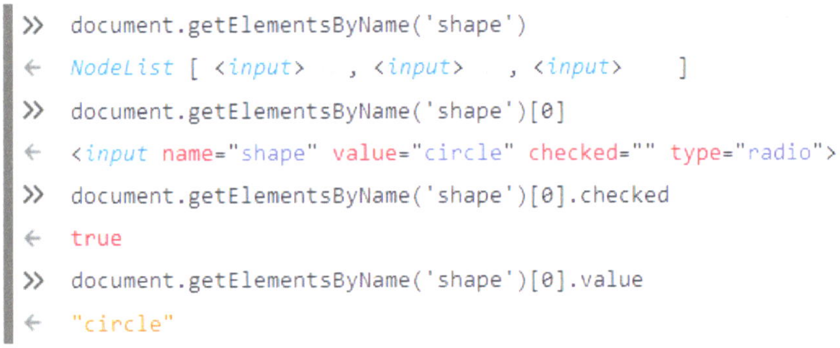

```
>>   document.getElementsByName('shape')
←    NodeList [ <input>    , <input>    , <input>    ]
>>   document.getElementsByName('shape')[0]
←    <input name="shape" value="circle" checked="" type="radio">
>>   document.getElementsByName('shape')[0].checked
←    true
>>   document.getElementsByName('shape')[0].value
←    "circle"
```

→   On the page, enter or select an integer in the spinner. In the command bar, enter the following expression:

```
document.getElementsByName('shapeTotal')[0].value
```

The output is the integer in a string that is in the spinner, as shown below.

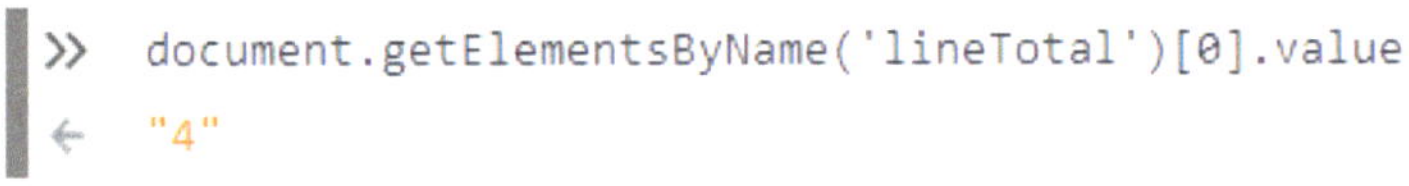

```
>>   document.getElementsByName('lineTotal')[0].value
←    "4"
```

Thus, if the value needs to be integer, call parseInt to convert the string to an integer. Enter the expression

```
parseInt(document.getElementsByName('shapeTotal')[0].value)
```

The output becomes a number without double quotation marks. See the output capture below.

```
>>  document.getElementsByName('lineTotal')[0].value
←  "4"
>>  parseInt(document.getElementsByName('lineTotal')[0].value)
←  4
```

## Workout 8-9

Based on the web page `input.html`, write a statement that accesses all the `input` elements with `type='radio'` in a button group named `'color'` and store the returned references in a variable `colorBTN`.

Write an expression for each of the following requests:

1. Get the second button from the reference nodelist

2. Get the check status of the second button

3. Get the associated value of the second button

Load `input.html` in a web browser. Test your expressions in the web console.

Make a screenshot for the outputs in the display pane.

## Reading Selection in Button Group

The page input.html consists of two radio button groups. For each button group, JavaScript needs to read the selection and validate it as well. A function can be declared for this purpose as it is common to every button group. After the function has been declared, we can simply call the function on each button group on the page.

The following function expression, `getSelectedButtonValue`, reads the selected button from a specific button group, referenced by `btnGroup`, and returns the associated value of the selected button.

```
1.  var getSelectedButtonValue = function (btnGroup){
2.          var i = 0;
3.          while (i < btnGroup.length && !btnGroup[i].checked) {
4.              i++;
5.          }
6.          return btnGroup[i].value;
7.  };
```

`while` loop is applied here to scan the button group. The variable `i` is the iterator. The loop condition connects two sub-conditions by `AND` operator:

     i < btnGroup.length **&&** !btnGroup[i].checked

The first sub-condition, `i < btnGroup.length`, tests if the current button is not the last button. If it is `false`, i.e., all the buttons have been scanned, the loop terminates. If it is `true`, proceed with evaluating the second sub-condition.

The second sub-condition is

```
!btnGroup[i].checked
```

which performs NOT with the operator ! to negate the value of btnGroup[i].checked. If the current button is checked, the sub-condition evaluates false and the entire loop condition is false, then the loop terminates and proceed to the next statement below the loop. If the current button is not checked, it evaluates true and the loop condition is true, then the loop increments the iterator and start the next iteration.

After the loop terminates, the value of the iterator i is the index of the checked button. The return statement at line 6

```
return btnGroup[i].value
```

will return the value of the checked button.

To call getSelectedButtonValue on a button group that is referenced by btnRef, write the following function call:

```
var selection = getSelectedButtonValue(btnRef);
```

On the page input.html, there are two button groups named shape and color. The following statements will store the user selections to two variables, shape and color, respectively.

```
var shapeBTN = document.getElementsByName('shape');
var colorBTN = document.getElementsByName('color');
var shape = getSelectedButtonValue(shapeBTN); //Read shape
var color = getSelectedButtonValue(colorBTN); //Read color
```

## Testing:

Load input.html in a web browser window. Open the web console.

In the command bar,

$\rightarrow$ Enter two following statements one by one:

```
Var shapeBTN = document.getElementsByName('shape')
getSelectedButtonValue(shapeBTN)
```

The output in the display pane is shown below.

```
>> var shapeBTN = document.getElementsByName('shape')
<- undefined
>> getSelectedButtonValue(shapeBTN)
<- "circle"
```

$\rightarrow$ Now, check the button 'Triangle' in the field box 'Pick a shape:' Enter

```
getSelectedButtonValue(shapeBTN)
```

This time, the output is "triangle".

## Handling Spinner

Given a spinner in the following input element

```
<input type="number" name="shapeTotal" min="1" max="10" />
```

To read the current value in the spinner, get the reference and access its attribute 'value'. Assuming this spinner is the first or the only HTML element whose name is 'shapeTotal', the following statements

```
var shapeTotal = document.getElementsByName('shapeTotal')[0];
var numShape = parseInt(shapeTotal.value);
```

will read the value from the spinner named 'shapeTotal', parse the value to an integer and store the integer in the variable numShape.

However, the use possibly has provided an invalid input which is not an integer between 1 and 10. If the script allows such invalid values and carries them to the subsequent statements, the page will not produce the right output. Input validation must be performed to help the user providing valid inputs.

Input validation can actually be achieved by utilizing both CSS rules and JavaScript.

### *CSS pseudo-class for invalid input*

CSS3 has new pseudo-classes which style several validation states such as valid, invalid, out-of-range and so on.

Recall that each input element has the attribute type that restricts input value to an acceptable data type. Recall thIn *Appendix C Common Values of the Attribute type for input Element*, common values are listed for the attribute type. In CSS3, pseudo-class :invalid will be activated if the content does not comply with the input's type setting.

For example, in an input element with type='number', any non-digit entry will activate :invalid to change the look of the input element. The new look can alert the user for invalid data entry, which is commonly a glowing border around the input element.

In css/input.css, there are two pseudo-classes with input.

- input:invalid specifies a look for invalid value.
  ```
  input:invalid {
      background-color: #f84c53;
      border: 2px solid #f84c53;
  }
  ```

- input:out-of-range defines the look when the user input is not in the range [1,10].
  ```
  input:out-of-range {
      background-color: greenyellow;
  ```

```
        border: 2px solid greenyellow;
    }
```

### *Register input event*

In JavaScript, the selection structure are often used for input validation. The following function expression, validateSpinner, is declared specifically for the spinner that is accessed by the reference shapeTotal.

```
1.  var validateSpinner = function () {
2.      numShape = parseInt(shapeTotal.value);
3.      if (Number.isNaN(numShape) || numShape > 10 || numShape < 1)
4.      {
5.          alertSpinner.style.display = 'block';
6.          return false;
7.      } else {
8.          alertSpinner.style.display = 'none';
9.          return true;
10.     }
11. };
```

Line 2 parses an integer from the current content of shapeTotal.

At lines 3 through 10 is an if-else statement. The if clause detects input values which are not integer or out of the range and shows the hidden alert below the spinner. The else clause hides the alert for valid input.

The conditional expression must be built in such a way that it is evaluated to true for an integer between 1 and 10 and false for any other values. The following comparision expression meets this requirement.

```
    Number.isNaN(numShape) || numShape > 10 || numShape < 1
```

The first part prevents a non-numerical input. The second part prevents a number greater than 10 and the third part prevents a number less than 1. Three parts are connected by OR operator.

As a function expression will not be triggered until JavaScript makes a call to it. To trigger validateSpinner everytime when the user enters or changes the spinner, we need to register an input event listener on the spinner 'shapeTotal' by the following statement

```
    shapeTotal.addEventListener('input', validateSpinner);
```

Thus, once a value change occurs in the spinner shapeTotal, it will trigger the action in the callback validateSpinner to validate the value.

## Interactions between JavaScript and HTML

Now we can open the script js/input.js.

```
1.    // Part 1: Access to the relevant HTML elements
2.    var target = document.getElementById('theme');
3.    var log = document.getElementById('log');
4.    var alertSpinner = document.getElementById('alertSpinner');
5.
```

```
6.    var submit = document.getElementsByName('submit')[0];
7.    var shapeBTN = document.getElementsByName('shape');
8.    var colorBTN = document.getElementsByName('color');
9.    var shapeTotal = document.getElementsByName('shapeTotal')[0];
10.
11.   var shape, color;//store user selections
12.   var numShape = 0;//reset total of shapes
13.   // Part 2: Functions
14.   var printShape = function (shape, color) {
15.       // Print a shape by adding div with shape and color as class names
16.       classname = shape + ' ' + color;
17.       newshape = "<div class=\'" + classname + "\'>" + numShape + "</div>";
18.       target.insertAdjacentHTML('beforeend', newshape);
19.   };
20.   var validateSpinner = function () {//Handle spinner
21.       numShape = parseInt(shapeTotal.value);
22.       if (Number.isNaN(numShape) || numShape > 10 || numShape < 1)
23.       {
24.           alertSpinner.style.display = 'block';
25.           return false;
26.       } else {
27.           alertSpinner.style.display = 'none';
28.           return true;
29.       }
30.   };
31.   var getSelectedButtonValue = function (btnGroup){//Read button selection
32.           var i = 0;
33.           while (i < btnGroup.length && !btnGroup[i].checked) {
34.               i++;
35.           }
36.           return btnGroup[i].value;
37.   };
38.
39.   function action() {// Define a callback for the submit button
40.       // Only print when numShape is between 1 and 10
41.       if (validateSpinner() === true) {
42.           shape = getSelectedButtonValue(shapeBTN);//Read shape
43.           color = getSelectedButtonValue(colorBTN);//Read color
44.           //Log
45.           msg = '<p class=\'log\'>Request for ' + numShape + ' shape(s). Printing...</p>';
46.           log.insertAdjacentHTML('afterbegin', msg);
47.           printShape(shape, color);// Print pattern
48.       }// End of if
49.   }
50.   // Part 3: Add Event Listeners
51.   // Register input event listener on the spinner 'shapeTotal'
52.   shapeTotal.addEventListener('input', validateSpinner);
53.
54.   // Register click event listener on submit button
55.   submit.addEventListener('click', action);
```

js/input.js

The statements in js/input.js can be divided into three parts.

→ Part 1: Before JavaScript starts interactions with HTML, it needs to get references to the HTML elements. Besides, it also needs to declare variables for storing intermediate values.

→ Part 2: This part contains function expressions and declarations.

- function expression: `printShape(shape, color)`

- function expression: `validateSpinner()`

- function expression: `getSelectedButtonValue(btnGroup)`

- function declaration: `action()`

→ Part 3: This part implements event-based interactions. Register a `click` event listener with the button `submit`. Register an `input` event listener with the spinner `shapeTotal`.

`validateSpinner` and `getSelectedButtonValue` have previously been discussed in the last two sections *'Handling Spinner'* and *'Reading Selection in Button Group'*.

### The function expression printShape

The function expression `printShape` is responsible for printing custom shape(s). It consists of the following two steps:

Step 1.  Take two arguments for `shape` and `color`,

Step 2.  Add a new `div` element to represent new shape(s) whose `class` name is determined by the given `shape` and `color` values.

```
14.    var printShape = function (shape, color) {
15.    // Print a shape by adding div with shape and color as class names
16.        classname = shape + ' ' + color;
17.        newshape = "<div class=\'" + classname + "\'>" + numShape + "</div>";
18.        target.insertAdjacentHTML('beforeend', newshape);
19.    };
```

Function: printShape

A new method `insertAdjacentHTML` is used here to insert the new element, as shown at line 18 of `js/input.js` in the following statement:

```
target.insertAdjacentHTML('beforeend', newshape);
```

This statement appends the new HTML content in `newshape` to the end of the target element `target`.

As scripted at line 2,

```
var target = document.getElementById('theme');
```

`target` is the reference to the element with the `id` value `'theme'`.

### Element.insertAdjacentHTML

This method is associated with the JavaScript object `Element`. The method is able to provide more options for insertion points than the `Element` property `Element.innerHTML`.

We have previously used `innerHTML` to replace the current HTML content in an HTML element with the new content. If we intent to add the new HTML content rather than replacing the old HTML content, the following statement

```
element.innerHTML = element.innerHTML + newContent;
```

will add `newContent` to the end of the current element content. The shortcut is

```
element.innerHTML += newContent;
```

To add the new content to the beginning of the current content, simply switch positions of the two operands in the operator `+`.

```
element.innerHTML = newContent + element.innerHTML;
```

However, if the new content needs to be inserted somewhere other than two ends, `Element.insertAdjacentHTML` is a method that we can choose. Also, this method call runs faster than updating `Element.innerHTML`.

To use this method, follow the syntax below.

Syntax

```
element.insertAdjacentHTML(position, newcontent);
```

`element` is a reference to the target HTML element; `position` is the position relative to the target element and it can take one of the following four strings.

-   `'beforebegin'`     : insert `newContent` before the target element.

-   `'afterbegin'`      : insert `newContent` directly after the beginning of the target element.

-   `'beforeend'`       : insert `newContent` at the end of the target element.

-   `'afterend'`        : insert `newContent` after the target element.

## Workout 8-10

Locate the files of *Example 8.1*. Rewrite the script `ex-8-forloop.js` by replacing `Element.innerHTML` with `Element.insertAdjacentHTML`.

### *Register listener on submit button*

After the user has provided all the required inputs, a click on the button PRINT NOW! should trigger the function `action` to print shape(s) to the target element `section#theme`. The trigger is implemented in the last line of `js/input.js` in the statement

```
55.   submit.addEventListener('click', action);
```

The callback is declared in the function `action`, as listed below.

```
39. function action() {// Define a callback for the submit button
40.       // Only print when numShape is between 1 and 10
41.       if (validateSpinner() === true) {
42.           shape = getSelectedButtonValue(shapeBTN);//Read shape
43.           color = getSelectedButtonValue(colorBTN);//Read color
44.           //Log
45.           msg = '<p class=\'log\'>Request for ' + numShape + ' shape(s). Printing...</p>';
46.           log.insertAdjacentHTML('afterbegin', msg);
47.           printShape(shape, color);// Print pattern
48.       }// End of if
49. }
```

Function: action

In the callback, the `if` statement calls `validateSpinner` to find out if the user has provided the valid value in the spinner. According to the evaluation result, there are two selections

Branch 1.    If the user input is valid, do the following operations:

1.    Call `getSelectedButtonValue` on `shapeBTN` to read user selection into `shape`

2.    Call `getSelectedButtonValue` on `colorBTN` to read color selection into `color`

3.    Print log paragraph

4.    Call `printShape` on `shape` and `color` to print the custom shape into the target area.

Branch 2.    If the user input is invalid, no action will be fired.

More discussions about registering events will be done in Chapter 9.

## Workout 8-11

Based on *Case 3.1* with the following script files

```
File Listing
        input.html,
        css/input.css,
        js/input.js
```

Modify `js/input.js` so that the page will print the user custom shape for n times and n is the user input in the field 'How many shapes?'

# A Mix of Decision and Loop

## Example 8.6

This example generates a random integer between 1 and 50 and gives the user 6 attempts to guess the number. A correct guess immediately halts the script with a success message. Each incorrect guess is followed by an alert box informing user whether the guess was too small or too big.

---

`File Listing`

> `js/for-1.js`

---

Run the script `js/for-1.js` in a Scratchpad window.

Are you able to guess the right number every time? Have you entered the median value each time?

The logic flow in this script is shown in the following diagram. A loop is marked in the grey area that contains two decision blocks in yellow and blue, respectively.

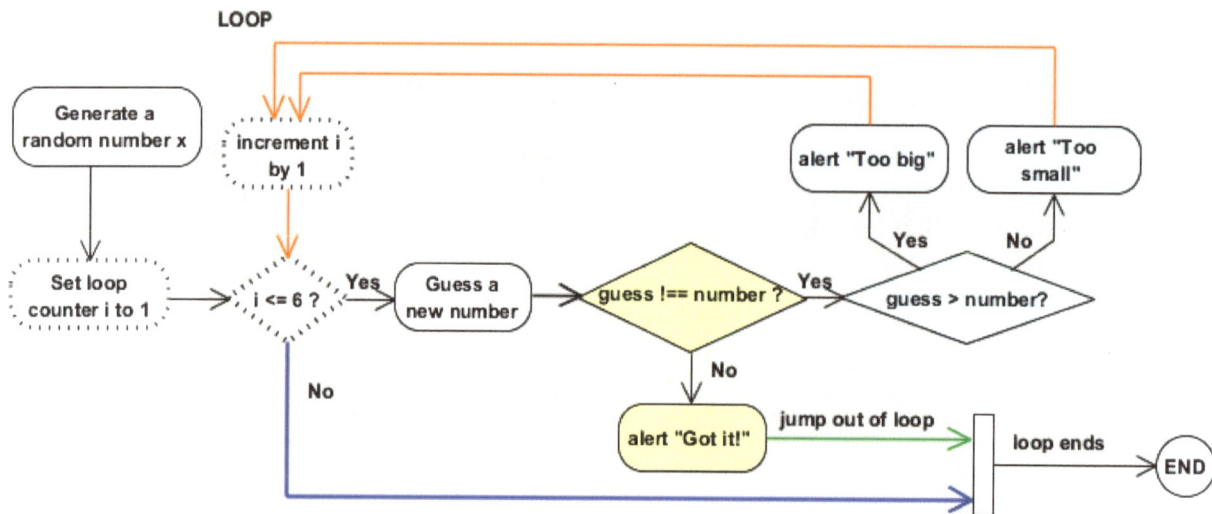

Read the diagram from left to right. The first step in the diagram is to generate a random integer in the range [x, y] for x = 1 and y = 50. Note that the two square brackets indicate both x and y being inclusive.

## Random Number Generation

Random number generation has a lot of applications in gambling, gaming, statistical sampling, computer simulation and cryptography. Random numbers can make a computer program behave unpredictably every time it is executed.

The expression

```
Math.floor(Math.random() * (y-x+1)) + x
```

generates a random integer in the range [x, y].

In the following, we will explain how this expression is constructed.

- The `Math.random` function is a built-in JavaScript PRNG function. PRNG is an algorithm that produces a random number. The `Math.random` returns a floating-point random number in the range `[0, 1)` that is, from `0` up to but not including `1`.

- To scale the output from `[0, 1)` to the range `[0, y-x+1)`, multiply it by y-x+1.

    ```
    Math.random() * (y-x+1)
    ```

- Apply `Math.floor` to convert a number to an integer. `Math.floor` returns the largest integer less than or equal to a given number. The expression

    ```
    Math.floor(Math.random() * (y-x+1))
    ```

    outputs a random integer in the range `[0, y-x]`.

- Next, scale the range to `[x, y]` by adding x

    ```
    Math.floor(Math.random() * (y-x+1)) + x
    ```

Thus, the following statement generates a random integer ranged in `[1, 50]` and stores it to the variable `number`

```
var number = Math.floor(Math.random() * 50) + 1;
```

## Set Up a Loop

After the random number generation, the logic flow in the diagram enters a loop which consists of three dotted shapes. The loop allows user to guess a number up to 6 times. In this case, the maximum iterations is already known as 6. Thus, `for` loop is preferred.

The following shows the statement structure with a loop counter `i` being initially set to one and incrementing in each iteration up to 6.

```
for (var i = 1; i <= 6; i++)
{
    [loop body: guess a number]
}
```

The initial expression sets the loop counter `i` to `1`. Conventionally, a loop counter is often named x, y or i, j, k and so on. The loop condition is `i <= 6`. The increment expression is `i++`.

For each `i` less than or equal to 6, the loop condition is evaluated to `true`, the interpreter will run the statement block between the curly brackets (in the loop body).

If the user has not made a right guess until the counter reaches 6, the loop terminates.

## Design Loop Body

What are the operations to be executed in each iteration?

During each iteration, the user makes a new guess and the browser displays a feedback to the user. If the guess is correct, the loop halts. At the end of each iteration, the counter `i` increments.

The following are the steps for making one guess.

Step 1.   Prompt the user to make a guess by entering an integer between **1** and **50**. **parseInt** converts the user input into **guess** as an integer.

```
var guess = parseInt(window.prompt('Enter guess #' + i + ' integer [1. . 50]'));
```

Step 2.   Then the first decision, represented by the yellow diamond, is made upon inequality between **guess** and **number** by the condition

```
guess !== number
```

Depending on the evaluation result, the execution flow splits into two branches for yes (**true**) or no (**false**), as shown in the following sub-diagram.

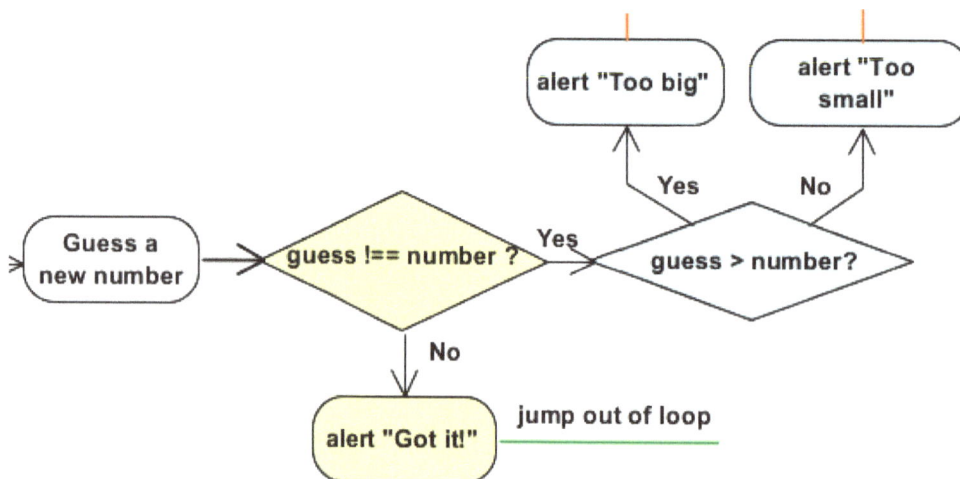

Branch 1.   (**false**) If **guess** is equal to **number**, alert the user a message **"Got it!"** and jump out of the loop.

Branch 2.   (**true**) Otherwise (else), it proceeds to the second decision point in the blue diamond, which evaluates the condition

```
guess > number.
```

Branch 1.   If **guess** is greater than **number**, alert **"Too big"**;

Branch 2.   Otherwise (else), alert **"Too small"**.

The following code will implement the steps in the sub-diagram above.

```
var guess = parseInt(window.prompt("Enter guess #" + i + " integer [1. . 50]"));
if (guess !== number)
    {
```

```
        if (guess > number) {
        alert("Too big");
        }
        else {
                alert("Too small");
        }
    }
    else {
        alert("Got it!");
        break;
    }
```

The color blocks correspond to the blue and yellow decision parts in the sub-diagram. The yellow part is the *outer* conditional statement; the blue part is the *inner* conditional statement.

### The keyword *break*

Note that the keyword break terminates the closest loop if the user has already guessed the right number.

> When a break statement occurs inside a loop, the loop immediately halts and the program control flow resumes at the next statement below the loop.

## Embed `if else` Statements into `for` Statement

Now we can copy the above `if else` statemsnt as loop body into the `for` statement. The complete script is js/for-1.js.

```
1.  var number = Math.floor(Math.random() * 50) + 1;
2.  for (var i = 1; i <= 6; i++)
3.  {
4.      var guess = parseInt(window.prompt("Enter guess #" + i + " [1. . 50]"));
5.      if (guess !== number)
6.      {
7.          if (guess > number) {
8.              alert("Too big");
9.          }
10.         else {
11.             alert("Too small");
12.         }
13.     }
14.     else {
15.         alert("Got it!");
16.         break;
17.     }
18. }
```

js/for-1.js

## Conditional Ternary Operator

As previously mentioned in Chapter 7 "*Conditional Ternary Operator*", both `if` and `if else` statements have a shortcut. The shortcut is a conditional operator which takes three operands.

We can rewrite js/for-1.js by means of two conditional operators.

## Example 8.7

File Listing

js/for-1-conditional-operator.js

```
1.    // Generate a random integer in [1,50]
2.    var number = Math.floor(Math.random() * 50) + 1;

3.    // Make a for statement for at most 6 iterations
4.    for (var i = 1; i <= 6; i++) {
5.        // Prompt the user for an integer
6.        var guess = parseInt(window.prompt('Enter guess #' + i + ' (1. . 50)'));
7.        // Make decisions by using conditional operator
8.        var result = (guess !== number) ? ((guess > number) ? 'Too big' : 'Too small') : 'Got it!';
9.        // Display the result to the suer
10.       alert(result);
11.       // If guess is right, break out of this loop
12.       if (result === 'Got it!') {
13.       break;
14.       }
15.   }
```

js/ for-1-conditional-operator.js

The new script is much shorter than its counterpart that uses if else statements because both decisions are condensed into three statements:

```
var result = (guess !== number) ? ((guess > number) ? 'Too big' : 'Too small') : 'Got it!';
alert(result);
if (result === 'Got it!') {
    break;
}
```

Within the first conditional operator ? in yellow, the blue part is an embedded conditional operator. Each of them is equivenlent to one if else statement in js/for-1.js.

## Workout 8-12

Write an expression that generates a random integer between 0 and 20 inclusive. *Hint*: The expression, `Math.floor(Math.random() * (y-x+1)) + x`, generates a random integer in the range [x, y].

## Workout 8-13

Modify *Example 8.3* to make the program alert a text if the user fails to guess the right number after six tries.

Below is a diagram for this new scenario. After the loop ends, two new steps are added in the dotted rectangle. The green diamond contains a conditional statement to check whether the guess is equal to the right number or not. If they are not equal, alert a text "You did not get the right number."

You can either use the script `js/for-1.js` or `js/guessNumber-conditional-operator.js` as the basis, or compose the new script from scratch.

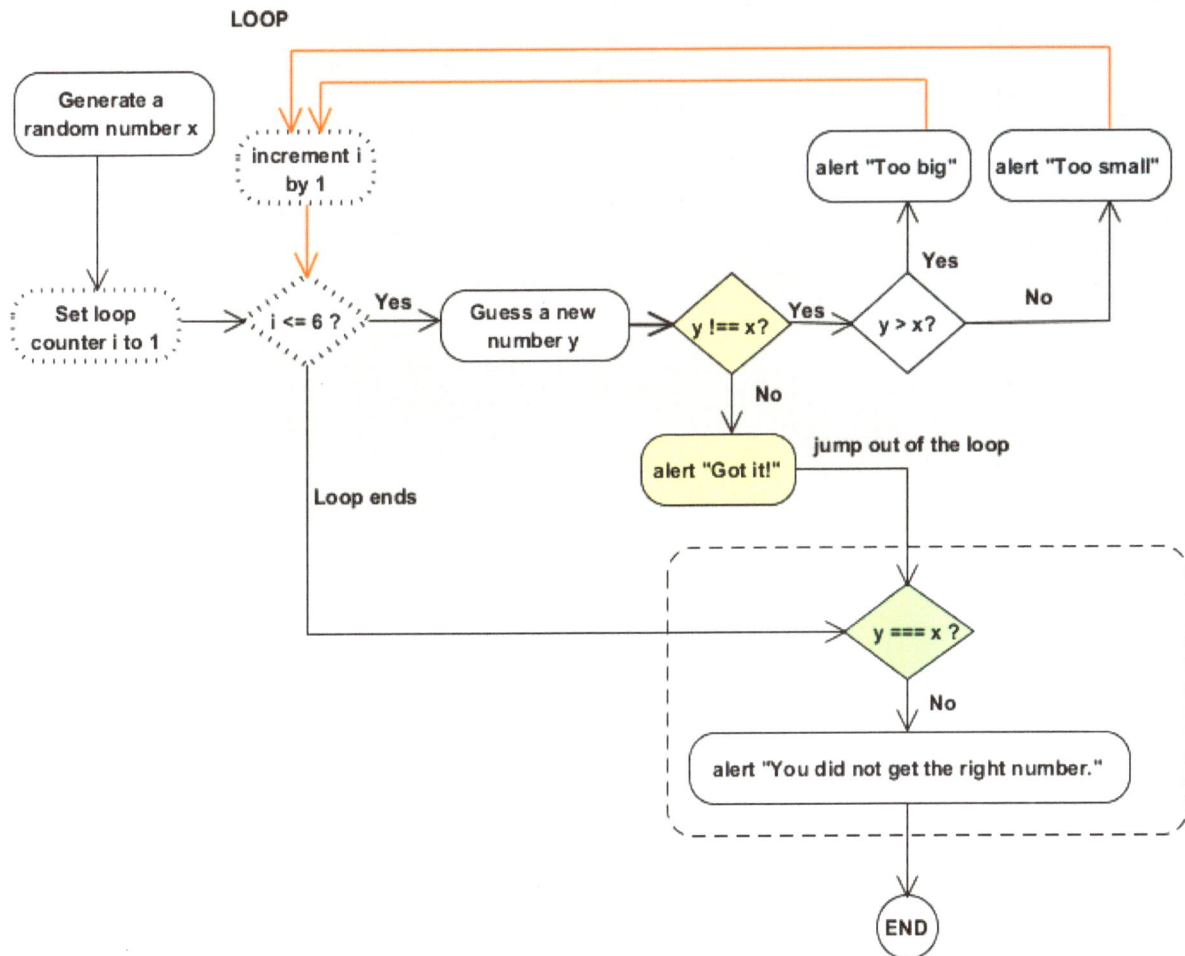

# Chapter 9    FUNCTION OBJECT

In JavaScript, a user-defined function is actually an instance of the JavaScript built-in object `Function`. As previously discussed in Chapter 4, a JavaScript object can have properties and methods. Therefore, JavaScript functions can have properties and methods too, alike any other objects.

This leads to the conclusion that we can declare one or more functions within a function. The inner functions are considered as the methods of the outer function. The following structure shows such a relationship between three functions.

Syntax

```
function funA([parameter(s)]) {

  [statement block]

  function funB ([parameter(s)]) {

    [statement block]

  }

  var funC = function ([parameter(s)]){

    [statement block]

  };

}
```

As `funA` encloses `funB` and `funC`, both `funB` and `funC` have function scope and can only be called locally by their name within `funA`. Neither `funB` nor `funC` are globally accessible outside of `funA` unless we use the keyword `new` to instantiate a new instance of `funA`.

Practically, we should be careful of nesting functions because improper use of them may cause performance issues.

This chapter will cover basics of the `Function` object and its properties. An example is given as an application of `Function` object.

## Table of Contents

# `Function` Properties

As previously indicated, a JavaScript function is an instance of the `Function` object. `Function` inherits properties and methods from JavaScript `Object`.

## Standard Properties

The `Function` object has several standard properties as listed below:

- `length`:       An integer that is the total number of arguments that are expected by the function

- `name`:       A string that is the name of the function

- `prototype`:       An object that inherits methods and properties from `Object.prototype.`

### Example 9.1

In a Scratchpad window, open `ch3/js/ex-3-4.js`. There are two function declarations, `reminder` and `calcArea`. In the browser window, open the web console. Enter the following four commands in order:

    &rarr; `calcArea`

    &rarr; `calcArea.length`

    &rarr; `calcArea.name`

    &rarr; `calcArea.prototype`

The output in the web console is shown below that displays the `Function` object `calcArea` for its properties, `length`, `name` and `prototype`.

```
>>  calcArea
←   function calcArea()
>>  calcArea.length
←   2
>>  calcArea.name
←   "calcArea"
>>  calcArea.prototype
←   Object { , 1 more… }
```

The last line in the output capture above is the value of the property `prototype`, `Object { , 1 more… }`. The value indicates that `prototype` is an object of two properties.

To display the details, click '`1 more`' in the output. A new right pane is open where the object is listed in a tree view with each line being a key/value pair.

Here, we only focus on the first property `'constructor'` with the value `'calcArea()'`. The property `'constructor'` is an object. To reveal the content in `constructor`, click the down arrow to the left of the key name `'constructor'`. The content is very similar to the object `calcArea`.

The prototype concept will not be elaborated on in this book. Next, we will discusss a special object, `arguments`, that is accessible within the scope of a JavaScript function.

# The Object arguments

In a JavaScript function, there is a local object named `arguments` that refers to the argument list from a function call. This object contains an entry for each argument passed to the function. For example, if a function call, `calcArea(5, 8)`, passes two arguments, then `arguments[0]` refers to the first argument, and `arguments[1]` to the second argument. `arguments.length` returns the total count of the arguments.

### Example 9.2

---

`FileListing`

      `js/object-arguments.js`

---

This example gives a function declaration `calcArea` with two formal parameters, `width` and `height`.

```
1.    function calcArea(width, height) {
2.        var area = width * height;
3.        for (var i = 0; i < arguments.length; i++) {
4.            console.log('arguments[' + i + '] = ' + arguments[i]);
5.        }
6.        if (typeof arguments[2] === 'string') {
7.            var html = '<h1>' + arguments[2] + '</h1>';
8.            var target = document.getElementsByTagName('body') [0];
9.            target.insertAdjacentHTML('beforeend', html);
10.       }
11.       return area;
12.   }
```

js/object-arguments.js

The code block between line 3 and line 10 accesses the local object `arguments`.

The `for` statement prints each defined argument in the web console.

If the third argument is passed in the function call and it is a string, the comparison expression

      `typeof arguments[2] === 'string'`

will be evaluated to `true` that enables the `if` statement to run its body. Thus, an `h1` element will be inserted to the current page in the active browser tab, at the position above the closing tag `</body>`.

## The typeof operator

The typeof operator returns a string that states the type of the unevaluated operand. The syntax is

```
typeof operand
```

Open the web console. In the command bar, enter the following expressions and watch the return for the type of each operand.

```
typeof "agile"
typeof ""
typeof a
typeof 37
typeof 3.14;
typeof(42)
typeof Math.LN2
typeof Infinity
typeof NaN
```

The following table lists some of the possible return values from the typeof operator.

| Type | Result |
|------|--------|
| Undefined | "undefined" |
| Null | "object" |
| Boolean | "boolean" |
| Number | "number" |
| String | "string" |
| Function object | "function" |
| Any other object | "object" |

Next, enter the following comparison expressions. Try to understand the evaluation result from each expression.

```
typeof "agile" === "string"
typeof "" === "string"
typeof a === "undefined"
typeof 37 === 'number';
typeof 3.14 === 'number';
typeof(42) === 'number';
typeof Math.LN2 === 'number';
typeof Infinity === 'number';
typeof NaN === 'number';
```

Now, we can test the function `calcArea` to experience how it changes its behavior upon arguments. Follow the steps below.

Step 1.     Open a new browser tab.

Step 2.     Open a Scratchpad window.

Step 3.     In the Scratchpad window, open `js/object-arguments.js`.

Step 4.     Click `Run` to run the script in the Scratchpad window.

Step 5.     Open the web console.

Step 6.     In the command line bar, enter:

```
calcArea(5, 8)
```

Watch the result from running this function call. It prints two arguments and the returned area value. There is no new `h1` element showing up at the web page because `arguments[2]` is `undefined` in this function call.

```
>>  calcArea(5, 8)
    arguments[0] = 5
    arguments[1] = 8
←   40
```

Step 7.     Now enter a new function call with three arguments:

```
calcArea(5, 8, 10)
```

The result is similar to the last one except with one more argument.

```
>>  calcArea(5, 8, 10)
    arguments[0] = 5
    arguments[1] = 8
    arguments[2] = 10
←   40
```

Even though `arguments[2]` is defined as `10`, the if statement will not run its body because the condition expects a string from `arguments[2]`.

Step 8.     Enter the following function call that passes a string in the third argument

```
calcArea(5, 8, "Octopus's Garden")
```

In addition to the argument list in the display pane, this function call will run the operations in the body of the `if` statement. A new text "Octopus's Garden" will appear at the web page.

```
>>  calcArea(5, 8, "Octopus's Garden")
    arguments[0] = 5
    arguments[1] = 8
    arguments[2] = Octopus's Garden
<-  40
```

# Embedded Functions

Recall that in *Case 1.1*, only the first car supports its button clicks. Apply `Function` object, we can implement button click events for all the cars in *Case 1.1*.

Before revisiting *Case 1.1 Cars*, let us learn how to use nesting functions in a simple photo-displaying page.

## Example 9. 3

Assuming we want to create a simple photo album of four cities as shown in the picture below.

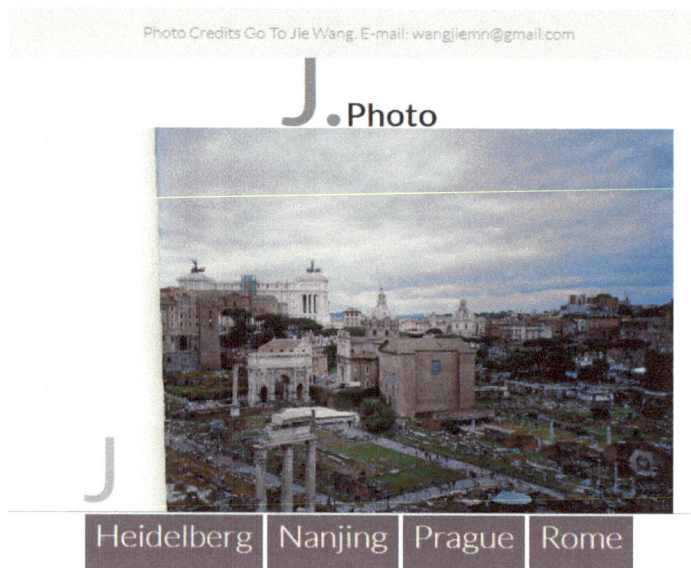

At the bottom of the page, there are four brown rectangles in a row with a city name above each. An element is considered as a button as long as it can trigger certain actions once the user clicks it. In the album, once the user clicks a button to select a city, the photo area above the button row should display the photo for the selected city.

### Step 1. Data resource

The resource for this album is a set of four photos, named `rome.png`, `prague.png`, `heidelberg.png` and `nanjing.png`.

## HTML and CSS

### Step 2. Design page

To make the page adapt to any number of city names, we will not include any specific city names in the HTML source code. Instead, use JavaScript to add each city to the web page. Each city is represented by an HTML element. A city name can be printed within an HTML element, `div`, `p`, `img` or others. In this example, we choose unordered list `ul` to list city names. The custom styles will make each `li` element appearing like a button. The original HTML source only contains an `ul` element where `li` elements will be written into by JavaScript.

The following table shows the design in three views: HTML element view, CSS style view and the content to be added to each element.

| HTML Element Tree View | CSS Style Tree View |
|---|---|
| ⊟ 🌀 HTML<br>　⊟ <> html<br>　　⊟ <> head<br>　　　<> title<br>　　　<> meta<br>　　　<> link<br>　　　<> meta<br>　　⊟ <> body<br>　　　⊟ <> footer<br>　　　　<> p<br>　　　⊟ <> header<br>　　　　<> h1<br>　　　<> div id=photo<br>　　　⊟ <> nav<br>　　　　<> ul id=list<br>　　　<> script | ⊟ ▦ Ids<br>　　▥ #photo<br>⊟ ▦ Imports<br>　　▥ url(https://fonts.googleapis.com/css?family=Lato:100,300,400)<br>⊟ ▦ Rules<br>　　▥ #photo<br>　　▥ body<br>　　▥ footer<br>　　▥ header<br>　　▥ header h1<br>　　▥ header h1:before<br>　　▥ nav<br>　　▥ nav li<br>　　▥ nav li:hover<br>　　▥ nav ul |

**Content Pieces & Their Associated Elements**

`<footer><p>`oto Credits Go To Jie Wang. E-mail: wangjiemn@gmail.com

`<header><h1>` Places Worth Visiting

*div#photo*

`<nav>`

*ul#list* Heidelberg   Nanjing   Prague   Rome
　　　　　　`<li>`　　`<li>`　　`<li>`　　`<li>`

In the HTML Element Tree View, the HTML elements are listed from top to down in the same order as they are written in the HTML source.

The body element encloses five level-1 elements: footer, header, div#photo, nav and script.

→ footer has a p element for showing relevant textual information.

→ header has an h1 element for page title.

→ div#photo is the photo area whose background image is set to a city photo.

→ nav element has an element ul#list.

　o　Inside ul#list, four li elements will be written by an external JavaScrip script.

→ script element makes a link to an external JavaScript file.

## Step 3. Create page

The implementation of the page has been provided. Download the following two script files and four image files. Load the page in a browser to see the initial album.

---

File Listing

> function-object.html
>
> css/function-object.css
>
> img/rome.png, img/prague.png, img/heidelberg.png, img/nanjing.png

---

```html
1.   <!DOCTYPE html>
2.   <html>
3.       <head>
4.           <title>Example: Function object</title>
5.           <meta charset="UTF-8">
6.           <link href="css/function-object.css" rel="stylesheet" type="text/css"/>
7.           <meta name="viewport" content="width=device-width, initial-scale=1.0">
8.       </head>
9.       <body>
10.          <footer>
11.              <p>Photo Credits Go To Jie Wang. E-mail: wangjiemn@gmail.com</p>
12.          </footer>
13.          <header>
14.  <h1>Photo</h1>
15.  </header>
16.          <div id='photo'></div>
17.          <nav>
18.              <ul id='list'></ul>
19.          </nav>
20.          <script src="js/function-object.js" type="text/javascript"></script>
21.      </body>
22.  </html>
```

---

function-object.html

---

```css
1.   @import url(https://fonts.googleapis.com/css?family=Lato:100,300,400);
2.   body {
3.       background: #FFFFFF;
4.       color: #888;
5.       margin: 0px;
6.       padding: 0px;
7.       font: 300 16px/22px "Lato", "Open Sans", "Helvetica Neue", Helvetica, Arial, sans-serif;
8.       text-align: center;
9.   }
10.  footer{
11.      background-color: #D3CFCA;
12.      border-bottom: 1px solid #FFFFFF;
13.      border-top: 1px solid #68778E;
14.      width: 100%;
15.  }
16.  header {
17.      height: 50px;
18.  }
```

```
19.   header h1 {
20.        color: #000;
21.        font-size: 2em;
22.        animation-duration: 3s;
23.        animation-name: slidein;
24.   }
25.   header h1:before {
26.        content: "J.";
27.        font-size: 3em;
28.        color: #888;
29.   }
30.   @keyframes slidein {
31.        from {
32.            margin-left: 100%;
33.            width: 100%;
34.        }
35.        to {
36.            margin-left: 0%;
37.            width: 100%;
38.        }
39.   }
40.   #photo {
41.        background-image: url(../img/rome.png);
42.        background-repeat: no-repeat;
43.        background-position: center center;
44.        background-size: contain;/*cover;*/
45.        transition: background-image 1s linear;
46.        height: 400px;
47.        border-bottom: 1px solid #68778E;
48.   }
49.   nav {
50.        border-bottom: 1px solid #98AFC7;
51.   }
52.   nav ul {
53.        list-style-type: none;
54.        margin: 0px;
55.         padding: 0px;
56.   }
57.   nav li{
58.        display: inline-block;
59.        height: 50px;
60.        margin: 2px;
61.        padding: 10px 10px 0px 10px;
62.        font-size: 2em;
63.        color: beige;
64.        background-color: #766369;
65.   }
66.   nav li:hover {
67.        background-color: #98AFC7;
68.        color: #FEFCFF;
69.   }
```

Note that the `id` selector `#photo` makes custom style rules for the photo area. A photo source is used to set the CSS property `'background-image'`. Initially, it is `url(../img/rome.png)` so that the photo area shows `rome.png` everytime when the album is loaded or refleshed in the browser.

Once a button is clicked, the triggered action should retrieve the `url` of the photo for the selected city and write the `url` to `'background-image'`.

## JavaScript

In this part, we work with JavaScript for interaction between the user and the album. As indicated in `function-object.html`, the external JavaScript is `js/function-object.js`.

Use either a code editor or Scratchpad. Create a new `js` file `'function-object.js'` in the subfolder `js`.

Follow the instructions below to edit this script file.

### Step 4. Store data

In order to access the given data resource in the program, we plan to store city names and photo names by the arrays `cities` and `photos`, respectively.

Enter the following two statements:

```
1.  var cities = ['Rome', 'Prague', 'Heidelberg', 'Nanjing'];
2.  var photos = ['rome.png', 'prague.png', 'heidelberg.png', 'nanjing.png'];
```

All array items are strings. The photos are named the same as city names except with the first letter capitalized. Each city has the same index in both arrays, say, to access `Rome` for its name and photo, use `0` in both arrays: `cities[0]` and `photos[0]`.

The following table shows how two arrays are paired to each other.

| index | 0 | 1 | 2 | 3 |
|---|---|---|---|---|
| cities[index] | 'Rome' | 'Prague' | 'heidelberg' | 'Nanjing' |
| photos[index] | 'rome.png' | 'prague.png' | 'heidelberg.png' | 'nanjing.png' |

### Step 5. Process data

Original data often needs cleaning by removing invalid or incorrect values. After preprocessing, data should be in appropriate formats for subsequent tasks. The sample album data in this example is very small and simple; neither cleaning nor preprocessing is needed.

One thing we can do is sorting cities by their names alphabetically. Sort both arrays in the same way to maintain their index relationship.

Enter the following statements at the end of the script:

```
3.  cities.sort();
4.  photos.sort();
```

After sorting, the position of each city has been changed in accordance with alphabetical order. The following table shows the arrays after sorting.

| index | 0 | 1 | 2 | 3 |
|---|---|---|---|---|
| cities[index] | 'heidelberg' | 'Nanjing' | 'Prague' | 'Rome' |
| photos[index] | 'heidelberg.png' | 'nanjing.png' | 'prague.png' | 'rome.png' |

### Step 6. Display data

As previously designed, each city is to be written into ul#list as a li element. To do so, firslty, get a reference to ul#list.

Enter the following statement at the end of the script:

```
5.  var list = document.getElementById('list');
```

At the end of ul#list, append a li element for each city in cities. Either Array.forEach or for loop can be used here for iterating over an array.

To implement this step by using Array.forEach, make the following method call

```
cities.forEach(function (element, index) {
    var htmlsource = '<li>' + element + '</li>';
    list.insertAdjacentHTML('beforeend', htmlsource);
});
```

An alternative is the for loop. The for statement is

```
6.  For (var index = 0; index < cities.length; index ++) {
7.      var htmlsource = '<li>' + cities[index] + '</li>';
8.      list.insertAdjacentHTML('beforeend', htmlsource);
9.  }
```

The two statement blocks do the same thing. You can add either block to the end of the script.

### Step 7. Test JavaScript code

After completeing all the previous steps, the script should create four li elements on the page.

It is a good practice to temporarily stop editing; instead, before moving to the next step, perform a page test to see if the page has been rendered to produce the new buttons.

Load function-object.html in a browser window. Four brown buttons should be placed below the photo. The button color changes if mouse hovers over a button. For this effect, refer to the CSS pseudo-class nav li:hover in the style sheets. If needed, debug the script utill the page is like the one below.

### *Step 8. Interact with HTML*

After all the cities have been inserted to the page, we can start the interaction part in JavaScript. The interaction in the album is limited to show an associated photo in the photo area for each button click.

A few questions need to be figured out before scripting the interaction.

Question 1. What are relevant HTML elements that will participate in the event?

- All the `li` elements

- `div#photo`

Question 2. How to get a reference to the relevant HTML elements?

```
var items = document.getElementsByTagName('li');
var photo = document.getElementById('photo');
```

Question 3. How many buttons are on the page? What is the expression that reads the totol number of the buttons?

- The property `length` returns the the total count of `li` elements
```
document.getElementsByTagName('li').length
```

Question 4. Does every button require to be bound with a click event?

- Yes.

- In JavaScript, to bind a `click` event to a target element for triggering a listener, the statement is
```
targetElement.addEventListener('click', listener);
```

The method `addEventListener` registers a `listener` on the `targetElement` for the event type `'click'`. `listener` can simply be a callback that carries out prescribed action.

Once an element is attached for a `click` event with a listener, the listener is only triggered when the user clicks the element. Once the listener is triggered, the action in the listener will be executed once.

Question 5.    What action needs to be performed after a click event has occurred?

- Get the image source of the selected city.

- Change the background image of `div#photo` to the image source

For example, assuming `imgsource = photos[1]`, the following statement will display `photos[1]` in the photo area.
```
photo.style.backgroundImage = 'url(\'img/' + imgsource + '\')';
```

<u>Question 6.</u>    <u>How many click events are needed on the album page?</u>

- As there are four cities, it implies four click events.

- A click event must trigger a listener specific to the target element with the matching index value and image source. The following table lists four click events as well as relevant data.

| Event # | 0 | 1 | 2 | 3 |
|---|---|---|---|---|
| Button click | Heidelberg | Nanjing | Prague | Rome |
| Selected city | 'heidelberg' | 'Nanjing' | 'Prague' | 'Rome' |
| Target element | items[0] | items[1] | items[2] | items[3] |
| Image source | photos[0] | photos[1] | photos[2] | photos[3] |

The following statements makes an event listener with the first button `items[0]`.

```
items[0].addEventListener('click', action);

function action() {
    var imgsource = photos[0];
    photo.style.backgroundImage = 'url(\'img/' + imgsource + '\')';
}
```

In general, to bind an event to a target element, take three basic steps.

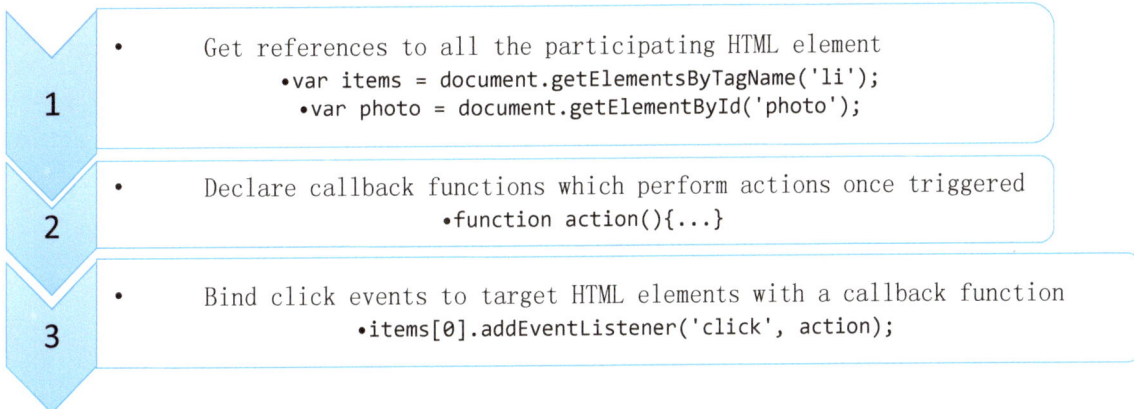

**1**
- Get references to all the participating HTML element
    - `var items = document.getElementsByTagName('li');`
    - `var photo = document.getElementById('photo');`

**2**
- Declare callback functions which perform actions once triggered
    - `function action(){...}`

**3**
- Bind click events to target HTML elements with a callback function
    - `items[0].addEventListener('click', action);`

To bind each city name to `click` event, apparently, we can make a copy of the block above for each button except for the index value ranging from 0 to 3. However, duplicating code is not a good practice; whenever it is possible, loop structure helps us make concise programs and even provides a program with a capability of handling new data without any code change.

In the next step, a solution will be given to automatically create a listener for each city without duplicate code.

## *Step 9 Compose script*

Now let us continue adding new statements to the script `js/function-object.js`.

Enter the statements from the following steps.

Step 1.   Get a collection of references to all li elements. At the end of the script, enter the statement

```
10.    var items = document.getElementsByTagName('li');
```

Step 2.   Get a reference to div#photo. At the end of the script, enter the statement

```
11.    var photo = document.getElementById('photo');
```

Step 3.   Declare a function showPhoto with two parameters item and imgsource. The function can register a click listener on a given target item in the 1st parameter. The listener updates background image by an image name imgsource in the 2nd parameter.

Enter the following statements at the end of the script:

```
12.    function showPhoto(item, imgsource){
13.        function action(){
14.            photo.style.backgroundImage = 'url(\'img/' + imgsource + '\')';
15.        }
16.        item.addEventListener('click', action);
17.    }
```

Note that at line 16,

```
        item.addEventListener('click', action);
```

The listener is a function named action. action is declared as a method within the function showPhoto. action specifies subsequent behaviors to be executed after a click event.

This makes an example of nesting functions.

showPhoto is the host (parent) function and action is the child function. The child function action is visible locally within the parent function showPhoto.

Thus, at line 16, action is passed as an argument to the method addEventListener.

Step 4.   Iterate over items to instantiate a new showPhoto instance for each li element.

Enter the following two statements at the end of the script:

```
18.    for (var index = 0; index < items.length; index++) {
19.        new showPhoto(items[index], photos[index]);
20.    }
```

In each iteration of the for statement, a new instance of showPhoto is instantiated by the statement

```
        new showPhoto(items[index], photos[index]);
```

The keyword new is applied to the previously declared constructor showPhoto to instantiate a new showPhoto instance.

Two values, items[index] and photos[index], are passed as the targe element and image source to the constructor showPhoto, making a new showPhoto instance.

As a result, during the construction of each new showPhoto instance, a new click listener is able to be bound to the target element referenced by items[index].

The script in this step gives us an example of Function object. Also, this shows a method that can be useful when multiple target elements need to be bound with the same listener except for a few different argument values.

In summary, we have completed the script js/function-object.js.

## Step 10. Test page

Download other image files for the album: img/heidelberg.png, img/nanjing.png, img/prague.png.

Now we should have the following files ready for testing.

---

File Listing

```
function-object.html,
css/function-object.css,
js/function-object.js
img/rome.png, img/heidelberg.png, img/nanjing.png, img/prague.png
```

Load function-object.html in a browser. Each button click will trigger displaying the matching photo for the selected city.

# *Cars* Revisited

In *Case 1.1*, we have registered a click event with two input buttons for the first car. The files in *Case 1.1* are listed below.

---

**File Listing**

> cars.html,
>
> css/car.css,
>
> js/cars.js, js/listCars.js,
>
> img/dodge.png, img/fordf150.png, img/chevrolet.png, img/ford.png

---

Open cars.html in a web browser. Recall the action that should be performed once a user clicks two buttons in the first car box.

## Event and Action

Open the script js/listCars.js in a code editor. Read Part 4 as liste below. Part 4 of js/listCars.js registers click events with both buttons of the first car cars[0].

```
1.    // ++++++++++++++++++++++++++++++++++++++++++++++++++++++++++++++
2.    // Part 4: Attach click event with two input buttons of cars[0]
3.    // ++++++++++++++++++++++++++++++++++++++++++++++++++++++++++++++
4.    // Get a reference collection of all elements with tag 'input'
5.    var inputs = document.getElementsByTagName('input');
6.    // Get a referecne collection of all elements with class name 'speed'
7.    var speeds = document.getElementsByClassName('speed');
8.
9.    function btnAccelerate() { // action for accelerating cars[0]
10.       var mph = parseInt(window.prompt('Enter an integer for acceleration rate:'));
11.       if (mph) { // if mph is valid and true, increase speed
12.           cars[0].accelerate(mph);
13.       }
14.       speeds[0].innerHTML = cars[0].currentSpeed + '<span class=\'mph\'>mph</span>';
15.    }
16.    function btnBrake() { // action for stopping cars[0]
17.       if (window.confirm("Stop?")) { // if user presses OK button in the confirmation window
18.           cars[0].brake();
19.       }
20.       speeds[0].innerHTML = cars[0].currentSpeed + '<span class=\'mph\'>mph</span>';
21.    }
22.
23.    // Define a click event for the 1st input element with the callback btnAccelerate
24.    inputs[0].addEventListener('click', btnAccelerate);
25.    // Define a click event for the 2nd input element with the callback btnBrake
26.    inputs[1].addEventListener('click', btnBrake);
```

The procedure in this part can be split into three steps.

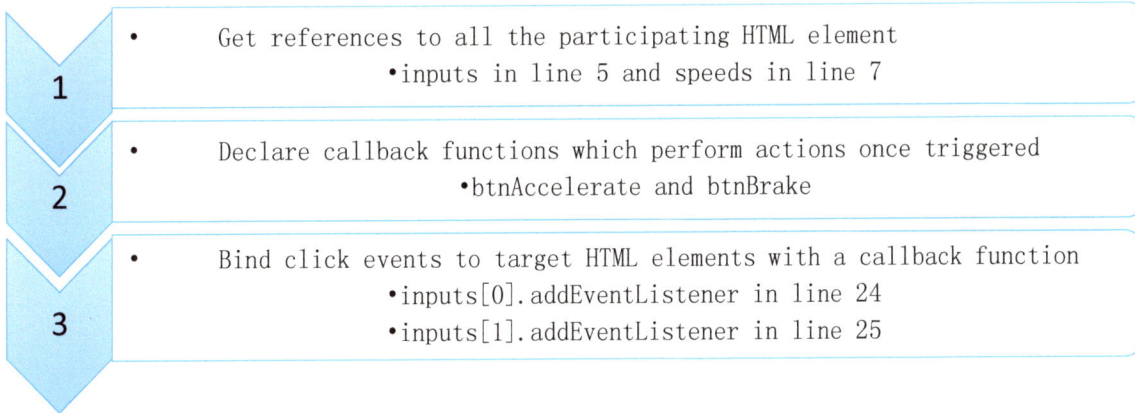

1 • Get references to all the participating HTML element
 • inputs in line 5 and speeds in line 7

2 • Declare callback functions which perform actions once triggered
 • btnAccelerate and btnBrake

3 • Bind click events to target HTML elements with a callback function
 • inputs[0].addEventListener in line 24
 • inputs[1].addEventListener in line 25

## Questions

Based on *Case 1.1*, answer the following questions:

Question 1. In the click event with the ACCELERATE button, what action should be performed?

Question 2. What is the name of callback in the event of the ACCELERATE button?

Question 3. List the HTML elements which participate in the click event for accelerating the car.

Question 4. In the click event with the STOP button, what action should be performed?

Question 5. What is the name of callback in the event of the BRAKE button?

Question 6. List the HTML elements which participate in the click event for stopping the car.

## Bind Event to Target

Now we want to implement the click event for all the cars by using the same method as the album page in *Example 9.3*. The method is based on Function object and nesting functions.

The following is a guide helping you complete the solution.

## Case 1.2

### Step 1. Copy and rename files

→ Copy cars.html to a new file cars-forloop.html

→ Copy js/listCars.js to a new file js/listCars-forloop.js

### Step 2. Edit the <script> tag

→ Open cars-forloop.html in a code editor. Locate the statement:

```
<script src="js/listCars.js"></script>
```

→ Replace js/listCars.js with js/listCars-forloop.js.

→ Save the file.

### Step 3. Load the page

Open cars-forloop.html in a code editor. Read the source code.

Also, load cars-forloop.html in a browser. Open the web console.

### Step 4. Answer questions

Based on the web page produced by cars-forloop.html, answer the following questions in order. Use the web console to run expressions or statements for testing the answer.

1.  List all the participating HTML elements.

2.  Write a statement to get a collection of references to all the input elements. Save the collection to a variable named inputs.

3.  Write an expression to access the length property of inputs. Run the expression in the web console to find the total number of the input elements.

4.  Among the input elements, what are the index values of the input elements having the text ACCELERATE?

5.  Among the input elements, what are the index values of the input elements having the text BRAKE?

### Step 5. Write the script

You will need to complete this step by yourself. Refer to Step 9 in *Example 9.3*. Modify js/listCars-forloop.js to implement two click events for each car on the page.

The final set of script files for *Case 1.2* should be named as below:

```
File Listing
        cars-forloop.html,
        css/car.css,
        js/cars.js, js/listCars-forloop.js,
        img/dodge.png, img/fordf150.png, img/chevrolet.png, img/ford.png
```

# Chapter 10  NESTING LOOPS & SUBPATTERNS

This chapter introduces a popular programming technique for nesting loops. In such a structure, the nesting loop is referred to as the outer loop and the nested loop is the inner loop. The outer loop takes control of the repetition times of the inner loop. We will apply nesting loops to *Case 3.1 Subpattern*.

## Table of Contents

# A Loop Within a Loop

Before applying nesting loops to *Case 3.1 Subpattern*, we will study several examples.

## Example 10.1

### File Listing

js/nesting-loop-1.js

Open a new browser window. Open a Scratchpad window. In the Scratchpad window, open the file `js/nesting-loop-1.js`. Click `Run`. The following output should appear in the browser window.

```
Outer Loop iteration # row = 1
123456
Outer Loop iteration # row = 2
123456
Outer Loop iteration # row = 3
123456
```

The output shows that this script prints the same sequence `123456` three times. The following is the script.

```
1.   // Get the reference to the 1st body element
2.   var target = document.getElementsByTagName('body') [0];
3.   // Erase the current content on the page.
4.   target.innerHTML ='';
5.   // Prepare html
6.   var prefix = '<p>Outer Loop iteration # row = ';
7.   var postfix = '</p>';
8.   var newline = '';
9.
10.  // Set up loop counter upper limits
11.  var outerMax = 3; // Set outer loop counter upper limit
12.  var innerMax = 6; // Set inner loop Counter upper limit
13.
14.  // Nesting Loops
15.  for (var row = 1; row <= outerMax; row++) {//Outer Loop
16.      //Make a new line
17.      newline = prefix + row + postfix;
18.      target.insertAdjacentHTML('beforeend', newline);
19.      //Inner loop
20.      for (var column = 1; column <= innerMax; column++) {
21.          target.insertAdjacentHTML('beforeend', column);
22.      }
23.  }
```

js/nesting-loop-1.js

The variables `outerMax` and `innerMax` set the upper limit for both loop counters. The nesting loops are between line 15 and line 23.

The outer `for` loop starts the first iteration with the loop counter `row` being 1. During each iteration of the outer loop,

- A new paragraph `newline` will be inserted to the end of the body element.

- The inner `for` loop between line 20 and line 22 will be executed once. It begins with the loop counter `column` being 1 and will repeat until `column` attains the value of `innerMax`, which is 6. During each iteration of the inner loop, the current `column` value will be inserted into the page, as shown at line 21. After the inner loop terminates, the sequence 123456 is completed on the page.

- As `outerMax` is initialized to 3, the inner loop will be repeated for three times. Thus, the page prints the same sequence for three times.

## Example 10.2

---

**File Listing**

js/nesting-loop-2.js

---

Open a new browser window. Open a Scratchpad window. In the Scratchpad window, open the file `js/nesting-loop-2.js`. Click Run. The output in the browser window should be a square of 9 rows by 9 columns.

```
123456789
123456789
123456789
123456789
123456789
123456789
123456789
123456789
123456789
```

Look at `js/nesting-loop-2.js` as below. Two changes have been made to the html string of `newline` and the value of `innerMax`. They are highlighted in yellow.

```
1.    // Get the reference to the 1st body element
2.    var target = document.getElementsByTagName('body') [0];
3.    // Erase the current content on the page.
4.    target.innerHTML ='';
5.    // Prepare html
6.    var newline = '<br />';
7.
8.    // Set up loop counter upper limits
9.    var outerMax = 9; // Set outer loop counter upper limet
10.   var innerMax = 9; // Set inner loop Counter upper limit
11.
12.   // Nesting loops
13.   for (var row = 1; row <= outerMax; row++) {//Outer loop
14.       //Make a new line
15.       target.insertAdjacentHTML('beforeend', newline);
16.       //Inner loop
17.       for (var column = 1; column <= innerMax; column++) {
18.           target.insertAdjacentHTML('beforeend', column);
```

```
19.        }
20.    }
```

## Workout 10-1

Modify `js/nesting-loop-2.js` to print the following right-triangle-like content on the page:

```
1
12
123
1234
12345
123456
1234567
12345678
123456789
```

Save the script into a new file named `js/nesting-loop-3.js`.

■ The sample output illustrates the relationship between the row number and the total number of columns in each row. Rows are identified by an integer, starting with **1** and incrementing for each new iteration. To make a right triangle, the total columns in a row equals its row number. The total number of rows is specified by `outerMax`. The following table shows this equality.

| Row number | 1 | 2 | 3 | 4 | 5 | 6 | ... | outerMax |
|---|---|---|---|---|---|---|---|---|
| Total of columns in the row | 1 | 2 | 3 | 4 | 5 | 6 | ... | outerMax |

Hint: Change the loop condition of the inner `for` loop.

## Workout 10-2

(Wikipedia) Floyd's triangle is a right triangular array of natural numbers, used in computer science education. It is named after Robert Floyd. It is defined by filling the rows of the triangle with consecutive numbers, starting with a 1 in the top left corner:

```
1
2   3
4   5   6
7   8   9   10
11  12  13  14  15
```

# Subpattern Revisited

Now let us revisit *Case 3.1 Subpattern*. The relevant files are listed below.

---

## File Listing

> input.html, css/input.css, js/input.js

---

We want to develop a new version *Case 3.2*. The new version has the similar main page as input.html except that the legend for the spinner is '*How many lines?*' The page provides the user with 12 subpattern options. The user can select a shape and a color to custom a subpattern. JavaScript will fill the rows of a right triangle with the custom subpattern.

On the left side of the page, a control section holds custom options, as shown in the leftmost screenshot below. Basically, the user requires to select a shape from the first button group, a color from the second button group and enters an integer in the text field for the toal number of lines. Then click PRINT NOW! to fire the action.

Below, the pictures in the middle and rightmost columns are some sample pattern prints. The actual print in each run depends on your selections.

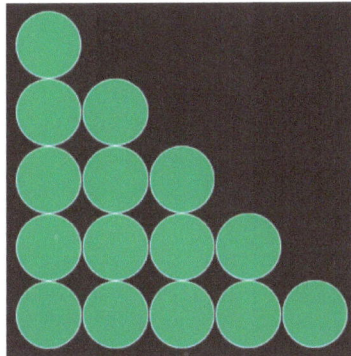

Comparing the sample print with the output from js/nesting-loop-3.js, both have the same structure in a right triangle if we neglect the smallest element. One uses custom shape and the other uses integers.

Thus, we can modify the function `printShape` in `js/input.js` by incorporating nesting loops. The outer loop is responsible for creating rows while the inner loop completes columns for each row by printing a subpattern shape for each column.

The previous `printShape` function in `js/input.js` only prints one subpattern shape, which is listed here.

```
var printShape = function (shape, color) {
// Print a shape by adding div with shape and color as class names
    var classname = shape + ' ' + color;
    var newshape = "<div class=\'" + classname + "\'>" + numShape + "</div>";
    target.insertAdjacentHTML('beforeend', newshape);
};
```

The new `printShape` function should fill in a row with subpatterns and shape rows into a right triangle. Declare `lineCount` for the total number of rows that the user has requested via the spinner. The following is a new `printShape` function.

```
var printShape = function (shape, color) {
// Print a shape by adding div with shape and color as class names
    var classname = shape + ' ' + color;
    var newshape = "<div class=\'" + classname + "\'></div>";
    var newline = '<p class=\'clear\'></p>';
    for (var row = 1; row <= lineCount; row++) {
        for (var column = 1; column <= row; column++) {
            target.insertAdjacentHTML('beforeend', newshape);//Make a new column
        }
        target.insertAdjacentHTML('beforeend', newline); //Make a new row
    }
};
```

## Case 3.2

The file set for `Case 3.2` is listed below.

### File Listing

```
subpattern.html,
css/subpattern.css,
js/subpattern.js
```

Load the main page `subpattern.html` in a browser window. Test the page.

## Workout 10-3

*Case 3.2* leaves an issue unresolved. After a pattern print has been created, if you click the button PRINT NOW! again, either with the current options or new options, a new print will continuously be appended to the previous one. In order to remove the old print, you have to click the reload current page button in the browser window to reflesh the page.

Resolve this issue.

Hint: You may consider to clean up the section #theme before making a new print.

.

# Chapter 11  TIME-BASED EVENTS

A loop enables a program to repeat a set of operations for a certain amount of times. A program can also be scheduled to respond after a time delay. Time-based events are mostly required for running time-sensitive operations either once or repeatedly.

JavaScript is both object-based and event-driven. The previous chapters have shown that JavaScript is object-based because it operates browser window, document object and HTML elements. JavaScript also manages events by user actions and time intervals.

In JavaScript, events include cursor movements, time lapse, button clicks, page loading and data entry.

This chapter will introduce relevant methods for managing time-based events. In a time-based event, the program runs or repeats a set of operations after the passage of time. The Window object can create time events using its methods setInterval, clearInterval, setTimeout and clearTimeout.

## Table of Contents

# Setting Up an Interval Timer

To set up a timer for triggering a task after every time interval,

Timer

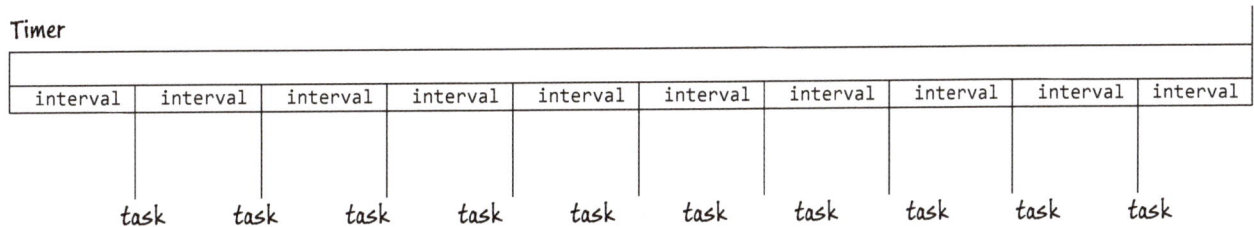

we can apply the method `window.setInterval,` using the following syntax.

Syntax

```
var intervalID = window.setInterval(functionName, delay[, parameter1, parameter2,…]);
```

This statement creates a timer that runs a task function at specified time intervals.

- `functionName` is the name of the callback function that defines operations to be fired.

- `delay` is the duration of each interval, which is a number in milliseconds (**1000** milliseconds = **1** second).

- If the task function has one or more parameters, list their names after `delay`. Separate parameter names must be separated by commas.

- `intervalID` is a unique numeric identifier of the timer. A timer identifier is required if the timer needs to be removed later by using the pairing method `clearInterval.`

## Example 11.1

File Listing

       `time-event.html, js/time-event.js`

Open `time-event.html` in the web browser. New paragraphs are showing up continuously one by one every second. This movement will not stop unless we close the browser tab or browser window.

```
1.    <!DOCTYPE html>
2.    <html>
3.        <head>
4.            <title>Time-based Event</title>
5.            <meta charset="UTF-8">
6.        </head>
7.        <body>
8.            <div id='output'></div>
9.            <script src="js/time-event.js" type="text/javascript"></script>
10.       </body>
11.   </html>
```

```
1.    var count = 0;
2.    var ref = document.getElementById('output');
3.    // Set up a timer for the action 'task'
4.    var intervalID = window.setInterval(task, 1000);
5.    // Declare the function task
6.    function task() {
7.        count ++;
8.        ref.insertAdjacentHTML('beforeend', "<p>Time interval   " + count + "</p>");
9.    }
```

In the script js/time-event.js,

> → count is a global variable and initialized to zero.

> → Lines 6 through 9 declares a function task. The function task increments count by one and inserts a new paragraph into the end of the HTML element 'output'.

> → Line 4 calls window.setInterval over two arguments, task and 1000.

>   1. The second argument 1000 specifies a time delay of 1000 milliseconds, equal to one second.

>   2. The first argument task specifies a callback to be fired after every 1000 milliseconds.

> → Line 4 also assigns an identifier, intervalID, to the created timer.

> → Line 8 calls the insertAdjacentHTML method to insert a new paragraph to the end of the HTML element div#output.

To terminate the new paragraph flow, we have to close the browser tab or window or the entire browser program. In order to avoid this action, we can clear the timer by calling another method window.clearInterval.

# Clearing an Interval Timer

To clear an existing interval timer, call `window.clearInterval` with the following syntax.

### Syntax

```
window.clearInterval(intervalID);
```

deletes a timer named `intervalID`. Prior to this method call, the name `intervalID` should have already been generated from calling `window.setInterval`.

### Example 11.2

### File Listing

```
clear-timer.html, js/clear-timer.js
```

To stop the continuous occurrence of new paragraphs in *Example 11.1*, we need to define a stop condition. During each task run, evaluate if the stop condition is satisfied; if so, clear the timer.

Open `clear-timer.html` in a browser window. The page should stop after printing the paragraph "*Time interval 10*". The new script is in `js/clear-timer.js`.

```
1.    var count = 0;
2.    var ref = document.getElementById('output');
3.    var intervalID = window.setInterval(task, 1000);
4.    function task() {
5.        count ++;
6.        ref.insertAdjacentHTML('beforeend', "<p>Time interval   " + count + "</p>");
7.        stopCount(); // Call stopCount to clear the timer
8.    }
9.    var stopCount = function () { // Declare the function stopCount
10.        if (count === 10) { // Check if count is 10; if so, clear the timer.
11.            window.clearInterval(intervalID);
12.        }
13.    };
```

js/clear-timer.js

The operations to clear the timer are specified in an anonymous function expression at lines 9 through 13, `stopCount`. `stopCount` examines if `count` equals `10`. If `count` is `10`, call `window.clearInterval` to clear the timer with the identifier `intervalID`.

The operations in `stopCount` must be run every time after the task has been completed. Thus, at line 7, add a function call to `stopCount` that will enable the time clearing process.

After the timer has been cleared, its associated task will not be triggered any more.

### Example 11.3

Now we can introduce a timer to *Example 8.1* that prints each star on a web page. After every 500 milliseconds, a new star appears on the page.

---

`File Listing`

> `stars-timer.html, css/stars-timer.css, js/stars-timer.js`

---

Before reading the scripts, open `stars-timer.html` in a browser window to see the timer has added a time delay before printing each star.

The script below, `js/stars-timer.js`, creates the timer and clears the timer as well.

```
1.    var stars = ["Alpha", "Beta", "Gamma", "Delta", "Epsilon", "Theta", "Chi", "Zeta", "Mu",
      "Eta"];
2.    var place = document.getElementById("stars");// Get a reference to the element 'stars'
3.    // Declare newline and initialize it to an empty string
4.    var newline = '';
5.    var index = 0; // Declare an array index for stars
6.
7.    // Set up a new timer intervalID to run printStar every 500 milliseconds
8.    var intervalID = window.setInterval(printStar, 500);
9.
10.   function printStar() {// Declare printStar
11.       newline = "<p>The star indexed by " + index + " is " + stars[index] + ".</p>";
12.       // Write newline into the element 'stars'
13.       place.insertAdjacentHTML('beforeend', newline);
14.       index++;
15.       stopPrint(); // Call stopPrint to determine whether to stop the timer or not
16.   }
17.   function stopPrint() {// Declare stopPrint
18.       if (index === stars.length) {// If index has increased to the last star, clear the timer
19.           window.clearInterval(intervalID);
20.       }
21.   }
```

js/stars-timer.js

---

$\rightarrow$ Line 2 retrieves the reference to the target HTML element where stars will be printed.

$\rightarrow$ Line 5 declares a global variable `index` to access array elements in `stars`.

$\rightarrow$ Line 8 sets up a timer named `intervalID` that fires an action `printStar` every `500` milliseconds.

- The action `printStar` is declared at lines 10 through 16, which

  - Creates a new HTML paragraph for the current star

  - Add the paragraph to the end of the target element

  - Increments `index` by one

  - Call `stopPrint` to decide whether the timer should be cleared or not

- The function `stopPrint` is declared at lines 17 through 20, which will clear the timer when `index` has pointed to the position after the last element in `stars`.

## Workout 11-1

Collect five pictures. Create a web page that insert a new picture every **1000** milliseconds until all the five pictures have been displayed on the page.

## Workout 11-2

Collect five pictures. Create a web page that contains an **img** element that displays one picture. Each picture is on-screen for 1000 milliseconds, then the next picture is shown. If all the three pictures have been displayed, go back to the first picture and start a new round. The page infinitely repeats this action.

# Subpattern Revisited

Recall *Case 3.2* that fills in a triangle with a custom subpattern. The nesting loop in *Case 3.2* is listed below. The outer loop creates each row and the inner loop completes all the columns for the row.

```
1.      for (var row = 1; row <= lineCount; row++) {
2.          for (var column = 1; column <= row; column++) {
3.              target.insertAdjacentHTML('beforeend', newshape);//Make a new column
4.          }
5.          target.insertAdjacentHTML('beforeend', newline); //Make a new row
6.      }
```

The statement at line 3 prints a shape for each column without delay. If we want to animate the process that one shape comes after another, an interval timer can produce a time delay between every two shapes.

What about starting an interval timer before printing each shape? Also, we want to make the timer stop immediately after the first interval. The following code implements this idea. At line 4, `setInterval` starts a timer with an interval of `300` milliseconds and a callback that deletes the timer.

```
1.      for (var row = 1; row <= lineCount; row++) {
2.          for (var column = 1; column <= row; column++) {
3.              window.clearInterval(intervalID);
4.              intervalID = window.setInterval(function () {
5.                  alert('running callback after the first interval..');
6.                  window.clearInterval(intervalID);
7.              }, 300);
8.              target.insertAdjacentHTML('beforeend', newshape);//Make a new column
9.          }
10.         target.insertAdjacentHTML('beforeend', newline);//Make a new row
11.     }
```

According to the order of the statements in the body of the inner loop, during each iteration, the page should alert the message at line 5 'running callback after the first interval..' Then, it prints a shape. The inner loop should alternate between alerting the message and printing a shape.

To test this solution, locate the files at the subfolder *case3*:

---
## File Listing

    subpattern-no.html, css/subpattern.css, js/subpattern-no.js

---

Open the main page `subpattern-no.html` in a web browser window. However, the actual result will not show an animation. Instead, the alert message pops up after the triangle is complete. This is caused by asynchrony of `setInterval`.

`window.setInterval` is asynchronous.

## Example 11.4

---
## File Listing

    js/asynchrony.js, js/asynchrony-callback.js

---

In the following script, according to the order that the statements have been written, the script intends to log four letters a, b, c, d in order. The letter b should display 200 milliseconds after a is displayed.

```
1.    console.log('a');
2.    var intervalID = setInterval(callback, 200);
3.    console.log('c');
4.    console.log('d');
5.
6.    function callback() {
7.        console.log('b');
8.        window.clearInterval(intervalID);
9.    }
```

js/asynchrony-callback.js

However, run the script `js/asynchrony-callback.js` in a Scratchpad window, the letter b will be the last one. That is because timer methods in JavaScript are asynchronous.

After the timer is set, JavaScript will not stay with the timer at line 2 until either an interval has passed or the timer is cleared. Instead, the execution flow goes to the next available statement, which is line 3 in this example. If an interval has passed, its associated callback will be executed; otherwise, JavaScript keeps executing the subsequent statements.

Sometimes, a simple callback can also be anonymous within a function call. See the following `js/asynchrony.js` which passes the entire callback declaration as an argument.

```
1.    console.log('a');
2.    var intervalID = setInterval(function () {
3.        console.log('b');
4.        window.clearInterval(intervalID);
5.    }, 200);
6.    console.log('c');
7.    console.log('d');
```

js/asynchrony.js

Therefore, in `js/subpattern-no.js`, once the timer has been set, JavaScript will continue to execture the next available statement in the loop body. The timer is moving forward and at the same time, tthe iterations keep generating new rows and columns. It appears that two tasks are progressing concurrently.

In this case, the nesting loop needs less time than the specified time interval 300 milliseconds; so the subpattern shapes will be all completed before the interval has passed.

In order to prevent the asynchronous execution order, the loop statements need to be replaced with other mechanisms. The following part will show one way to gurantee the previous interval has completed before starting the next repetition, assuming that the execution time of the callback is shorter than the interval (here 300 milliseconds).

### The function action

Set the interval timer as the last step in the function `action` that is the callback in the `click` event with the `submit` button. The box below shows the function `action` which has two method calls at line 9 and line 10 to clear the existing timer and start a new timer on the callback `printShape` for every delay.

```
1.  function action() {//Function: a callback for submit button
2.      if (validateSpinner() === true && typeof intervalID==="undefined") {
3.          shape = getSelectedButtonValue(shapeBTN);//Read shape
4.          color = getSelectedButtonValue(colorBTN);//Read color
5.          //Log
6.          msg = '<p class=\'log\'>Request for ' + lineCount + ' line(s). Printing...</p>';
7.          log.insertAdjacentHTML('afterbegin', msg);
8.          // Clear and start timer
9.          window.clearInterval(intervalID);
10.         intervalID = window.setInterval(printShape, 300, shape, color);
11.     }
12. }// End of action
```

At line 10,

```
    intervalID = window.setInterval(printShape, 300, shape, color);
```

the last two arguments, `shape` and `color`, are passed to the callback `printShape`.

At line 2, the conditional expression in the `if` statement contains a sub-condition

```
    typeof intervalID==="undefined"
```

which evaluates `true` if no timer has previously been started yet. It evaluates `false` if a timer has been set earlier and the button click will not trigger any operation.

### The function printShape

After the previous interval has completed, the callback `printShape` should print a subpattern shape for the specific `shape` and `color` values. The declaration is shown below.

```
1.  var printShape = function (shape, color) {//Function: Print a shape
2.      classname = shape + ' ' + color;
3.      makeLine(); //Decide to print a new line or not
4.      htmlsource = "<div class=\'" + classname + "\'></div>";
5.      target.insertAdjacentHTML('beforeend', htmlsource);
6.      columnCounter++;
7.      stopPrint(); //Decide to stop timer or not
8.  };
```

When printing a subpattern shape, we must make two decisions:

→ Before printing: Whether the current row is complete and a new row needs to be created. This decision is made by calling the function `makeLine` at line 3 of `printShape`

→ After printing: Whether all the rows have completed and clear the timer thereafter. This decision is made by calling the function `stopPrint` at line 7 of `printShape`.

The variables to be declared for counting rows and columns are

```
var lineCount = 0; // The total rows to be requested
var rowCounter = 0; // row counter: #lines
var columnCounter = 0; // column counter: #shapes in a line
```

lineCount is read from the spinner named lineTotal, which is the total lines that the user has requested.

rowCounter should increment after inserting a new HTML paragraph, representing a new row.

columnCounter should increment after printing a new shape, representing a new column, as shown at line 6 in the function printShape.

### The function makeLine

The condition that determines whether the current row has completed or not is

```
columnCounter === rowCounter
```

because for each row, the column size equals the index number of the row. This has been explained in *Case 3.2*.

```
1.    var makeLine = function () {// Print a new HTML paragraph representing a new row
2.        if (columnCounter === rowCounter) {// The current row is complete?
3.            columnCounter = 0; // Reset the column counter
4.            target.insertAdjacentHTML('beforeend', '<p class=\'clear\'></p>');// Create a new row
5.            rowCounter++; // Increment rowCounter
6.        }
7.    };
```

### The function stopPrint

The following condition evaluates true if the row counter equals lineCount and the current row has completed.

```
rowCounter === lineCount && columnCounter === rowCounter
```

The declaration of stopPrint is shown below.

```
1.    var stopPrint = function () {// Clear timer once all rows are complete.
2.        if (rowCounter === lineCount && columnCounter === rowCounter) {
3.            window.clearInterval(intervalID);
4.        }
5.    };
```

The complete case is named Case 3.3 with the following files.

## Case 3.3

### File Listing

```
subpattern-delay.html,
css/subpattern.css,
js/subpattern-delay.js
```

Load the main page `subpattern-delay.html` in a web browser window. The animation effect is enabled on the page. However, the PRINT NOW! button only responds to the first click. The user has to reload the page for each new print.

## Workout 11-3

Consider *Case 3.3* where the PRINT NOW! button only reacts to the first click. Change the program such that the user can request a new print without reloading the page.

# Setting a Time Delay

As previously discussed, `window.setInterval` repeats a task until `clearInterval` stops it. If the task only requires one execution, `window.setTimeout` is a better option. `setTimeout` creates a time delay and `clearTimeout` clears the delay.

Syntax

```
var timeoutID = window.setTimeout(functionName, delay[, parameter1, parameter2,…]);
window.clearTimeout(timeoutID);
```

- `window.setTimeout` runs a function after a specified time delay in milliseconds.

- It returns a numeric identifier `timeoutID`. `timeoutID` is required by `window.clearTimeout`.

- `window.clearTimeout` stops the timer named `timeoutID` before timeout.

The following example shows that `setTimeout` is asynchronous.

## Example 11.5

File Listing

js/timeout.js

Run the script in a Scratchpad window.

```
1.  console.log('a');

2.  window.setTimeout(function () {
3.    console.log('b');
4.  }, 500);

5.  console.log('c');

6.  window.setTimeout(function () {
7.    console.log('d');
8.  }, 500);

9.  console.log('e');
```

js/timeout.js

# Creating a Time Event

Combination of setTimeout with setInterval can be used to implement time-based applications such as making animation effects. For instance, during a time frame of 10 seconds, a task needs to be done once every 1 second; at the end of the frame, some operations need to be performed.

The corresponding execution flow is shown in the following table. The task will be repeated 10 times as there are 10 times 1000 milliseconds in a frame of 10000 milliseconds. The stop operations will only run one time after 10000 milliseconds have elapsed. Due to the fact that timer methods are asynchronous, if it takes more than the interval time to run the task, unexpected results may occur, depending on the program logic.

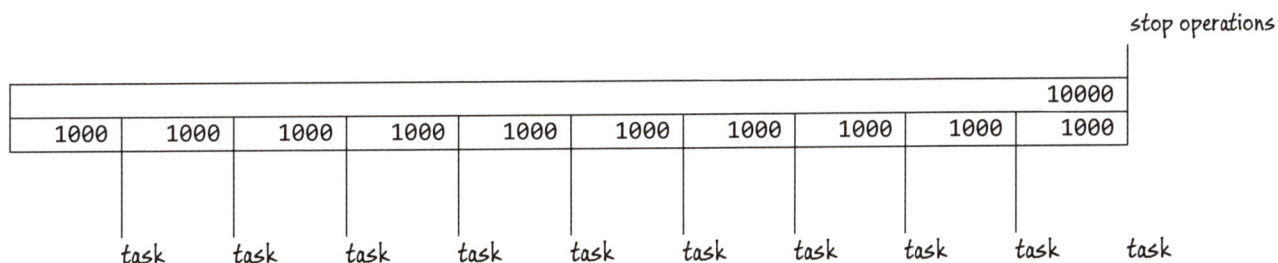

Below is a script template that sets up such a time event.

**Template 1  Time Event**

```
1.    // Block 1: Declare required data for setting a time event
2.    var frame = ms1; interval = ms2;
3.    var frameID, intervalID;
4.    // [other data declarations and initializations]
5.    // Block 2: Define the time event
6.    var start = function (stop, frame, task, interval) {
7.        window.clearTimeout(frameID);
8.        frameID = window.setTimeout(stop, frame);
9.        intervalID = window.setInterval(task, interval);
10.   };
11.   // Block 3: Declare the action that needs to be repeated after each interval
12.   var task = function () {
13.       //[tasks]
14.   };
15.   // Block 4: Declare the action that needs to be executed after the time frame ends
16.   var stop = function () {
17.       window.clearInterval(intervalID);
18.       window.clearTimeout(frameID);
19.       //[additional tasks needed]
20.   };
21.   // Block 5: Create an instance of the time event and start it
22.   start(frame, stop, interval, task);
```

The template is functionally broken down into five blocks. Assuming ms1 is the time duration in milliseconds of the entire time frame, ms2 is the time duration in milliseconds of each time interval.

# Initialize a Time event

The first block declares initial data that is required for setting a time event. It declares two timer named `frameID` and `intervalID` as well as two time periods, `frame` and `interval`, in milliseconds. If any additional initial data are needed, include them in this block.

The third block declares a function `task`, containing the action to be repeated after each time interval.

In the fourth block, the stopping operations are stored in a function `stop`, along with two statements at line 17 and line 18 which clears two timers named `timeoutID` and `intervalID`.

Together, these three blocks specify a time event scenario.

# Construct the Time Event

The second block constructs the time event in a function `start`. The function `start` manages and controls the execution flow in the time event.

Line 7 clears `timeoutID` if it exists.

```
window.clearTimeout(frameID);
```

Line 8 starts a timer `frameID` and calls `stop` after the timer stops.

```
frameID = window.setTimeout(stop, frame);
```

Line 9 starts a timer `intervalID` and calls `task` after each interval lapses.

```
intervalID = window.setInterval(task, interval);
```

The execution sequence of line 8 and 9 is illustrated in the following diagram.

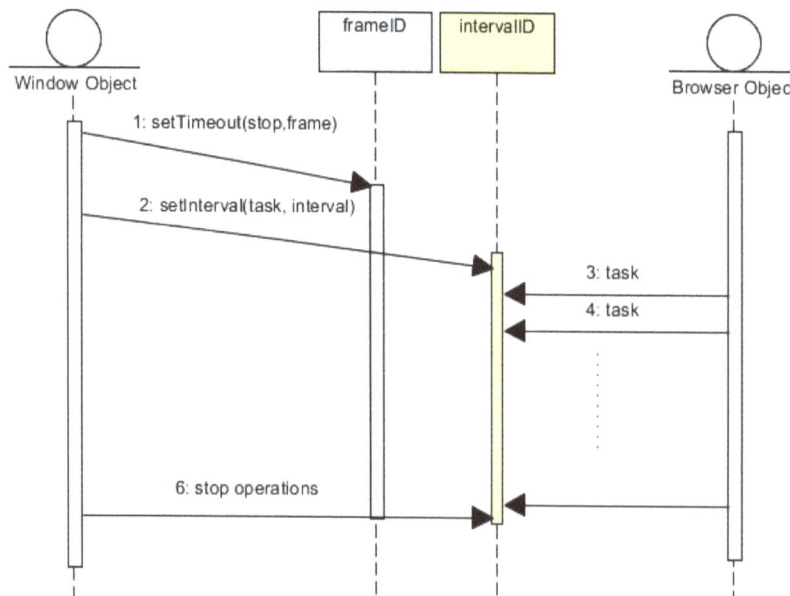

The diagram contains

  – Two objects, window and browser, in circle

  – Two variables, frameID and intervalID, in rectangle

  – Several function calls in labeled lines

The function call lines are placed from top to bottom in the same order that they are fired in the program.

Blue and yellow vertical bars indicate the lifetime of frameID and intervalID, respectively. The blue bar should last for 10000 milliseconds. The time distance between every two task-calling lines, such as 3:task and 4:task, is 1000 milliseconds.

## Implement the Time Event

The last block is a function call

```
start(stop, frame, task, interval);
```

which starts the time event by calling start with four arguments.

> When applying this template to a specific problem, the function task needs to be declared. The operations that are scheduled after the timer stops can be written into the function stop. Any preconditions can be placed into the function start.

In the following parts, let us apply this time event template.

# Case Study – King Zoo

In this case, during a given time frame of `12300` milliseconds, for every `300` milliseconds, an animal is moved to a zoo. Once timeout, a summary report is printed at the bottom of the web page.

## Case 4.1 King Zoo

The files of *Case 4.1* are stored in the folder `case4`.

### File Listing

        zoo.html, css/zoo.css, js/zoo.js,

        img/cat.png, img/camel.png, img/crocodile.png, img/elephant.png, img/hawk.png,

        img/kangaroo.png, img/lion.png, img/ostrich.png, img/panda.png, img/sheep.png,

        img/tiger.png, img/zebra.png

Open `zoo.html` in a web browser window. Animals will be coming one after the other. The expected view will be similar to the screenshot below, except that for each page load, animals would be different because each is randomly selected from twelve species.

## Step 1. Outline a zoo area

The header element displays the zoo name. The content in the zoo is enclosed by a section element having the id value 'zoo', which embeds two div elements; each has a class selector to specifiy the width. The wireframe is shown below.

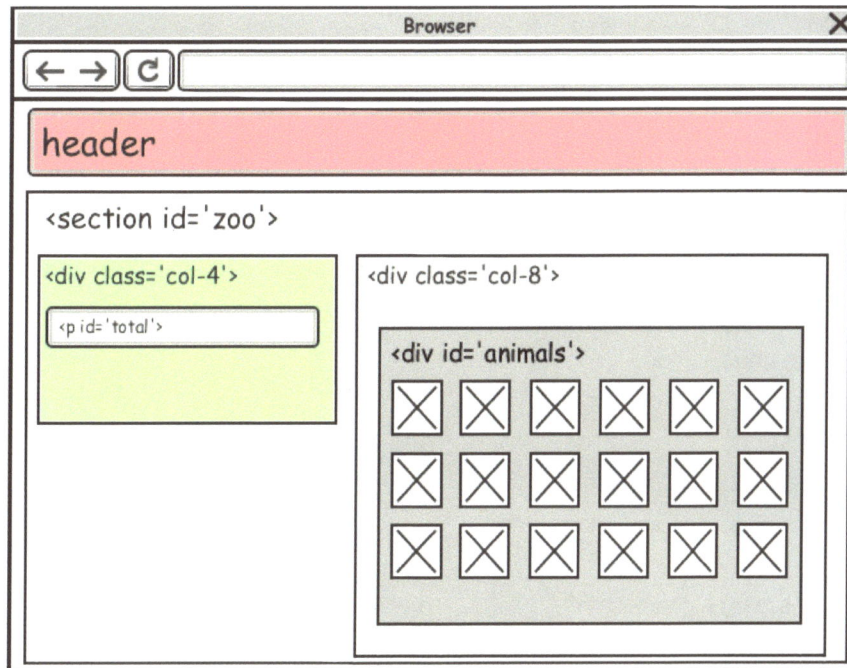

On the right column of the page, inside the element div#animals, each small square with a cross represents an animal to be added to the zoo. These small boxes are not included in the HTML source; instead, they will be added by JavaScript after the page has been loaded in the browser. The following is the HTML source that creates the same layout as the wireframe above.

```
1.  <!DOCTYPE html>
2.  <html>
3.     <head>
4.         <title>Time-based Event</title>
5.         <meta charset="UTF-8">
6.         <link href="css/zoo.css" rel="stylesheet" type="text/css"/>
7.     </head>
8.     <body>
9.         <header>KING ZOO</header>
10.
11.        <section id="zoo">
12.            <div class="col-4">
13.                <div id="alert">
14.                    <p id='total'></p>
15.                </div>
16.            </div>
17.            <div class="col-8">
18.                <div id="animals"></div>
19.            </div>
20.        </section>
```

```
21.
22.            <script src="js/zoo.js" type="text/javascript"></script>
23.     </body>
24. </html>
```

The associated style rules are declared in `css/zoo.css`.

The `class` selectors beginning with `'col-'` defines 12 different percent width values if the screen size is greater than 768 pixels. They are responsive for tablets and mobile phones.

Two @media rules are made for two viewport sizes, 768 pixels or less and 480 pixels or less. In this case, for both viewport sizes, all the selectors have 100% screen width.

```
/* For desktop: */
.col-1 {width: 8.33%;}
.col-2 {width: 16.66%;}
.col-3 {width: 25%;}
.col-4 {width: 33.33%;}
.col-5 {width: 41.66%;}
.col-6 {width: 50%;}
.col-7 {width: 58.33%;}
.col-8 {width: 66.66%;}
.col-9 {width: 75%;}
.col-10 {width: 83.33%;}
.col-11 {width: 91.66%;}
.col-12 {width: 100%;}
@media only screen and (max-width: 768px) {
    /* For tablets: */
    [class*="col-"] {
        width: 100%;
    }
}
@media only screen and (max-width: 480px) {
    /* For mobile phones: */
    [class*="col-"] {
        width: 100%;
    }
}
```

## Step 2. Model animal species

There are twelve species; each is represented by an image. Each new animal is randomly picked from these twelve species.

Firstly, store their names in an array `species`

```
var species = ['camel', 'cat', 'crocodile', 'elephant', 'hawk', 'kangaroo', 'lion', 'panda',
'ostrich', 'sheep', 'tiger', 'zebra'];
```

### *Style an animal*

Each animal is caged in a `div` element. To place an animal in a `div` element, the `div` element must be subject to two sets of style rules.

- Common properties over all the species are described in a `class` selector `.animal`.

```
.animal{
    display: block;
    float: left;
    width: 70px;
    height: 70px;
    margin: 5px; padding: 5px;
    background-size: 100%; // fit the background image to the position area
}
```

- The styles specific to an individual species are declared in a `class` selector of the same name as the species. Each species-relevant `class` selector sets the species image as background image. The following 12 class selectors.

```
.cat {background-image: url(../img/cat.png);}
.camel {background-image: url(../img/camel.png);}
.crocodile {background-image: url(../img/crocodile.png);}
.elephant {background-image: url(../img/elephant.png);}
.hawk {background-image: url(../img/hawk.png);}
.kangaroo {background-image: url(../img/kangaroo.png);}
.lion {background-image: url(../img/lion.png);}
.ostrich {background-image: url(../img/ostrich.png);}
.panda {background-image: url(../img/panda.png);}
.sheep {background-image: url(../img/sheep.png);}
.tiger {background-image: url(../img/tiger.png);}
.zebra {background-image: url(../img/zebra.png);}
```

The `url` of each image file is relative to the `css` file.

If the images are not stored in the `img` folder, change the `url` values.

For instance, to model a tiger in a `div` element, the HTML source should be

```
<div class='animal tiger'></div>
```

For other animals, simply replace `'tiger'` with other species name.

## Step 3. Randomly select a species & create a new animal

After a 300-millisecond interval, JavaScript should randomly select a species and add a new animal to the zoo.

As previously discussed in Chapter 8 *Random Number Generation*, the expression

```
var type = Math.floor(Math.random() * 12);
```

generates a random integer between 0 and 11.

`species[type]` retrieves a species name from the array `species`, so `species[type]` should be assigned to the `class` attribute of the new animal.

The following statement will create the HTML content for a new animal `newanimal`.

```
var newanimal = "<div class=\'animal " + species[type] + "\'></div>";
```

## Step 4. Add the new animal to zoo

The following statements adds `newanimal` to the zoo area `div#animals`.

```
var ref = document.getElementById('animals');
ref.insertAdjacentHTML('beforeend', newanimal);
```

## Step 5. Initialize a time event

Now, let us follow *Template 1 Time Event*. In the first block of the template, we need to set up initial data.

```
var frameID, intervalID;
var interval = 300; frame = 12300;
var count = 0;
var species = ['camel', 'cat', 'crocodile', 'elephant', 'hawk', 'kangaroo', 'lion', 'panda',
'ostrich', 'sheep', 'tiger', 'zebra'];
```

The variable `count` is used for counting the animals. It increments by one for each new animal.

## Step 6. Generate the function `task`

The task to be fired after each interval is declared in the function `task`.

```
var task = function () {
    var ref = document.getElementById('animals');
    count ++;
    var type = Math.floor(Math.random() * 10);
    var newanimal = "<div class=\'animal " + species[type] + "\'></div>";
    ref.insertAdjacentHTML('beforeend', newanimal);
};
```

## Step 7. Generate the function `stop`

After time has run out, a summary should be printed to the HTML element `p#total`. These summarizing operations should be written into the function `stop`.

```
var stop = function () {
    window.clearInterval(intervalID);
    window.clearTimeout(frameID);
    var summary = "During " + frame/1000 + " seconds, " + count + " animals have moved into
the zoo. Be sure to provide them with three meals per day.";
    var ref = document.getElementById('total');
    ref.insertAdjacentHTML('afterbegin', summary);
};
```

## Step 8. Fire the Event

To start the event, make the following function call

```
start(frame, stop, interval, task);
```

## Step 9. Deploy the Template

Organize the parts from the previous steps into `js/zoo.js`, as printed below.

```
1.   var frameID, intervalID;
2.   var interval = 300; frame = 12300;
3.   var count = 0;
4.   var species = ['camel', 'cat', 'crocodile', 'elephant', 'hawk', 'kangaroo', 'lion', 'panda',
     'ostrich', 'sheep', 'tiger', 'zebra'];
5.   var start = function (stop, frame, task, interval) {
6.       window.clearTimeout(frameID);
7.       timeoutID = window.setTimeout(stop, frame);
8.       intervalID = window.setInterval(task, interval);
9.   };
10.  var stop = function () {
11.      window.clearInterval(intervalID);
12.      window.clearTimeout(frameID);
13.      var summary = "During " + frame/1000 + " seconds, " + count + " animals have moved into
     the zoo. Be sure to provide them with three meals per day.";
14.      var ref = document.getElementById('total');
15.      ref.insertAdjacentHTML('afterbegin', summary);
16.  };
17.  var task = function () {
18.      var ref = document.getElementById('animals');
19.      count ++;
20.      var type = Math.floor(Math.random() * 12);
21.      var newanimal = "<div class=\'animal " + species[type] + "\'></div>";
22.      ref.insertAdjacentHTML('beforeend', newanimal);
23.
24.  };
25.  start(stop, frame, task, interval);
```

## Workout 11-4

Copy the folder case4 to your computer.

In the script zoo.js, add a new function that counts the total number of a species in the zoo.

Save the new script to a new file: zoo-ex.js.

In zoo.html, modify the src value of the element script in zoo.html and save the new HTML to zoo-ex.html.

The complete file set should include the following scripts:

### File Listing

zoo-ex.html, css/zoo.css, js/zoo-ex.js,

img/cat.png, img/camel.png, img/crocodile.png, img/elephant.png, img/hawk.png,

img/kangaroo.png, img/lion.png, img/ostrich.png, img/panda.png, img/sheep.png,

img/tiger.png, img/zebra.png

The page zoo-ex.html has the same function as zoo.html. In addition, after the timer stops, it should provides the user with an interface to retrieve the total number of animals for a species.

*Hint:*

The structure of zoo-ex.js is given below. The new additions are highlighted in brown. At the end of the function stop, a function extra is called. The declaration of extra starts at line 25.

```
1.    var frameID, intervalID;
2.    var interval = 300; frame = 12300;
3.    var count = 0;
4.    var species =
      ['camel','cat','crocodile','elephant','hawk','kangaroo','lion','panda','ostrich','sheep','tige
      r','zebra'];
5.    var start = function (frame, stop, interval, task) {
6.        window.clearTimeout(frameID);
7.        timeoutID = window.setTimeout(stop, frame);
8.        intervalID = window.setInterval(task, interval);
9.    };
10.   var stop = function () {
11.       window.clearInterval(intervalID);
12.       window.clearTimeout(frameID);
13.       var summary = "During " + frame/1000 + " seconds, " + count + " animals have moved into
      the zoo. Be sure to provide them with three meals per day.";
14.       var ref = document.getElementById('total');
15.       ref.insertAdjacentHTML('afterbegin', summary);
16.       extra();
17.   };
18.   var task = function () {
```

```
19.        var ref = document.getElementById('animals');
20.        count ++;
21.        var type = Math.floor(Math.random() * 12);
22.        var newanimal = "<div class=\'animal " + species[type] + "\'></div>";
23.        ref.insertAdjacentHTML('beforeend', newanimal);
24.
25.    };
26.    var extra = function(){
27.        // statements
28.    };
29.    start(frame, stop, interval, task);
```

You need to complete the declaration of the function extra, which is supposed to return the total number of a species in the zoo. A do while statement is recommended for the function extra; however, other loop types will also work. The following provides a sample logic for the function extra in three steps.


**do {**

Step 1. Display a prompt, listing all species available in the zoo and asking the user to enter a species name.

> For example, "There are ten species: 'camel', 'cat', 'crocodile', 'elephant', 'hawk', 'kangaroo', 'lion', 'panda', 'ostrich', 'sheep'. \n If you want to know the total of a species, enter the species name. We will count for you. : "

Step 2. Respond to the user in an alert displaying the total number of the requested species.

> (*Hint*: The species is distinguished by the name of their associated class selector.)
> Recall the method getElementsByClassName. The following statement will return a collection of all of the html elements having a specific class name 'animal cat'.
>
> ```
> var refs = document.getElementsByClassName('animal cat');
> ```
>
> If the species name is stored in a variable type, then rewrite the statement above to
>
> ```
> var refs = document.getElementsByClassName('animal' + type);
> ```

refs.length will return the total number of elements in the collection refs.

Step 3. Display another prompt window, asking whether the user wants to know the total number for another species.

> a. If the user answers with yes, the function will repeat the action by going back to step 1.
>
> b. If the user answers with no, the function will exit.

**} while ([loop condition]);**

[loop condition] in the while statement is a placeholder that you need to write a condtional expression that controls the loop to continue or terminate.

# Chapter 12   REVISITING

# ROLES AT THE SCENE

We have learned that decisions and loops empower a computer program to respond to users upon their input. Time events can create timers which apply a time schedule to repeat an action on a web page until the timers are cleared.

In this chapter, we will apply these techniques to the last version of *Roles at the Scene* in *Case 2.3*. We plan to restructure the program and augment its functionality. In the current version *Case 2.3*, the role can only move one step further each time; with the new version, the role is capable of continuously moving.

## Table of Contents

Locate the following files from the last version in *Case 2.3*.

---

**File Listing - Case 2.3**

```
scene-1-switch.html,
css/scene.css,
js/Role-1-switch.js, js/playRoles-1.js,
img/dogface.png, img/cat.png
```

---

Open the main page `scene-1-switch.html` in a browser window. Recall that the page displays two animal roles, `dog` and `cat`. Both roles can make one movement towards the direction that the user has commanded.

The new version is in *Case 2.4*.

## Case 2.4

The script set of *Case 2.4* is stored in the folder `case2`, including the following files.

---

**File Listing - Case 2.4**

```
scene-2.html,
css/scene.css,
js/Role-2.js, js/playRoles-2.js,
img/dogface.png, img/cat.png
```

---

To see the new occurrences in the new version, open `scene-2.html` in the browser window. The cat keeps falling down until reaching the floor, then it will return to the ceiling and fall down again. A new alert box appears every a few seconds. Upon entering an integer into the alert box, the dog will move one step toward the indicated direction.

This chapter will describe how these new logics are programmed.

# Briefing Upgrades

The following is a briefing of the upgrades in two groups, either enhancing the capibilities of the `Role` object or improving the execution flow of the program.

To enhance the `Role` object,

* Upgrade 1.    Add a new capability `Role.hitWall(bottom, maxleft)` which sets the rules when the role hits a wall, ceiling, floor, left or right. The valid active area is outlined by two parameters `bottom` and `maxleft`. `bottom` sets the maximum distance from the top and `maxleft` sets the maximum distance to the right.

* Upgrade 2.    Augment the existing method `Role.move(direction)` by incorporating `hitWall`. The augmented method will need two more parameters `bottom` and `maxleft` that are required by `hitWall`. The new method `Role.move(direction, bottom, maxleft)` enables the role to adjust the position upon hitting a wall of its active area.

* Upgrade 3.    Add a new behavior `Role.fall(bottom, maxleft)` which enables the role to move one step down and check if it hits the bottom wall; if so, send the role back to the ceiling with a random left position less than `maxleft`.

To improve the execution flow,

* Upgrade 4.    Add a new callback function `fall(index)` that enables the role, referenced by `roles[index]`, to run the method `Role.fall` to move one step down.

* Upgrade 5.    Add a new function `startTimeEvent(task, interval, roleIndex)` that schedules a time event for the role, referenced by `roles[roleIndex]`, to repeat the function `task` after each time interval. `startTimeEvent` returns the timer ID.

* Upgrade 6.    Create a time event for the `dog`. After every 6 seconds, the `dog` peforms the task `moveRole`, i.e., the user sends a direction command to the `dog` and the `dog` moves one step to that direction.

* Upgrade 7.    Create a time event for the `cat`. After every 20 milliseconds, the `cat` executes the task `fall(index)`. An infinite repetition of `fall(index)` will make an illusion that the `cat` keeps falling down.

The following parts will describe how these upgrades are implemented.

# Augmenting the Role

Firstly, we will power up the `Role` object by offering it three new capabilities. Each capability will be written as a new method into the contructor `Role`.

## Upgrade 1: Role.hitWall

This new method, `Role.hitWall`, is responsible for detecting if a role hits a wall and if so, calculating a new top or left position. The upperlimits for the top and left position are predefined in two parameters `bottom` and `maxleft`. `bottom` sets the maximum distance from the top and `maxleft` sets the maximum distance to the right.

The implemention is given below. Each `if else` statement is used for processing one occasion.

```
1.      this.hitWall = function (bottom, maxleft) {
2.          // Calculate a new left or top position once hitting a wall
3.          // maxleft is the furthest left position that a role can go.
4.          // bottom is the deepest distance a role can go down.
5.
6.          // Check if hitting the ceiling or floor
7.          if (parseFloat(this.top) >= bottom) { // floor
8.              this.top = bottom + 'px';
9.          } else if (parseFloat(this.top) <= 0) { // ceiling
10.             this.top = 0 + 'px';
11.         }
12.
13.         // Check if hitting the left or right wall
14.         if (parseFloat(this.left) <= 0) { // left wall
15.             this.left = 0 + 'px';
16.         } else if (parseFloat(this.left) >= maxleft) { // right wall
17.             this.left = maxleft + 'px';
18.         }
19.     };
```

Role.hitWall (bottom, maxleft)

## Upgrade 2: Role.move

In the method `Role.move`, incorporate the wall hitting function to adjust position once the role hits a wall. This can be simply done by adding a statement to call the method `Role.hitWall`, which is displayed at line 24 of the script below.

```
1.      this.move = function (direction, bottom, maxleft) {
2.          // Read the current position
3.          var left = parseFloat(this.left);
4.          var top = parseFloat(this.top);
5.          var speed = this.speed;
6.          // Update the position according to direction and speed
7.          switch (direction) {
8.              case 0:
9.                  top = top - speed;
10.                 break;
11.             case 1:
12.                 left = left + speed;
13.                 break;
14.             case 2:
15.                 top = top + speed;
16.                 break;
17.             case 3:
18.                 left = left - speed;
19.                 break;
20.             default:
21.                 window.alert("Wrong command!");
22.         }
23.         // If hitting a wall?
24.         this.hitWall(bottom, maxleft);
25.         // Move the role to the new position
26.         this.setPosition(left, top);
```

```
27.          };
```

Role.move (direction, bottom, maxleft)

## Upgrade 3: Role.fall

The last new capability is to enable the following operations:

Step 1.    Move the role one step down.

Step 2.    Check if the top position is not less than bottom and determine whether the role hits the bottom wall or nor.

Step 3.    If the role hits the bottom wall, write 0px to the property key top and write a random position less than maxleft to the property key left.

Step 4.    Move the role to the new position.

The implementation of the method is shown below.

```
1.          this.fall = function (bottom, maxleft) {
2.              // maxleft is the furthest left position the role can go.
3.              // bottom is the deepest position from the top that the role can go down.
4.              this.move(2, bottom, maxleft); // Move the role a step down
5.              if (parseFloat(this.top) >= bottom) { // When hitting the bottom,
6.                  this.top = 0 + 'px'; // Send the role back to the ceiling,
7.                  this.left = Math.random() * maxleft + 'px'; // Randomize a left position less than
        maxleft.
8.              }
9.              this.setPosition(this.left, this.top); // Move the role to the new position
10. };
```

Role.fall (bottom, maxleft)

Now we have completed all of the three upgrades to the Role. The new Role constructor is printed below as in js/Role-2.js.

```
1.  var Role = function (ref, avatar, left, top, showup, speed) {
2.      this.ref = ref;
3.      this.avatar = avatar;
4.      this.left = left + 'px';
5.      this.top = top + 'px';
6.      this.showup = showup;
7.      this.speed = speed;
8.
9.      this.setup = function () {
10.         this.ref.style.left = this.left;
11.         this.ref.style.top = this.top;
12.         this.ref.style.backgroundImage = "url(" + avatar + ")";
13.         this.ref.style.visibility = this.showup;
14.     };
15.
16.     this.setVisibility = function (showup) {
17.         this.showup = showup;
```

```
18.          this.ref.style.visibility = showup;
19.      };
20.
21.      this.setPosition = function (left, top) {
22.          this.left = left + 'px';
23.          this.top = top + 'px';
24.          this.ref.style.left = this.left;
25.          this.ref.style.top = this.top;
26.      };
27.
28.      this.hitWall = function (bottom, maxleft) {
29.          // Calculate a new left or top position once hitting a wall
30.          // maxleft is the furthest left position that a role can go.
31.          // bottom is the deepest distance a role can go down.
32.
33.          // Check if hitting the ceiling or floor
34.          if (parseFloat(this.top) >= bottom) { // floor
35.              this.top = bottom + 'px';
36.          } else if (parseFloat(this.top) <= 0) { // ceiling
37.              this.top = 0 + 'px';
38.          }
39.
40.          // Check if hitting the left or right wall
41.          if (parseFloat(this.left) <= 0) { // left wall
42.              this.left = 0 + 'px';
43.          } else if (parseFloat(this.left) >= maxleft) { // right wall
44.              this.left = maxleft + 'px';
45.          }
46.      };
47.
48.      this.move = function (direction, bottom, maxleft) {
49.          // Read the current position
50.          var left = parseFloat(this.left);
51.          var top = parseFloat(this.top);
52.          var speed = this.speed;
53.          // Update the position according to direction and speed
54.          switch (direction) {
55.              case 0:
56.                  top = top - speed;
57.                  break;
58.              case 1:
59.                  left = left + speed;
60.                  break;
61.              case 2:
62.                  top = top + speed;
63.                  break;
64.              case 3:
65.                  left = left - speed;
66.                  break;
67.              default:
68.                  window.alert("Wrong command!");
69.          }
70.          // If hitting a wall?
71.          this.hitWall(bottom, maxleft);
72.          // Move the role to the new position
```

```
73.          this.setPosition(left, top);
74.      };
75.
76.      this.fall = function (bottom, maxleft) {
77.          // maxleft is the furthest left position the role can go.
78.          // bottom is the deepest position from the top that the role can go down.
79.
80.          this.move(2, bottom, maxleft); // Move the role a step down
81.          if (parseFloat(this.top) >= bottom) { // When hitting the bottom,
82.              this.top = 0 + 'px'; // Send the role back to the ceiling,
83.              this.left = Math.random() * maxleft + 'px'; // Randomize a left position less than
    maxleft.
84.          }
85.          this.setPosition(this.left, this.top); // Move the role to the new position
86.      };
87.
88. };
```

js/Role-2.js

## Updating the Execution Flow

The upgrades numbered 4 through 7 are relevant to the execution flow in the main script `playRoles.js`.

* Upgrade 4.

Add a new callback function `fall(index)` that enables the role, referenced by `roles[index]`, to run its method `Role.fall` for one time.

```
function fall(index) {// The role, referenced by roles[index], jump one step down.
    roles[index].fall(bottom, right);
}
```

* Upgrade 5.

Add a new function `startTimeEvent(task, interval, roleIndex)` that schedules a time event for the role, referenced by `roles[roleIndex]`, to repeat the function `task` after each interval. `startTimeEvent` returns the timer ID.

The implementation for this new function is given below.

```
function startTimeEvent(task, interval, roleIndex) {
    var intervalID;
    window.clearInterval(intervalID);
    intervalID = window.setInterval(task, interval, roleIndex);
    return intervalID;
}
```

The syntax with the statement highlighted in blue,

```
intervalID = window.setInterval(task, interval, roleIndex);
```

needs an explanation for the third argument `roleIndex`.

When the `callback` function in a time event has input parameters, list those parameters after the second parameter `interval`. In this statement, `roleIndex` will be passed to the `callback` function `task` as an argument.

*Upgrade 6.*

Create a time event for the dog. After every 6 seconds, the dog peforms the task `moveRole`, i.e., the user sends a direction command to the dog and the dog moves one step towards the indicated direction.

Firstly, we need to declare variables to store intervals and timer IDs.

```
// Declare an array for time intervals
var interval = [];
// Declare an array for timer IDs
var intervalID = [];
```

Next, we can specify an interval of 6 seconds.

```
interval[0] = 6000;
```

Call `startTimeEvent` with three arguments by the statement

```
intervalID[0] = startTimeEvent(moveRole, interval[0], 0);
```

that creates an interval timer which repeats the function `moveRole` after each interval. Recall that `moveRole(index)` is a function in `js/playRoles.js` that sends a direction command to `roles[index]` and the role moves one step to that direction.

*Upgrade 7.*

Create a time interval event for the `cat` to repeat the task `fall(index)` every `20` milliseconds.

The same as the statements in the last upgrade except for the index of the role and the name of task to be repeated. The index of the role cat is `1`. Firstly, assign `20` milliseconds to `interval[1]`.

```
interval[0] = 6000;
```

Then call `startTimeEvent` with three arguments

```
intervalID[1] = startTimeEvent(fall, interval[1], 1);
```

An infinite repetition of `fall(1)` will make an illusion that the `cat` is falling down.

## The new script

The following is the new script in `js/playRoles-2.js` with the new code highlighted in yellow.

```
1.    // ++++++++++++++++++++++++++++++++++
```

```
2.    // Part 1: Declare Global variables
3.    // ++++++++++++++++++++++++++++++++++
4.    var bottom; // Height of game area
5.    var right; // Width of game area
6.    var xini; // Initial left position
7.    // Declare an array for role names
8.    var roleNames = [];
9.    // Declare an array for role avatar images
10.   var roleAvatars = [];
11.   // Declare an array for speed
12.   var speed = [];
13.   // Declare an array for role instances
14.   var roles = [];
15.   // Declare an array, prex, to store the left position of each role
16.   // which is the horizontal distance to the left wall.
17.   var prex = [];
18.   // Declare an array, prey, to store the top position of each role
19.   // which is the vertical distance to the top wall
20.   var prey = [];
21.   // Get a reference to div#scene
22.   var scene = document.getElementById('scene');
23.   // Declare an array for time intervals
24.   var interval = [];
25.   // Declare an array for timer IDs
26.   var intervalID = [];
27.
28.   // ++++++++++++++++++++++++++++++++++
29.   // Part 2: Implement a specific case
30.   // ++++++++++++++++++++++++++++++++++
31.   // Give names
32.   roleNames = ['dog', 'cat'];
33.   // Give resource files for avatar
34.   roleAvatars = ['img/dogface.png', 'img/cat.png'];
35.   // Assign each role with a speed
36.   speed = [5, 3];
37.
38.   // Set size of scene: bottom, right, xini
39.   setArea(630, 220, 120);
40.   // Set the initial left and top for role[0]
41.   prex[0] = xini;
42.   prey[0] = bottom; // bottom
43.   // Set the initial left and top for role[1]
44.   prex[1] = Math.random() * xini;  // a random horizontal distance between 0(inclusive) and
         xini(exclusive)
45.   prey[1] = 0; // top
46.   // Call functions
47.   insertHTMLelements();
48.   createRoles();
49.   placeRoles();
50.
51.   //Create a time event for the dog.
52.   //After every 6 seconds, send a direction command to the dog and the dog moves one step to
         that direction.
53.   interval[0] = 6000;
54.   intervalID[0] = startTimeEvent(moveRole, interval[0], 0);
```

```
55.
56.   //Create a time event for the cat.
57.   //After every 20 milliseconds, the cat falls one step down.
58.   interval[1] = 20;
59.   intervalID[1] = startTimeEvent(fall, interval[1], 1);
60.
61.   // +++++++++++++++++++++++++++++++++
62.   // Part 3: Function Declarations
63.   // +++++++++++++++++++++++++++++++++
64.   function setArea(vbottom, vright, vxini) {
65.       bottom = vbottom; // Height of game area
66.       right = vright; // Width of game area
67.       xini = vxini; // Initial left position
68.   }
69.
70.   function insertHTMLelements() {// Display roles at scene
71.       var content = '<div id=\'roles\'>';
72.       // Append every role to HTML content
73.       roleNames.forEach(function (element, index) {
74.           // Compose the HIML string that creates a div element for a role name.
75.           content = content + '<div class=\'role\' id=\'' + element + '\'></div>';
76.       });
77.       // Update the HTML source within the scene
78.       scene.innerHTML = content + '</div>';
79.   }
80.
81.   function createRoles() {// Create a role instance for each name in roleNames
82.       roleNames.forEach(function (element, index) {
83.           roles[index] = new Role(document.getElementById(element), roleAvatars[index], 0, 0,
        'hidden', speed[index]);
84.       });
85.   }
86.
87.   function placeRoles() {// Place each role in the scene
88.       roles.forEach(function (element, index) {
89.           element.setup();
90.           element.setPosition(prex[index], prey[index]);
91.           element.setVisibility('visible');
92.       });
93.   }
94.
95.   function moveRole(index) {// Command a role to move around
96.       var direction = null;
97.       var input = window.prompt("Command " + roleNames[index].toUpperCase() + ": \n Four
      standard commands denoted by 0, 1, 2 and 3: \n 0. Run up \n 1. Run right \n 2. Run down \n
      3. Run left. \n Enter an integer [0,3] for the command: ");
98.       direction = parseInt(input);
99.       roles[index].move(direction);
100.  }
101.
102.  function fall(index) {// The role, referenced by roles[index], jump one step down.
103.      roles[index].fall(bottom, right);
104.  }
105.
```

```
106.  function startTimeEvent(task, interval, roleIndex) {// Create an interval timer for a role to
        repeat a task forever
107.      var intervalID;
108.      window.clearInterval(intervalID);
109.      intervalID = window.setInterval(task, interval, roleIndex);
110.      return intervalID;
111.  }
```

js/playRoles-2.js

# Designing New Scenarios

After completing all the upgrades, the new version *Case 2.4* is stored in the following files:

## File Listing – Case 2.4

scene-2.html,

css/scene.css,

js/Role-2.js, js/playRoles-2.js,

img/dogface.png, img/cat.png

All of these resources are listed in two tree views. In the following, the left tree lists all the keys of `Role` in `js/Role-2.js`. The right tree lists all the global variables, `HTML` elements and functions in `js/playRoles-2.js`.

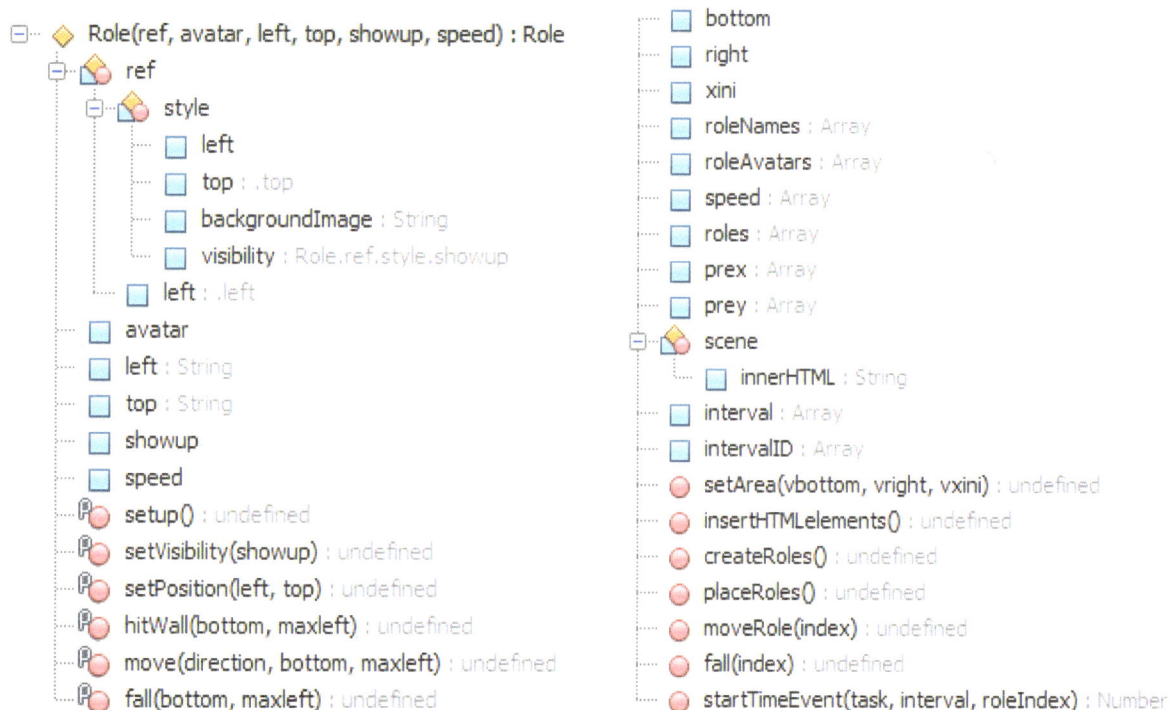

The blue squre indicates the property key or variable or element property.

The red circle indicates the method key or function.

The icon of three overlapped shapes indicates the `HTML` element.

Based on these existing resources, data, object and functions, we can create various scenarios by changing the execution logics in the main script `js/playRoles-2.js`. However, be aware that new resources such as new variables, methods and functions will most likely be required for more complex logics.

## Example 12.1

For example, we can make a simple scenario where both roles, `dog` and `cat`, keep falling down. Keep the same time event with the `cat`.

We set the interval for the `dog` role to `100` millisecond

```
var interval = [100, 20];
```

In addition, we change the `callback` task in the time event with the `dog` to `fall`:

```
intervalID[0] = startTimeEvent(fall, interval[0], 0);
```

With these two changes to the script `js/playRoles-2.js`, we have completed a new scenario *Case 2.5*, which are implemented by the following scripts.

## Case 2.5

### File Listing

```
scene-3.html,
css/scene.css,
js/Role-2.js, js/playRoles-3.js,
img/dogface.png, img/cat.png
```

Open `scene-3.html` in a browser window. It is obvious that dog's motion is not smooth. We can fix this by adjusting the speed value and the interval that is associated with `dog`.

## Workout 12-1

Based on *Case 2.4 Roles at the scene*, create new resources to allow a role to possess more running skills besides falling down, such as running up, running left or right. Implement a scenario that both dog and cat keep falling down until receiving a command that asks the role to change the running direction.

APPENDICES

# Appendix A. Common CSS Properties and Their Equivalent Names in JavaScript

| CSS | JavaScript | CSS | JavaScript |
|---|---|---|---|
| background | background | font | font |
| background-attachment | backgroundAttachment | font-family | fontFamily |
| background-color | backgroundColor | font-size | fontSize |
| background-image | backgroundImage | font-variant | fontVariant |
| background-position | backgroundPosition | font-weight | fontWeight |
| background-repeat | backgroundRepeat | height | height |
| border | border | left | left |
| border-bottom | borderBottom | letter-spacing | letterSpacing |
| border-bottom-color | borderBottomColor | line-height | lineHeight |
| border-bottom-style | borderBottomStyle | list-style | listStyle |
| border-bottom-width | borderBottomWidth | list-style-image | listStyleImage |
| border-color | borderColor | list-style-position | listStylePosition |
| border-left | borderLeft | list-style-type | listStyleType |
| border-left-color | borderLeftColor | margin | margin |
| border-left-style | borderLeftStyle | margin-bottom | marginBottom |
| border-left-width | borderLeftWidth | margin-left | marginLeft |
| border-right | borderRight | margin-right | marginRight |
| border-right-color | borderRightColor | margin-top | marginTop |
| border-right-style | borderRightStyle | overflow | overflow |
| border-right-width | borderRightWidth | padding | padding |
| border-style | borderStyle | padding-bottom | paddingBottom |
| border-top | borderTop | padding-left | paddingLeft |
| border-top-color | borderTopColor | padding-right | paddingRight |
| border-top-style | borderTopStyle | padding-top | paddingTop |
| border-top-width | borderTopWidth | page-break-after | pageBreakAfter |
| border-width | borderWidth | page-break-before | pageBreakBefore |
| clear | clear | position | position |
| clip | clip | float | cssFloat |
| color | color | text-align | textAlign |
| cursor | cursor | text-decoration | textDecoration |
| display | display | filter | filter |
| text-decoration: blink | textDecorationBlink | text-transform | textTransform |
| text-decoration: line-through | textDecorationLineThrough | top | top |
| text-decoration: none | textDecorationNone | vertical-align | verticalAlign |
| text-decoration: overline | textDecorationOverline | visibility | visibility |
| text-decoration: underline | textDecorationUnderline | width | width |
| text-indent | textIndent | z-index | zIndex |

# Appendix B. Reserved Words and Names used by JavaScript

## Reserved Words:

| | | | | | |
|---|---|---|---|---|---|
| abstract | debugger | final | instanceof | protected | throws |
| boolean | default | finally | int | public | transient |
| break | delete | float | interface | return | true |
| byte | do | for | let | short | try |
| case | double | function | long | static | typeof |
| catch | else | goto | native | super | var |
| char | enum | if | new | switch | void |
| class | export | implements | null | synchronized | volatile |
| const | extends | import | package | this | while |
| continue | false | in | private | throw | with |

## Predefined Names:

| | | | | | |
|---|---|---|---|---|---|
| alert | decodeURI | frameRate | layer | outerWidth | secure |
| all | decodeURIComponent | function | layers | packages | select |
| anchor | document | gctClass | length | pageXOffset | self |
| area | element | hasOwnProperty | link | pageYOffset | setInterval |
| array | elements | hidden | location | parent | setTimeout |
| assign | embed | history | Math | parseFloat | status |
| blur | embeds | image | mimeTypes | parseInt | String |
| button | encodeURI | images | name | password | submit |
| checkbox | encodeURIComponent | isFinite | NaN | pkcs11 | taint |
| clearinterval | escape | isNaN | navigate | plugin | text |
| cleartimeout | eval | isPrototypeOf | navigator | prompt | textarea |
| clientinformation | event | java | Number | propertyIsEnum | top |
| close | fileUpload | JavaArray | Object | prototype | toString |
| closed | focus | JavaClass | offscreenBuffering | radio | undefined |
| confirm | form | JavaObject | open | reset | unescape |
| constructor | forms | JavaPackage | opener | screenX | untaint |
| crypto | frame | innerHeight | option | screenY | valueOf |
| Date | frames | innerWidth | outerHeight | scroll | window |

## Names of Event Handlers:

| | | | | |
|---|---|---|---|---|
| onbeforeunload | oncontextmenu | onkeypress | onmousemove | onreset |
| onblur | onerror | onkeyup | onmouseout | onsubmit |
| ondragdrop | onfocus | onload | onmouseover | onunload |
| onclick | onkeydown | onmousedown | onmouseup | |

# Appendix C. Common Values for the Attribute `type` of the `input` Element

| `type` Value | Description |
| --- | --- |
| checkbox | A checkbox |
| color | A color picker |
| date | A date control (year, month and day (no time)) |
| datetime-local | A date and time control (year, month, day, hour, minute, second, and fraction of a second (no time zone) |
| email | A field for an e-mail address |
| file | A file-select field and a "Browse..." button (for file uploads) |
| hidden | A hidden input field |
| image | An image as the submit button |
| month | A month and year control (no time zone) |
| number | A field for entering a number |
| password | A password field (characters are masked) |
| radio | A radio button |
| range | A control for entering a number whose exact value is not important (like a slider control) |
| reset | A reset button (resets all form values to default values) |
| search | A text field for entering a search string |
| tel | A field for entering a telephone number |
| text | Default. Defines a single-line text field (default width is 20 characters) |
| time | A control for entering a time (no time zone) |
| url | A field for entering a URL |
| week | A week and year control (no time zone) |

# TABLE OF EXAMPLES

## TABLE OF EXAMPLES

# TABLE OF CASES

## TABLE OF CASES

# TABLE OF WORKOUTS

TABLE OF WORKOUTS

# REFERENCES

[1] JavaScript | MDN - Mozilla Developer Network. https://developer.mozilla.org/en-US/docs/Web/JavaScript

[2] Jon Duckett, JAVASCRIPT & JQUERY interactive front-end web development

[3] Make a shape in a single HTML element. https://css-tricks.com/examples/ShapesOfCSS/

# CREDITS

[1] www.vectoropenstock.com/terms-and-conditions/

[2] Vecteezy.com

[3] http://www.thefreeicon.com/

[4] Ford Pickup Truck Sketch from VectorHQ.com

[5] http://www.freepik.com/free-vector/dog-breed-collection-in-flat-design_834959.htm. Designed by Freepik

[6] http://www.freepik.com/free-vector/cute-forest-animals_787689.htm. Designed by Freepik

# ABOUT THE AUTHOR

Jie Wang is an associate professor in computer information systems. She received a M.Eng. in electrical engineering and holds a Ph.D. degree in computer science. Her teaching interests cover computer information systems, information technology, computer science, informatics and data science. Her research interests include data and computational issues arising from information systems including information management and data mining, information privacy, social media and user-generated content analysis. Her work has led to a total of more than 40 publications in refereed journals and conference proceedings with the topics encompassing data privacy, data mining and applied mathematics among others.